Richard Aldington & H.D.

Richard Aldington

& H.D.

The Early Years in Letters

Edited with an introduction and commentary by
Caroline Zilboorg

INDIANA UNIVERSITY PRESS   *Bloomington & Indianapolis*

Manufactured in the United States of America

Library of Congress Cataloging-in-Publication Data

Aldington, Richard, 1892–1962.
    Richard Aldington and H.D. : the early years in letters / edited with an introduction and commentary by Caroline Zilboorg.
        p.   cm.
    Includes index.
    ISBN 0-253-36868-5 (cloth : alk. paper)
    1. Aldington, Richard, 1892–1962—Correspondence.   2. H.D. (Hilda Doolittle), 1886–1961—Correspondence.   3. Authors, English—20th century—Correspondence.   4. Poets, American—20th century—Correspondence.   I. H.D. (Hilda Doolittle), 1886–1961.
II. Zilboorg, Caroline Crawford.   III. Title.
PR6001.L4Z547   1992
821'.91209—dc20
[B]   91-70

1 2 3 4 5   96 95 94 93 92

all Holdings information.

‗ers

‗: H. D. (Hilda
‗chors, English—20th centu

— Available

Contents

List of Illustrations

Preface

This project grew out of a firm conviction that biography is important. The raw material of a life, and in this case two lives, is of inestimable value in understanding the art that is created as a result of those lives. Biography consists of a synthesis of raw material, selection and annotation, commentary and analysis. Neither H.D. nor Aldington have been served well by biography, and their reputations and their art as a result have been considerably obscured and misconstrued. These difficulties have their source in part in the writers' own work: H.D.'s autobiographical fiction, particularly *Bid Me to Live*, has encouraged readers to see her life as she at various times and for varying purposes chose to portray it. Her memoirs, notably *End to Torment* and *Tribute to Freud*, are also idiosyncratic and, valuable as they are, should not be confused with the whole truth. Aldington's novels, particularly *Death of a Hero*, also have strong autobiographical components, and his memoir, *Life for Life's Sake*, is notable in part for its omissions.

In the book which follows I have chosen not to draw on the authors' fictional treatments of their own experiences except when I felt it was necessary, and then I have so noted it. Similarly, I have used their memoirs sparingly. I have also avoided relying on biographies (notably Janice Robinson's *H.D.: The Life and Work of an American Poet* and Barbara Guest's *Herself Defined: The Poet H.D. and Her World*, and Charles Doyle's *Richard Aldington: A Biography*), which have drawn heavily on H.D.'s and Aldington's novels, often confusing autobiographical fiction and primary sources. I have also avoided using H.D.'s unpublished novels "Asphodel" and "Paint It To-Day" (virtual *romans à clef*, but written it would seem for Bryher, and thus biased accounts in which much of importance is omitted). Other unpublished material is also suspect: for example, written testimony H.D. submitted to an English court during divorce proceedings in 1937 intentionally created false impressions and contained obvious untruths in order to bring about a legal settlement with as little difficulty as possible. I have tried my best to avoid using such material as well.

Realizing that even with letters one is reading a particular version of reality, I have nonetheless chosen to base the biography and commentary in this edition on the wealth of previously unpublished correspondence by and concerning both H.D. and Aldington. It seems to me that in letters, the reader is always aware by their very nature of writer and intended audience. Thus, while correspondence has a created voice and a shaped truth, the reader is conscious of both and the consequent burden of interpretation. In this context, the letters which follow reveal a particularly powerful view of the relationship between H.D. and Aldington.

Some information that the reader of this correspondence might want is no longer available. Aldington refers often to volumes in the library he and H.D. shared, but these books were separated, lent, sold, and have otherwise failed to survive as a collection. Books in H.D.'s later library are now at the Beinecke at Yale, but it contains few volumes before the early twenties; the same is true of Bryher's library, which includes many of H.D.'s books and is now housed in a building dedicated to it on the grounds of Perdita Schaffner's home in East Hampton, New York. Although Alister Kershaw has kept several books Aldington owned at the time of his death in 1962, Aldington's library has not been preserved.

The reader might also have been aided by Aldington's military service record, but this, too, is unavailable: German bombing of London during the Second World War destroyed many early records at the Ministry of Defense. H.D.'s side of the early correspondence is also unavailable (see Introduction).

I have chosen to translate most of the foreign language material in Aldington's letters, excepting the most obvious French phrases. He used French often and at length, frequently idiomatically or employing somewhat dated military slang. Additionally, his command of French in the teens was nowhere near so good as it would become in the twenties and during his later years, when he lived entirely in France. His Italian, Spanish, and Latin as well as French I have translated in notes as less distracting to readers able to read these languages with ease; Greek I have translated within brackets in the text as a courtesy to most readers now unable to read it otherwise.

I have also included two appendices: the Biographical Appendix identifies in some detail the people to whom Aldington often refers, and the Periodical Appendix identifies frequently mentioned periodicals.

Acknowledgments

I could not have completed my work without the help of the following libraries. Special acknowledgment is made to the following libraries for permission to publish or quote from material in their collections; they are cited in the book by the letters indicated.

BL   The Beinecke Rare Book and Manuscript Library, Yale University
BM   The British Library
UL   The Brotherton Library, University of Leeds
UCLA   The University Library, University of California, Los Angeles
        Special Collections, University of Chicago
        The Fales Library, New York University
        Firestone Library, Princeton University
        Grasselli Library, John Carroll University
HRC   The Harry Ransom Humanities Research Center, University of Texas
          at Austin
HU   The Houghton Library, Harvard University
HL   The Huntington Library, San Marino, California
        Rare Book and Special Collections Library, University of Illinois, Ur-
          bana-Champaign
        The Imperial War Museum, London
UIL   The University of Iowa Libraries, Iowa City
        The Lilly Library, Indiana University
        Lincoln Library, Lake Erie College
        Special Collections, Middlebury College
        The Ministry of Defense, Hayes, Middlesex
        University Libraries, University of Minnesota, Minneapolis
SIU   The Morris Library, Southern Illinois University
        Mugar Memorial Library, Boston University
        Olin Library, Cornell University
PRO   The Public Record Office, Kew, Richmond
UR   The University of Reading Library, Reading
        The Royal Signals Museum, Blandford Camp, Dorset
TU   The Rare Book and Manuscript Collection, Temple University
UV   Special Collections, University of Victoria

All of Aldington's letters to H.D. are published here by the generous permission of the Yale Collection of American Literature, the Beinecke Rare Book and

Manuscript Library, Yale University. All letters from H.D. and Aldington to Amy Lowell are at HU; all letters from Aldington to Frank Stewart Flint are at HRC; all unpublished letters from Aldington to John Cournos are at HU; all quotations from H.D.'s letters to John Cournos are from unpublished letters at HU unless otherwise noted; all letters to Clement Shorter are at UL. All letters from H.D. and Aldington to Bryher are at BL; all letters from Bryher to H.D. are also at BL. "Refuge from War," by Harriet Monroe, first appeared in *Poetry*, © 1918 by the Modern Poetry Association, and is reprinted by permission of the Editor of Poetry.

A portion of the Introduction appeared in the *H.D. Newsletter* as "H.D. and R.A.: Early Love and the Exclusion of Ezra Pound," Vol. 3, No. 1, 26–34.

Special acknowledgment is made to the following for permission to publish or quote from previously published or unpublished material: Alister Kershaw, literary executor for Richard Aldington; Perdita Schaffner, literary executor for H.D. and Bryher; New Directions; Dundas and Wilson, Trustees, Limited, agents for the estate of Cecil Gray; David Wilkinson; and Ann Monroe Howe, literary executor for the estate of Harriet Monroe.

I am particularly grateful to several people who have encouraged me in my work. A. Walton Litz at Princeton University has been inspiring and generous; this project began during the summer of 1987 when I received a grant from the National Endowment for the Humanities and participated in a seminar which he directed. I am grateful to the National Endowment for the opportunity to work at Princeton and for the colleagues I met there whose warm responses to my research helped to shape it; I am specifically indebted to Carol Gilbertson and Andrew Kappel. Particular librarians have gone beyond the call of regular duties to be helpful: Shelley Cox, Rare Book Librarian at the Morris Library at Southern Illinois University at Carbondale; Martin Taylor in the Department of Printed Materials at the Imperial War Museum in London; Patricia Willis, Curator of the Yale Collection of American Literature at the Beinecke, and the entire staff at the Beinecke, especially Richard Hart and Steven Jones. Thanks also to the staff at the Paul Nash Trust. I am also grateful to the staff at Indiana University Press who helped with the details of manuscript preparation. Scholars with a committed interest in H.D.'s work have encouraged this edition in its various stages; Diana Collecott, Susan Friedman, Eileen Gregory, and Robert Spoo deserve special thanks. Scholars with a committed interest in Aldington have also supported me in many valuable ways; I am very grateful to Fred Crawford and David Wilkinson. This book would never have been written without the kindness, warmth, good sense, and pioneering work of Norman Gates, to whom I am deeply indebted for his understanding of Aldington and unstinting encouragement. I must thank Catherine Aldington for her kindness in approving the publication of her father's correspondence, and I am grateful to Perdita Schaffner, who gave me permission to publish H.D.'s letters and who has been gracious and interested from the very beginning.

ACKNOWLEDGMENTS

I owe a special debt to Alister Kershaw, whose friendship to me has gone beyond his role as Aldington's literary executor. His kindness to me and my family during our visits to Maison Sallé; his wife Jelka's good humor and good food; his own sharp wit, wide knowledge and interests have all been immeasurably valuable. I also owe another debt of friendship to Louis Silverstein, who catalogued the H.D. papers at the Beinecke and has since taken a special interest in scholars who come to New Haven to examine the wealth of those and related papers. The many good meals taken with him and Monty Montee at Silverleigh; the evenings spent with Louis at his computer; the hours of good talk and his many letters have all contributed greatly to this project.

I am grateful to my four young children (Austin, Tobias, Elodie, and Miranda Nevin), who have always respected their mother's work and understood the traveling and time away from them that it necessitated. To my husband, Tom Nevin, who never typed a word of the manuscript but throughout the project cared about Aldington and H.D. and supported me with innumerable acts of proofreading, translating, research, listening, and love, I am more thankful than I can ever say.

Richard Aldington & *H.D.*

Introduction

ichard Aldington began to write almost daily letters to his wife, Hilda Doolittle Aldington (H.D.), as soon as he entered the British army on June 24, 1916. She wrote to him nearly as frequently, and the intense correspondence between them continued until his demobilization in mid-February of 1919. They wrote to each other less often from mid-February through April of 1919 and sporadically into the 1920s, resuming a limited exchange of letters between 1929 and 1932. They resumed the correspondence in 1937, their letters becoming more frequent and continuing, often twice a week, until H.D.'s death on September 27, 1961.

Not all of these letters have survived, but the astounding number (nearly 1,200) which have revealed the development over a span of more than forty years of two complex people who never ceased to care deeply about each other. The missing letters are also a part of the story, for as Alister Kershaw, Aldington's literary executor and a close personal friend, suggests, while Aldington "wasn't in the habit of piously preserving every letter he ever received . . . hers would have been infinitely precious to him."[1] H.D. similarly valued Aldington's letters; in her autobiographical novel *Bid Me to Live* (1960), Aldington appears as the character Rafe Ashton, who brings back to Julia (H.D.) on his leaves all the letters she has written to him.[2]

But something happened to this early correspondence. In light of Kershaw's statement, Aldington's purposeful destruction of letters from H.D. seems uncharacteristic, but in the early 1950s H.D. reported to her friend and admirer Norman Holmes Pearson that "during the first war she had written Richard every day, and he had sent back the letters periodically for her to keep, along with his to her. 'There was a trunkful.' When she left the apartment, she left the books + letters behind; then when they met for the first time [after 1919] in Paris [in May 1929] . . . , she asked what had become of them, + he said he had destroyed them all."[3] On the basis of Aldington's letters to H.D. during the war, it is easy to imagine her concern about the revelation of their private contents. Aldington in his turn may also have felt that the intimacy and loss the letters recorded were too powerful for him to preserve. Thus he apparently did destroy their letters of 1916 and 1917, which he would have recovered from H.D.'s flat along with books and other papers she had stored there, as well as her letters to him after March of 1918, which he would have had with him when he moved to a cottage in Hermitage, Berkshire, in December of 1919. When at the end of 1920 he moved to Malthouse Cottage in Padworth, his charwoman's daughter recalled over sixty years later:

> . . . he left a lot of papers, and all the things that were left behind him saying what will happen to him in wartime. . . . Saying about his wife and all the things about his wife. My mother destroyed those. Really, they were letters about him and his wife . . . to Mr. Aldington . . . from her to him. . . . there were piles and piles of papers left. He left the whole lot behind and Mother said, "What's that?" . . . and he said to my mother, "Would you burn that for me?" So she said, "Yes, certainly." And she said [to the daughter, then aged eleven], "Well, look at this!" And then, in the end, she destroyed them.[4]

Such destruction of correspondence and papers, however upsetting to future readers, was also for Aldington a natural part of the cleaning up occasioned by his numerous and sometimes unanticipated moves from one residence to another. For example, Aldington left Malthouse Cottage precipitously in August 1928, for Italy: his friend Alec Randall was recovering from typhoid fever near Rome and his wife wired Aldington with an urgent invitation to visit him during his convalescence.[5] Aldington had planned to host Glenn Hughes, an American scholar interested in imagism, during September; in his absence, he lent Malthouse Cottage indefinitely to Hughes and his family. He periodically requested papers from Hughes during the winter of 1928–29, but he did not decide to give up the cottage until the end of November 1928, effective at the end of February 1929.[6] As a result Aldington disposed of and relocated his books, papers and other possessions from a distance and left much to be burned at the discretion of others, for he remained on the continent throughout 1929. If all the early letters between Aldington and H.D. were not burned by Mrs. Brown in 1920, it seems likely that they were destroyed during this later period.

The letters which follow are thus one side of the early correspondence: Aldington's letters to H.D. between April 1918 and December 1920. This was a pivotal and important time in both writers' lives, a dramatic and intense period personally, socially, and historically. These years would test their love for each other and challenge their ideas of art and the future, calling into question all of their earlier decisions and commitments. The letters are deeply embedded in their biographies—not merely literary, philosophical, or topical exchanges—and an overview of both writers' lives before 1918 seems in order.

Aldington was born in Hampshire on July 8, 1892. He and his two sisters and brother grew up in the south of England in Portsmouth, Dover, and the surrounding countryside. His childhood does not appear to have been a particularly happy one: in his memoir, *Life for Life's Sake* (1941), he repeatedly and at length details the constraining middle-class life that oppressed him as a boy, experience that he treated bitterly and with understandable censure in "Childhood," a poem which first appeared in *The Egoist* in 1914.

His parents were not really sympathetic to his nature, although each had enough awareness of the young Aldington's personality to realize his developing values and misunderstand them. His mother appears to have been especially difficult in this respect. A domineering woman who aspired to "culture" as socially defined at the turn of the century, May Aldington seemed to her son throughout his life an affected, pretentious, and hollow person whose sentimentality and materialism came to represent all that he abhorred in England. She wrote several romantic novels, and evidently drank to the point of being unpredictable and unreliable. Aldington's deep hostility toward her developed into his notion of the "bad" mother who appears regularly in his fiction: Mrs. Winterbourne, for example, in *Death of a Hero* (1929); Mrs. Withers in *The Colonel's Daughter* (1931); Mrs. Reeves in *Seven against Reeves* (1938). By implication, Aldington developed simultaneously an ideal of the "good" mother, based not so much on direct experience as on wide reading of both early twentieth-century psychology (Havelock Ellis, for instance) and literature, English, continental, and classical. This notion of the "good" mother was also an imaginative response to the feminism with which he was in close contact after he moved to London.

Aldington's father, in contrast, appears to have been a rather weak man for whom his son felt an abiding affection and intellectual affinity. A middle-class solicitor, Albert Aldington had little business acumen or ambition, and his son resented his lack of direction and consequent hypocrisy. But Aldington also saw him as a victim of Victorian English culture, and respected his wide and independently acquired knowledge of history and letters. His father made some effort to launch Aldington's literary career, and on June 7, 1910, wrote on his behalf to St. Loe Strachey, editor of *The Spectator*:

> I have a son between 17 + 18, of whom one of our greatest living writers [George Bernard Shaw, to whom Aldington's mother had sent a sample of his work] has declared that "he has literary ability enough for anything," + as I am therefore anxious to obtain for him an atmosphere that would be congenial, it has occurred to me that possibly you might be able to find him a position that would be mutually satisfying.
>
> As an old lover of the classics I can vouch for the boy's ability in that direction. His knowledge of French is good, of art excellent, of English literature, for his age quite remarkable. His productions, particularly in poetry are equally distinctive, + withal, he is tall, muscular + can do a twenty mile walk any day of the week.[7]

Albert Aldington's large library with its strong collection of Elizabethan and Romantic poets as well as classical and European authors was a rich treasure for the young Aldington; it was there he grounded himself early in literature and the past.

The other solace of Aldington's childhood was nature. He relished the countryside in the south of England, its flowers, hills, chalk cliffs, and sea. As a youth,
he became a great walker, setting out on long hikes over the downs and through
the villages in the rural South Foreland. His approach to nature was at once
sensual and scientific, imaginative and precise. He enjoyed swimming and dreamy
afternoons in the sun as well as counting the miles he walked and collecting
butterflies. These two tendencies—the passionate and the analytical—come to
characterize his responses to all aspects of life: literature was simultaneously a
personal, private, emotional experience and something to take a well-reasoned
public stand on; love was intimate, sexual, and overwhelming as well as spiritual,
and yet something one could analyze and consider responsibly.

There is obviously a potential conflict here, and it was one which Aldington
never fully resolved in his relationships with others, in his own art, or in his
critical and biographical work. He was increasingly conscious of these tensions in
his personality, yet the gusto with which he approached life, often combining
seriousness with humor, his sensibility with sense, made him many lasting friends
and not-so-lasting lovers. His own account of himself in 1929 in response to a
questionnaire sent out by *The Little Review* captures these contrasting aspects of
his personality while it conveys the apparent arrogance and even off-handedness
of this man who was emotionally private and scrupulously truthful about his own
feelings as well as sensitive and widely read:

1. What would you most like to do, to know, to be? . . .
2. Why wouldn't you change places with any other human being?
3. What do you look forward to?
4. What do you fear most from the future?
5. What has been the happiest moment of your life? The unhappiest? . . .
6. What do you consider your weakest characteristics? Your strongest?
7. What things do you really like? Dislike? . . .
8. What is your attitude toward art today?
9. What is your world view? . . .
10. Why do you go on living?

Aldington responds:

1. A. To write a poem.
    B. Greek.
    C. Ninon de Lenclos.[8]
2. Because 'tis better to endure those ills we know than to fly to others that
    we know not of [*Hamlet*, act 3, scene 1].
3. Telling England what I really think of it.
4. Having to take a job.

5. A. Losing my virginity. B. Lying with a virgin.
6. A. Honesty. B. Independence. C. Ha! ha! D. He! he!
7. A. Women's. B. Puritans.
8. Enlightened benevolence.
9. Despair.
10. Pour écraser l'infâme [to crush the infamous].[9]

Aldington's hellenism, his knowledge of French literature and language, his love of Shakespeare, his feminism, his respect for art, his enjoyment of sexuality and personal freedom, his hostility toward England and hypocrisy, his forthrightness and privateness, however masked by brash humor, are all readily apparent here. Almost twenty years earlier, when at eighteen he first came to London in the autumn of 1910 to attend University College, his character was well-formed and his academic knowledge advanced; the experiences he would have in the next decade deepened and complicated the man who appears above in *The Little Review* in 1929.

Aldington completed only one year at University College before his family's financial indiscretions forced him to leave to earn his own living. The academic year was not particularly intellectually quickening for him—he had already covered more ground on his own than most entering students—but he pursued Greek with diligence and enthusiasm; Aldington always worked intensely with care, precision, and a clear plan. He pursued and mastered Greek, Latin, French, and Italian in this fashion. After leaving University College, he received for a while a small allowance from his parents, which enabled him to support himself as a journalist and to begin to publish his poetry in British periodicals. He lived simply during the summer and fall of 1911, and began to associate with London's bohemian fringe. Early in 1912 Aldington met Brigit Patmore; through her he met Ezra Pound, who had come to London in 1908, and soon after Aldington attended a party at Patmore's where he met H.D.

H.D. did not become publicly known as "H.D." until Pound, as *Poetry*'s foreign correspondent, signed her poems "H.D. 'Imagiste' " before sending them off to Harriet Monroe in the early fall of 1912. In January 1913, H.D.'s first poems appeared in *Poetry*, where Aldington's work had appeared two months previously. In the table of contents, she is listed as "H.D., 'Imagiste,' " although the poems in the text are attributed merely to "H.D." She never again appears as "H.D., 'Imagiste' "; when Monroe publishes her a second time in February of 1914, she appears as "H.D." both in the table of contents and in the text. "H.D." was a literary persona, however, like the others she variously assumed (Rhoda Peter, D.A. Hill, Delia Alton, John Helforth), and when Aldington met her at Mrs. Patmore's, she was Hilda Doolittle, just as after her marriage she was always Hilda Aldington.

H.D. was born in rural Bethlehem, Pennsylvania, on September 10, 1886.

When she was nine, her father, Charles Doolittle, left his position as professor of astronomy and mathematics at Lehigh University for a comparable position at the University of Pennsylvania; the family moved to Upper Darby, five miles west of Philadelphia. Here H.D. grew up in the countryside near a busy city, attending private schools in Philadelphia, then commuting to Bryn Mawr for a year and a half (October 1905 through January 1907). In 1908–1909, she enrolled at the University of Pennsylvania in the college course for teachers, but she did not pursue the program.

From a previous marriage, Charles Doolittle had two sons, and with his second wife, Helen Wolle Doolittle, produced three more, one older than H.D. and two younger. H.D. thus defined herself in a predominantly masculine and professional household. She was sympathetic with her mother as the only other female and as a woman also defined by her relationships with the males in the family. Her mother appears, however, to have been somewhat passive and busy, having put aside her own interests in painting and music in order to assume the more conventional roles of wife and mother to a large family. She was a maternal and warm woman, religious but not fanatic, and supportive of her daughter in her intellectual aspirations and later unconventional life. H.D. was her father's favorite child, yet Charles Doolittle seems a preoccupied and cerebral figure in H.D.'s childhood. A serious man of real prominence in his field, he worked hard at odd hours in the Flower Observatory, and apparently had little time for active family life. He, too, however, encouraged his only daughter's formal education, particularly in science and mathematics, and must have approved an independence of spirit and seriousness of purpose that characterized the maturing H.D., who could romp with ease through the fields and woods near her home, hold her own with her brothers, and pursue academically French, German, Latin, and Greek as well as literature and the natural sciences.

The essentially rural experience of H.D.'s childhood fostered the intense sensitivity to nature which she shared with Aldington. She enjoyed the independence she gained as the result of being the only girl among boys in a large family in which she was encouraged both to excel physically and intellectually and to develop a spiritual response to the world. Particularly close to her brother Gilbert, two years her senior, she also had many female friends in the neighborhood and at school, but seems to have sought out particular friends who became confidantes for periods of time, sharing with her especially intimate and private experiences of a personal and often spiritual nature.

Thus H.D. like Aldington valued self-reliance and freedom. Her need for confidantes, however, distinguishes her from him in a significant respect, for although Aldington valued intimacy and deeply enjoyed close relationships, he seems to have been more self-contained than H.D., less willing to reveal himself to others, more controlled, less emotionally raw. This important difference explains in part why Aldington appears to have developed few intimate friends by the time he met H.D. in 1912; it also speaks to the difference in experience that H.D., six years Aldington's senior, brought to their relationship.

An account of Aldington's youth is an account of solitary experience and mentors: parents, occasionally sensitive teachers, older men who shared with him their libraries and wider knowledge of art, languages, nature, history, and Europe. An account of H.D.'s life before 1912 is often an account of intense relationships with other people: her parents (who both seem to have been closer to her and more powerful influences in her life than Aldington's in his), her brothers, and particular friends. The most important of these early friends were Ezra Pound and Frances Gregg.

H.D. met Pound in 1901; she was fifteen and he a year older and already a freshman at the University of Pennsylvania. The two shared excellent educations which they both valued, having gained them both formally and informally, and a special sensitivity to poetry. They were young, exuberant, and independent people who enjoyed each other's company at social gatherings and during solitary walks in the woods. Just as later H.D. would turn repeatedly in her writing to her relationship with Aldington, fictionalizing him not only in *Palimpsest* (1926) and *Bid Me to Live* but in numerous other works and even in *Helen in Egypt*, the long poem published just before her death in 1961, so Pound also figures prominently in her writing throughout her life: he is the central figure in *End to Torment*, a memoir written in 1958, a character in *Helen in Egypt*, George Lowndes in *Hermione*, written in 1926–27. H.D.'s relationship with and eventual engagement to Pound (which seems to have been, like his engagements to other women, periodically official and unofficial) were interrupted several times by his work at Hamilton College, his term of college teaching in Indiana, and his travels in Europe, but she maintained an intense relationship with him into 1912. When H.D. left America for France in July of 1911, she traveled with Frances Gregg and her mother, and finally saw for herself the Europe which Pound must have described to her in great detail. In September she left the continent for England where she again, after Frances Gregg's departure for America in the autumn of 1911, resumed her close friendship with Pound.

H.D.'s relationship with Gregg began in 1910 when they met in Philadelphia and continued through the fall of 1911. Like Aldington and Pound, Gregg is fictionalized in H.D.'s work, appearing as Fayne Rabb, for example, in *Hermione*, which is also dedicated to her. Gregg, for a time a student at the Pennsylvania Academy of Fine Arts, shared with H.D. an interest in poetry, but her relationship with H.D. seems to have been more sensual than intellectual, more passionate than cerebral, in contrast to H.D.'s relationship with Pound, which appears to have consisted of a great deal of emotionally charged philosophical discussion of themselves and of literature and art. H.D.'s friendship with Gregg was sexual in a way not evident in H.D.'s romantic friendship with Pound. If we can trust H.D.'s own fictionalized account of her relationship with him in *Hermione* as well as her memories of him in *End to Torment,* Pound was not finally an effectively passionate lover; despite some physical exchanges of intimacy, it seems unlikely that they ever slept together.[10] H.D.'s lesbian relationship with Gregg, on the other hand, seems to have fulfilled her sexually, at least for a time.[11]

Both friendships were fraught with difficulties, however, for all three participants had powerful personalities which tended to vie with each other for dominance rather than complement each other in mutual fulfillment and balance. Neither relationship permitted H.D. much independence and in their intensity evidently embroiled the partners in psychological tensions instead of evoking complementary and shared thoughts and feelings. Matters were made increasingly complex for H.D. by the intermittent and overlapping pace of these two friendships and by the simultaneous romantic attraction Pound and Gregg briefly shared with one another.

By the time Aldington and H.D. met in early 1912, they were both free and independent writers on their own in London. Through Pound, Aldington was beginning to meet other young poets and artists and to establish himself as a participant in England's modernist movement. Brigit Patmore and Aldington were having a passing affair.[12] She was not happy with her insensitive and impecunious husband, and had sought out young bohemian artists as an alternative society. Born in 1883, she was two years older than Pound, three years older than H.D., and nine years older than Aldington; she was thus seeking out interesting if slightly younger contemporaries who had chosen less conventional paths for themselves than she had initially begun to follow. Patmore was also consciously rebelling against a philandering, Victorian husband and a traditional married life. That she was a mother with two young sons gave her a privileged status as an experienced woman that enabled her to create a salon of sorts and to live her life with a measure of freedom not conceded to unmarried women in 1912. She enjoyed the full advantage of her special position.

H.D.'s affair with Frances Gregg was essentially over: early in 1912 Gregg began a lifelong romantic friendship with John Cowper Powys, and in April married his close friend Louis Wilkinson. She did invite H.D. to join her and her new husband on their European honeymoon, but Pound with some effort dissuaded H.D. from accompanying them. By 1911 Pound had begun courting Dorothy Shakespear, whom he married in April of 1914, and his relationship with H.D. had become more fraternal than romantic. Aldington, H.D., Pound, and Patmore met often in London in the early months of 1912. H.D. had decided to remain in England and to work on her writing; a small allowance from her parents gave her a measure of security and permitted her to spend long hours reading at the British Museum and relishing a city rich in art and literature. Patmore found her charming and sexually attractive, and probably encouraged her own lover in his attentions to H.D. out of a genuine willingness to foster romantic relationships but also impulsively as a way of loving H.D. vicariously through him. Aldington needed little outside encouragement, and H.D. responded to him as a colleague, an intellectual equal, and a romantic partner. Pound liked to introduce people; he liked to bring young artists together, to quicken one person with another, to send new work to editors, to electrify the chemistry of a gathering. He was often brilliant in doing all these things; he was more awkward in his reactions to the consequences of what he had done: initially cordial working relationships with editors often became after a time impossible, and he alternatively perplexed and outraged friends and acquaintances when he no longer controlled their activities. From his perspective, people seemed to have changed, or to be different from the way he had initially perceived them, or to be acting oddly. He never quite grasped that H.D. and Aldington were falling in love with each other, but he was finally willing to accept, even if he could not understand, their partnership.

In the spring of 1912 Aldington was working hard to establish himself as a literary critic and poet and was also regularly writing articles on subjects of more general interest. With the small monthly allowance from his parents, he managed to support himself. After H.D. left for a visit to France in May of 1912, an enamored Aldington soon joined her. Pound was also in Paris that summer and the three sometimes toured the city together, although H.D. and Aldington were clearly at this point close companions and their relationship was deepening. They went regularly together to museums and their shared experience of both visual and literary art was an obvious element in their romance. H.D. showed her diary to Aldington, and during these months in Paris, it occasionally even became a joint enterprise: on May 28, 1912, Aldington wrote humorously in the diary about the art they were seeing; on July 4, in response to a painting they had both seen in the Louvre, he composed a sonnet, "Angelico's Coronation," and dedicated it "To H.D." In the octave he remarks on the Christian painting's attraction for him, its delicacy and calm; in the sestet, he rejects the peace of Fra Angelico for a hellenic life and love:

> . . . the blithe wild earth,
> Scurry of satyr-hooves in dewy lands,
> Pan-pipes at noon, the lust, the shaggy fur,
> White bosoms & swift Dionysiac mirth.[13]

H.D. and Aldington thought of themselves as "Greeks"; on June 15 H.D. noted in her diary that they had spent the morning in the Luxembourg Gardens, "R deep in Greek choruses—H—sketching cast of Gladiator—" They probably also consummated their love that summer. On June 10, H.D. recorded in her diary that when Pound joined them for tea, she said to him, " 'You see I am taking your advice.' (The advice weeks since in Luxembourg gardens 'You better marry Richard')." On the facing page is a poem by H.D. beginning "I love you. . . ."

Aldington in officer's uniform, probably taken in London in late 1917 or early 1918.

H.D., probably taken in late 1917 at 44 Mecklenburgh Square.

The diary also reveals the emotionally intense but formally conventional poems both H.D. and Aldington were producing. They are writing on the Greek or personal subjects that would become characteristic of their mature poetry, but in strict meter and rhyme, formal elements both would soon reject for the vers libre of early modernism.[14] After their return to London in August, H.D. and Aldington went back to their respective work. In late September of 1912 their now famous encounter in the British Museum tearoom or in a nearby tea shop probably occurred: H.D. showed her poems to Pound and he, impressed with what he read, signed them "H.D. 'Imagiste' " and sent them off in October to *Poetry*.

Three of Aldington's early poems, also written before Pound labeled him an "Imagiste," appeared as imagist works in *Poetry* in November 1912; H.D.'s poems appeared in January 1913. The two were by no means established poets from this time forward, but their debut in *Poetry* was a significant introduction of their verse to serious readers who sensed a new awakening of poetry at the very beginning of the modernist movement. Both H.D. and Aldington had published poems in newspapers,[15] but neither had received the critical consideration both would receive from now on. The translations on which each would work—free, poetic, and impressionistic renditions of Greek verse, more precise and conventional translations of contemporary French prose—became parallel if not occasionally collaborative efforts from this point, and their shared discussions of books and each other's work became an integral part of their increasingly intimate relationship.

In October of 1912 H.D. left for another trip to the continent. She spent some time in Paris, where she saw Pound, who was also briefly there, before travelling south in Italy to meet her parents, Margaret Snively, and her father, who had made the trip to Europe with them. The Snivelys were neighbors of the Doolittles in Upper Darby and Margaret had been a close friend of H.D.'s since girlhood. The Doolittles missed their only daughter, whom they had not seen for fifteen months, and were curious and probably somewhat concerned about what she was doing and her future plans. They landed at Genoa on October 14; on October 18 they left for Florence, stopping at Pisa on the way.[16] The Doolittles and the Snivelys saw the sights; Mrs. Doolittle bought H.D. a dress; H.D., Professor Doolittle, and Margaret took Italian lessons together until the end of November. On December 2, the Snivelys left Florence for Nice, where Dr. Snively, an Episcopalian minister, had an appointment; Margaret remained there with her father until his death in January 1914, when she moved to England.[17] On December 4, 1912, the Doolittles took the train from Florence to Rome. On December 5, they began their sightseeing, and Mrs. Doolittle noted that there was "—mail for Hilda."

In H.D.'s absence, Aldington worked furiously in London, managing before the end of the year to persuade A.R. Orage, editor of *The New Age*, to accept a proposed series of articles on Italy. With this small measure of security he left

London for the continent, arriving in Rome in mid-December. H.D. and Aldington did not return to London until August of 1913, and their eight months of
traveling essentially together, primarily in Italy but also in France, took them as
far south as Naples. This period was not the family visit that Pound felt the
Doolittles expected;[18] Aldington was increasingly in love with H.D. and she increasingly inclined to him, although according to Pound H.D. was influenced by
her parents[19] and Aldington finally needed Pound's permission to pursue his
courtship seriously.[20] Even as late as May 1913, Pound observed rather insistently
that despite H.D.'s time alone with Aldington, "she doesn't seem much more in
love"; with patent obtuseness, Pound declared the next day, "I think they *must*
be in love."[21]

They were in love. Pound is not a particularly reliable source for this period.
H.D. in her few surviving letters to others from this time tended to write of the
sights and climate she experienced and does not mention Aldington.[22] Aldington
is similarly discreet in his many postcards to his father and sisters during his
travels, never once mentioning the Doolittles or H.D. by name nor even indicating that he is courting someone; his postcards refer to his work, the sights he
is seeing, the weather, his changes of address.[23] Both writers are also reticent
about this period in their later autobiographical work. H.D. does not discuss this
trip in *End to Torment*, for example, which focuses on her early relationship with
Pound. In *Life for Life's Sake*, Aldington writes that he left London in December
because of the fog as well as because of a postcard from "a friend in Genoa"
(clearly H.D.) telling him that in Italy the blossoming almond trees " 'will be full
out in a few weeks.' "[24] He does not mention spending most of his trip abroad
with H.D., but focuses instead on amusing characters, local sights, and the fine
climate in conveying the beauty and delight he discovered during these months
in the south. He indicates with only slight ambiguity that it is Italy he is in love
with rather than a woman, writing that

> we can never quite regain the first fine careless rapture of discovering Italy. Perhaps
> the course of true love runs all the truer for not being smooth; and very possibly
> my enjoyment of these wanderings was made keener because I had been forced to
> wait so long, overcome difficulties and take risks. In spite of very high expectations
> I was not disappointed.[25]

While Aldington is writing here of his affection for Italy and his financial con-
straints, he is also I think equating the experience of Italy with the realization of
his love for H.D. He implies that their relationship, despite their insecure fi-
nances and the presence of other people and even of other lovers, was like the
almond trees on the postcard about to come into full bloom. Further, H.D. had
for years identified herself with trees. Pound may well have called her "Dryad" as
early as the poem "The Tree," which he wrote for her and gave to her bound

together with the other poems in "Hilda's Book" in 1907; surely Aldington called her "Dryad" in 1913. Thus the "friend's" postcard increases in significance and becomes an erotic invitation to join H.D. in Italy.

It is important to see the Aldingtons' marriage as a love match between equals. The Aldingtons' courtship deserves particular attention because of its misrepresentation by Pound and its at best oblique presentation by Aldington and H.D. themselves. A detailed account vividly reveals their love and its development. On December 12, 1912, Mrs. Doolittle notes that H.D. was spending time with her "English friends"; on December 16, Mrs. Doolittle writes, "Hilda had tea with her English friends," Aldington presumably among them by this time. Mrs. Doolittle's travel diary for 1912–13 is an important source for understanding Aldington's and H.D.'s early love. She was clearly an outsider, but her entries are regular and specific though brief and generally without commentary. The details reveal the texture of H.D.'s and Aldington's days and Mrs. Doolittle's affectionate encouragement of their courtship. While Pound's version suggests all sorts of tensions within and without the relationship, Mrs. Doolittle's diary conveys a much happier and smoother friendship. On December 18, she noted that "Hilda was feeling particularly well." On December 20, she mentioned Aldington for the first time: "Hilda out with R.A." H.D. seems to have spent much of each day sightseeing with Aldington, occasionally with her father and mother, but generally without them. By December 24, Mrs. Doolittle was calling him "Richard." When the Doolittles left Rome for Naples on February 12, 1913, Aldington followed two days later, and he and H.D. resumed their pattern of days out together at museums and local sights, then tea and dinner at which her parents might join them. When Professor and Mrs. Doolittle left Naples for Venice on March 6, she noted that "H. and R.A. came on later train." On March 14, the Doolittles and Aldington took a boat to Capri, then traveled across the island to Anacapri, where they all stayed.

Throughout their travels Mrs. Doolittle seems to have been quite close to her daughter. She evidently accepted and respected H.D.'s intimacy with Aldington, confining her maternal solicitude to buying H.D. nice clothing: she purchased her daughter a dress in Florence (October 25, 1912), blue fabric for another dress in Rome (December 9, 1912), and material "for Hilda's new nightdress" in Capri (March 19, 1913). On March 23, Mrs. Doolittle wrote "make plans—Hilda remains here [at Anacapri] while we [the Doolittles] go to Sicily." The Doolittles took the boat to Naples on March 25, went on to Sicily, returning to Naples on April 11, then taking the train to Rome. On April 14, the Doolittles arrived for a brief stay in Bologne, finally reaching Venice on April 17. H.D. and Aldington remained unchaperoned in Anacapri for six weeks; Mrs. Doolittle's diary reveals no signs that she was the least upset with her daughter's decision nor could she have been the least deluded about the intimacy of H.D.'s relationship with Aldington. Mrs. Doolittle regularly noted her correspondence with her daughter, and letters and postcards passed constantly between them throughout March and April of 1913. On May 4, Mrs. Doolittle wrote, "Ezra P.—looked for us—found us here [in Venice]—we came back to the hotel together—he had dinner with us—stayed until midnight." On May 5, "Ezra called this afternoon + had dinner again with us." The impression conveyed is that Pound was rather lonely. On May 7, H.D. and Aldington arrived in Venice, and during the next week they and Pound and the Doolittles spent time together; on May 8, "Ezra gave a gondola party this evening . . . wonderful! Hilda and Richard in one + E + I in another—back 11:30—" Professor Doolittle left for the Untied States on May 15. On May 21, Mrs. Doolittle was again devoting herself to her daughter's wardrobe: "Bought blue crepe for blouse for Hilda—have nearly finished it."

Aldington seems to have grown quite close to Mrs. Doolittle in late May and June. He and she and H.D. traveled together to attend a Bach festival at Verona on May 30, moving on from there to Lake Garda on June 4. On June 5, Mrs. Doolittle noted that she "Had a long row on lake with Richard"; on June 6, she was making and having a dressmaker make clothes for H.D.; on June 7, "Richard took me out boating"; on June 10, "after dinner Richard took us on the lake—moonlight + very beautiful—" On June 22, 1913, they left the lake for Verona, where Professor Doolittle met them on June 25; Aldington went with them partway, then continued on to Paris. On July 6, H.D. left her parents in the Alps for Paris; her mother commented, "I know H. will enjoy settling down for a little but we shall miss her."

The Doolittles went on to tour Switzerland, Austria, and Germany; Aldington and H.D. spent the rest of July together in Paris. After their return together to London in early August, they moved into separate flats at Churchwalk, Kensington: H.D. lived at Number 6, Aldington at Number 8; Pound lived at Number 10. The Doolittles arrived in London on September 4 and were greeted by H.D. and Aldington. Professor Doolittle soon became ill, however, and the Doolittles stayed in town only long enough to celebrate H.D.'s twenty-seventh birthday on September 10 before going on to Bournemouth, where it was thought Professor Doolittle could best recover. On September 19, Mrs. Doolittle recorded: "Eventful day. Richard and Hilda came for the day to talk about the future— Such a lovely time + I am happy for them both!" She added exuberantly that she felt "happy + peaceful!!"

On September 28, the Doolittles returned to London to "prepare for [H.D.'s] marriage." H.D. and her mother went shopping daily for "towels +c." and "to get Hilda's things together" (September 30, 1913). On October 18, 1913, in the presence of Pound and the Doolittles, Aldington and H.D. were married. Shortly after the wedding, her parents returned to the United States and the Aldingtons together moved into a flat of their own at 5 Holland Place Chambers; Pound soon moved, too, into a flat just across the hall.

Pound's intrusive presence during the Aldingtons' courtship and the early months of their marriage was disconcerting and sometimes awkward for them. The direct influence Pound had on H.D.'s formative work before 1908 was, like their engagement, long since over, and H.D. had grown into a poet in her own right. After the Greggs' departure for America in the autumn of 1911, she had begun regular and disciplined work on her poetry, spending daily hours reading in the British Library, starting on her translations as exercises in language, experimenting with free verse and classical material. A significant part of Aldington's and H.D.'s attraction for each other was their independently arrived at but shared ideas of poetry: its subjects, purposes, techniques, language, emotional effects. The many versions of Pound's initiation of imagism all suggest that when he read H.D.'s poems over the famous tea, they appeared new to him: he was apparently not familiar with them in earlier drafts, and his enthusiasm arose in part because of his genuine surprise at what he immediately claimed in his naming of H.D. and the movement as his own discovery and invention. It seems likely that he read Aldington's poems at the same meeting.[26]

The Aldingtons and Pound were active participants in the exhilarating literary ferment in this prewar period in London. Their many mutual friends—Ford Maddox Hueffer (later Ford), Violet Hunt, May Sinclair, Frank Flint, John Gould Fletcher, John Cournos, Brigit Patmore—contributed to the development of early modernist verse in the many informal discussions about art which occurred not only in tea shops but in Soho restaurants, at evening parties at Brigit Patmore's, and at each other's flats. Still, Aldington and H.D. were working together intimately in an atmosphere of mutual exchange and influence that was particularly important to them personally and to the shaping of their poetry. In his desire to direct and to control, and sometimes by his mere presence, Pound was an intruder. Aldington recalled in Life for Life's Sake that in the spring of 1912, "Ezra had been butting in on our studies and poetic productions, with alternative encouragements and the reverse, according to his mood,"[27] and H.D., too, remembered in End to Torment her disconcerted surprise when she discovered Pound examining the apartment across the narrow hall from the Aldingtons'; he was looking for a place to live with Dorothy Shakespear after their wedding: "I found the door [to the opposite flat] open one day before they were married, and Ezra there. "What—what are you doing?" I asked. He said he was looking for a place where he could fence with Yeats. I was rather taken aback when they actually moved in. It was so near." She added rather pointedly, "But we went soon after [in January 1915] to Hampstead. . . . After that we did not see much of Ezra and the Kensington group. . . ."[28]

Initially with Pound's help, but soon quite independently of him Aldington and H.D. established themselves as writers in these prewar years. The New Freewoman, owned and edited by Dora Marsden with help from Harriet Shaw Weaver, had become interested in imagism through Pound's influence. Rebecca West devoted an article to the movement in the issue of August 15, 1913; the next issue

(September 1, 1913) included poems by Aldington, H.D., and other imagist poets as well as an article by Hueffer ("On Poetry") and "In Meter," by Pound, in which he discussed Robert Frost's *A Boy's Will* and verse by D.H. Lawrence and Walter de la Mare. More of Aldington's poems appeared on September 15, and he began to write book reviews for *The New Freewoman* with the October 1 issue. Thereafter Aldington wrote topical articles on English life, new art, and modern literature. Pound also appeared as a regular writer of columns on art and poetry, and although H.D.'s work did not again appear in *The New Freewoman*, even three stories by Frances Gregg were published there on December 1, 1913. Aldington and H.D. had found in this periodical a very small but influential outlet for their ideas and work, and by the end of the year Aldington had carved out a place for himself on its staff.

In January of 1914, *The New Freewoman* changed its name to *The Egoist* and Aldington's name was listed as assistant editor on its masthead. Pound continued to exert influence at the paper, but his work came to appear here less and less often, and Aldington's regular reviews and translations begin to reveal his wide interests in continental (particularly French) and classical literature as well as in modernist writing. Poems by Aldington appeared in *Poetry* in January 1914; two poems by H.D. appeared there in February. In the same month, with Pound as editor, *Des Imagistes*, an anthology of imagist poetry, was published in the United States; Aldington and H.D. were well represented with several poems each.

The Aldingtons had come to know Amy Lowell, also represented in *Des Imagistes*, primarily through correspondence. By the spring of 1914 they were exchanging letters regularly, and Pound's control of the imagist movement as editor, advertiser, and general advocate was waning while his place in the Aldingtons' personal life was becoming increasingly cumbersome. In a letter in Aldington's hand but signed by both him and H.D., Aldington wrote to Amy Lowell that Pound lay on their couch and claimed he had "cerebral gout." Aldington added only half humorously, "Perhaps Ezra is a little cracked."[29] When Lowell visited London in the summer of 1914, she met the Aldingtons frequently and plans began for a second imagist anthology. Pound refused to participate, explicitly in reaction to Amy Lowell, whom he rejected out of hand on account of her corpulence, patrician Boston background, and inconsistently strong verse. Psychologically, Pound needed to maintain a control that true group effort denied, and he redirected his energies elsewhere with some superiority and hostility. Aldington points out additionally in *Life for Life's Sake* that Lowell "was fed up with Ezra. So were others."[30]

In fact, Aldington was chiefly in charge of the subsequent imagist anthologies that appeared in 1915, 1916, and 1917. While some of the contributors were American (Lowell, H.D., and Fletcher), most of the poets whose work appeared in these collections were either British (Aldington, Flint, and D.H. Lawrence) or were living in England at the time.[31] Through Amy Lowell, the Aldingtons met Lawrence in July of 1914, and their intellectual and personal friendship with him became important for both of them.

The Aldingtons' marriage seems to have been a good one in 1914 and 1915. They managed to extricate themselves in large measure from past relationships and to work and love together as a couple. H.D. became pregnant in August of 1914 and despite the war, Aldington did not feel immediately threatened: Britain had no military draft at the time. He published his first book of verse, *Images*, in 1915, and both he and H.D. turned more and more toward a rural life beyond the intense war atmosphere of London. They moved in January of 1915 from Kensington to a larger flat in Hampstead, and their letters to others during this period speak of frequent trips to "the country," generally to Surrey (where James Whitall had a house) or Rye (where Aldington's parents lived) or west toward Devon and Cornwall and the country Aldington had known affectionately in childhood. The new apartment in Hampstead also offered them more than a physical distance from central London. Aldington wrote to Amy Lowell on February 1, 1915: "We like it much better out here as we have a larger flat with a real bathroom & a kitchen. I surprise my useless American wife with my skill & accuracy in cooking potatoes & mending chairs—they are admirable avocations for clearing one's mind & in this clearer atmosphere, away from Kensington squabbles & intrigues I feel more hopeful. . . ."

In May, the Aldingtons' child was born dead, an extremely traumatic experience which continued to haunt them both for years. This was a pivotal time in their marriage and deserves attention at length not only in the context of the Aldingtons' immediate personal lives but in terms of the larger social events which were inextricably related to both H.D.'s and Aldington's understanding of the child's death and their relationship at this point.

Britain declared war against Germany on August 4, 1914, and the continental Europe with which Aldington identified himself—particularly France and Italy—became embroiled in battles whose horror soon outbalanced the instant patriotism and enthusiastic enlistment of huge numbers of men in the late summer. The Battle of the Marne occurred on September 5 through 12; First Ypres followed in October. The Germans bombed the Yorkshire coast on December 16; the first airship raid on England came on January 19, 1915. Aldington had no hallowed respect for British institutions nor any special political objection to Germany, but he felt an obligation to the other men of his generation who were fighting and dying. For Aldington the war would always be a personal experience, and although he had little in common with his fellow soldiers, he would always feel a deep bond of male companionship and respect beyond intellectual affinity with those who had participated in the First World War.

The declaration of war created a somewhat different situation for H.D. She loved her husband deeply and supported his responses to the war, but she was an American woman, and the United States would not enter the war for three more years. Like Aldington, she had no strong political feelings, but direct participation in the war was not for her as a woman either an opportunity or a direct threat. The possibility of returning to the States for the duration became a constant question intensified by her husband's conscription in 1916. Thus the war introduced tensions into their marriage, for it stressed their differences in nationality and gender; it also replaced the social and intellectual atmosphere of prewar London, which had nourished their relationship, with a political and military consciousness antithetical to both their natures but directly affecting them.

The first years of their companionship occurred during an era of feminist ferment to which both of them were sympathetic. Suffragette riots and demonstrations characterized the period, and the issue of votes for women came to a head early in 1912. The House of Commons rejected the franchise on March 28, 1912, and a second time on May 6, 1913. *The New Freewoman* was a clearly feminist paper which was not founded as a platform for early modernist literature but as a forum for feminist and related causes. *The New Freewoman*, like its predecessor in 1911, *The Freewoman*, and its successor *The Egoist*, published articles on birth control, female and male sexuality and sexual preference, childbirth, women's economic situation, free love, and the suffragette movement. These were all issues in the air and in the press, and H.D. and Aldington not only knew about them but characteristically responded to them in personal terms.

Years later, in one of his six novels, *Very Heaven*, Aldington reveals through a central character much like himself the effect of the feminism of this period on a man's notion of womanhood. The young Christ Heylin addresses the woman with whom he has fallen in love:

> "Let's admit that the attraction between us is a sexual one. If it weren't for our sex, we'd be no more than friends. It's the fact of sexual desire which compels us to seek each other, which gives us this sense of ecstatic happiness. I'm not going to fall into the common literary sublimation, and pretend to myself and you that I want you and adore you for something you're not. I don't want you to be a blessed damosel or even a sweet girl graduate in golden hair. You're not a violet by a mossy stone or one of the brightest stars in all the heavens. Under that pretty blue gown of yours is the naked body of a human woman. I rejoice in it. I'm glad you're a real woman, I want you as a woman. I know that you are exquisitely and wonderfully made of millions of cells, that your heart keeps them alive by beating blood to them, that there are subtle chemical processes in you, that you have periods, that you have a womb and ovaries and breasts. And all that is the true wonder, the real beauty, the miracle of wonders, that you are you!"[32]

This sort of awareness in all likelihood informed Aldington's attitudes toward sexuality and female identity in the early years of his marriage to H.D.; he was certainly no traditional or conventional male. The atmosphere of conformity and the impression of a nation in uniform encouraged both Aldington and H.D. to turn inward, to withdraw, to retreat. Neither had an affinity for large groups anyway; both could be aloof and shy, though they had good friends during these years: John Cournos was friendly with both of them, though particularly close to H.D., while Frank Flint became Aldington's intimate intellectual companion and confidante.

The baby's death resulted in a breakdown of the conventional unit of father, mother, and child and bonded H.D. and Aldington more intensely to each other as individuals who had shared a painful experience. They were both private people, but Aldington did write to Amy Lowell of their loss on May 21, 1915; after a paragraph about business matters, he confesses:

> I have been rather distressed, because Hilda was delivered of a little girl still-born, about 2. am. this morning. She (Hilda) was in a good nursing home & had an obstetrical specialist. I haven't seen the doctor, but the nurse said it was a beautiful child & they can't think why it didn't live. It was very sturdy but wouldn't breathe. Poor Hilda is very distressed, but is recovering physically.

The experience also made Aldington aware of how fragile H.D. could be. Her distress was natural, of course, but he sensed as well as shared her acute grief while realizing that he was somehow tougher, more able to handle emotional pain. From this point on in their relationship, Aldington assumed a role as protector not evident earlier. He was always a champion of H.D.'s poetry when she was more hesitant about its strengths, but now he became aware that she also sometimes needed someone as a buffer between her and the harshness of reality, the brutality of experience that could harm her more easily than it could him. By nature more practical and organized than she, he seems to have decided upon a conscious retreat from London into the country. When H.D. left the nursing home on June 11, they immediately drove to Surrey, not returning to London until late August. That winter, however, they gave up their flat in Hampstead and moved to Devonshire, where they remained until after Aldington entered the army.

Aldington had considered enlisting in the national wave of patriotism following Britain's declaration of war, but because of a hernia operation in 1908, which he mentioned to an induction officer enlisting men at a local armory, he was told that it was unlikely that he would be passed as medically fit to train with the first troops going abroad. This brief vision of military bureaucracy and masses of men milling about was sufficient to deter him in any event; for a short while, he still felt disposed to serve, but by December of 1914, he felt personally threatened and oppressed by the war atmosphere and wrote to Lowell on December 7:

> This war is killing us all, Amy. As Gourmont says our word is "wait"; but the daily waiting, the anxiety, the constant strain is making us all "old." Only just over four months! And those last four months seem immeasurably longer to me than all the

rest of my life. I cannot concentrate my mind for long enough on beautiful things to be able to write good poetry—there is too much at stake in Belgium and France for me to forget them long. For this is the great war, the war of democracy against autocracy, of the individual against the state, of the Anglo-Latin civilization against the Prussian, even of vers libre against academic meters! . . . If we lose I don't see the use of my going on with my work—logically I should have to become a professional soldier. So you see, I can't work well at present.

If 1915 was a transitional year during which the Aldingtons withdrew in large measure from the intensities of bohemian London and turned inward and toward each other, 1916 promised imminent conscription and more challenging changes in their situation. The war atmosphere may have threatened Aldington's creative powers, but actual combat would threaten his life. Many options, all disruptive, presented themselves: the Aldingtons both seriously considered going to the United States for the duration.[33] Aldington persuaded his father, then working as a minor official in the ministry of munitions, to try to get him immediately into officers' training, where impersonal army life might be less brutalizing, but his father could do little.[34] Aldington made a variety of legal arrangements granting H.D. power of attorney should he be wounded, declared missing in action, or killed, and wrote a will.[35] They debated whether he should enlist so as to have perhaps some choice in how he would serve, or wait until the eventual passage of the conscription act and take his chances.[36] H.D. considered leaving for Philadelphia alone when her husband entered the army; she feared the possible forced labor during which able women without families might be compelled to work in factories or otherwise support the war effort.[37]

In February of 1916, the Aldingtons moved from Hampstead to a small cottage in north Devon. They had little money, but found the country an escape of sorts. H.D. wrote to Amy Lowell: "You see, this war period, our *joint* income is about 3 pounds a week—we live here extremely comfortably on it." The pressures of war still intruded, however, and H.D. continues: "I can not write you what I think, feel + know about this terrible war. We are all weakened by this continual strain!" Before she closes, referring to her baby's death, she adds that she finds that things have been particularly stressful since she was "ill" the previous year.[38]

In March a draft of the Military Service Act of 1916 was passed; in May *Some Imagist Poets, 1916* appeared; on May 24 conscription of married men began. By June 1916 there were 1,400,000 British troops on an eighty-mile battlefield in France. With conscription imminent, Aldington accepted the inevitable, and in order to be with his friend Carl Fallas, "so that at least . . . [they each] should have someone to talk to,"[39] Aldington and Fallas enlisted together in late May as infantry privates in the Eleventh Battalion of the Devonshire Regiment. After a brief respite, he and Fallas were inducted in late June and sent to train in Worget Camp in Wareham, Dorset.

The period between February and June of 1916 was a particularly significant one for H.D.'s and Aldington's marriage. H.D. was recovering somewhat from the trauma of losing their child and was preparing her first volume of poems for publication; Constable accepted the book by the end of February, although because of paper shortages it did not appear until the fall. She and Aldington took long walks on the Devonshire hills, and in the spring and summer regularly swam naked with friends in a nearby stream. John Cournos frequently visited from London and introduced them to his acquaintances, Carl and Florence Fallas, who lived in the neighborhood. Both Aldingtons responded sensitively to the raw nature surrounding them and enjoyed the independence and freedom of rural life. They were writing poetry and working together on translations. There seems to have been an aura of abandon about these months as well as an atmosphere of impending doom; a sense of frivolity and danger; a combination of productive mental and physical exertion and self-indulgence. This period was the beginning of H.D.'s flirtatious letters to Cournos, in which she told him in turn how much she cared for her husband and how close she and Cournos were to each other spiritually and sensually. Aldington was alternately resigned and frantic. On the one hand he was concerned about H.D. and made practical plans for their present and future life; on the other he was no longer able to protect her from their impending separation or his own anticipated suffering.

While H.D. was fragile and easily emotionally shaken in that experiences often affected her unusually deeply and over a long period of time, she was also a perceptive woman of great intelligence whose good sense could often co-exist with, if it could not curb, her intense emotional responses. She was domestically impractical, a poor speller, and impulsive, and sometimes seemed to function on an airy plane that at best could be called "spiritual," at worst childish and irresponsible; but she was also an energetic and well-disciplined poet with a broad sense of humor and the intelligence to understand both people and ideas. She was stronger than those who tried to protect her sometimes thought she was; she could if necessary rise to the occasion that demanded her inner strengths.

Aldington, in contrast, was more practical, also intelligent but more assertive, firm, and clear about his convictions. The sensitivity and passionate joy he brought to experience were aspects of his character he tended to save for private and intimate sharing. He was vulnerable and capable of deep emotional responsiveness, but tended to cover his sensitivity with good humor, camaraderie, and hard work. He was tender and sensual, but preferred to shelter this part of his nature not out of concern for his public appearance but out of a sense of self-protection.

And he was young. At twenty-three he was literary editor of an influential journal, a poet whose work appeared regularly in America and England, co-editor of several anthologies of imagist verse, a budding literary critic and translator; he was a married man, ready to assume the responsibilities of fatherhood, and felt that everything he cared about would soon be destroyed or put in limbo for an indefinite period, perhaps never again to be recovered. Many of the lofty ideas he and H.D. shared about art and relationships seemed irrelevant or unrealizable in the world of 1916. They had always believed in "free love," in their own union as greater than any other relationship, even a sexual one, either could have. They were not prepared for the emotional havoc such naive ideas can create when put into action. People do dumb things under pressure, but if Aldington's affair with Flo Fallas during that spring and summer was foolish in retrospect, it was not merely impulsive; rather, it can be understood as an attempt to put into practice—as time seemed to be running out—an idea both he and H.D. were convinced was realistic and fair.

Aldington's attraction to Flo Fallas seems to have been almost exclusively sexual. Soon after he met her in March of 1916, he wrote to Frank Flint about how erotic she appeared to him, but he also shared his resolve not to sleep with her, feeling that such an act would disturb H.D.[40] By June he wrote Flint that he and Flo had twice consummated their attraction, but he was jocular, sharing with Flint his fleeting panic when the postman knocked at the Fallases' door while he and Flo were in bed together. He did not mention her again in letters to Flint; indeed a deep respect and love for H.D. are repeatedly conveyed. The affair was disturbing to H.D., but Aldington evidently did not consider his feelings for Flo Fallas so serious as his wife sometimes suspected them to be.

H.D.'s letters to John Cournos reveal her response. She was not initially hurt, but felt that if the affair with Flo were something that Aldington wanted or needed, then she approved. She did not at first consider it a serious attraction or a threat or a particularly disturbing fact. By the fall, however, she was fearful that perhaps it was a more serious relationship, although there was little evidence for this conclusion and Aldington assured her that her concern was unfounded. She wrote Cournos that Aldington had written to her: " 'Hang Flo & damn Carl. . . . For God's sake, love your Faun . . .' "[41]

Neither H.D. nor Aldington fully realized the repercussions an affair might have. It introduced further tensions into an already difficult situation and resolved nothing, although it did partially assuage some of Aldington's frustrations with the military by providing a fleeting distraction. While Aldington was apparently fairly open and he hoped clear with H.D. about his feelings for Flo Fallas, H.D. was more concerned than she felt she could let him know; she felt ironically that she had to protect him from the brutality of soldiering and war and serve as a peaceful, comforting, and inspiring center for him. She wanted to be supportive at a time when much of his identity was stripped from him. Their relationship was precious to them both, and the fact of Aldington's affair, with whatever feelings he may have had for Flo Fallas, faded away.

Army life was devastating to Aldington. He felt isolated from the other men, not superior so much as unbridgeably different. As a professional poet who managed to earn a living by exposing his soul in language and who shared his ideas and perceptions of literature and life with others through the relatively safe medium of the written word, scrubbing filthy floors and peeling potatoes was anesthetizing labor. The long hours of physical drill left little time or energy for reading or writing, and while he soon came to appear extraordinarily physically fit, he also seemed hurt and emotionally hollow. As he had anticipated in his letter to Amy Lowell, the army brutalized the poet in him. He wrote to Flint in July, "I am on the go from 5:30AM to 7PM & have only time for one note as a rule & that goes to H.D."[42] In the same month he wrote Cournos that he hoped by diligent work and perhaps through the influence of friends to gain a promotion that would keep him in England for further training. He continued only half jokingly: "There is just a chance; and I do want to live, for my own sake, of course, but also for H.D.'s. What would she do without me?"[43] Later in July in an undated letter he wrote Cournos again:

> Yesterday I had a horrible experience, which please don't tell H.D. In the morning I was down for Officers Mess Fatigue. I had to beat carpets, clean windows, polish forks and spoons and, worst of all, scrub floors. I don't mind scrubbing like tables & [?] which Carl [Fallas] and I do for our beat every morning. But at this fatigue I was put to scrub the stone floor of one of the filthiest kitchens I ever saw in my life. It was deep with grease, soot and mess of all kinds. The bucket was greasy & the scrubbing rags so unspeakably filthy & slimy that it made me nauseated to touch them and I shuddered every time I had to plunge my hand into the pail of loathsome, greasy water. For a while it broke me, old chap, and I'm not too ashamed to tell you that for a moment or two I just bent my head & sobbed. It was so bitter a humiliation, so sordid a Golgotha. . . . I am very glad that I am not an officer, very glad. It is so much better to be hurt than to hurt.
>
> Do please keep this from H.D. I wouldn't have her know for worlds. . . .

Aldington needed here to share his experience with one of the few people he now thought of as his close friends; the others were Frank Flint, Alec Randall (whom he had met at University College and who now worked in military intelligence) and H.D. Simultaneously, however, he wanted to hide his suffering from H.D., to protect her if he could, identifying himself with her, for he would have avoided his own pain if it had been possible. What he could not avoid himself, he could at least try to prevent from hurting H.D. He continued to feel overwhelmingly reduced by the military experience. He wrote to Cournos on August 14, 1916:

> You must try to forgive my silence. On weekdays I have so little energy after work that I can only write one letter & that nearly always goes to H.D. . . .
> . . . don't, *don't* let yourself be shoved into this. Better retire to U.S. for 6 months or so, than get this soul-destroying mechanism on to you.

Aldington was always closer to Amy Lowell than was H.D., although he often found her presumptuous and overbearing, and he even confided in her during this period. On June 30, he wrote her of his entry into the army: "I am afraid poor Hilda is very lonely without me; I feel the separation very keenly." In August he wrote: "H.D. has been truly wonderful; her affection and unselfish devotion have been the prop of my existence." He thanked her for a recent letter which "helped me to get through a hard day"; he told her that there was much about the details of his life that he felt he could not share with her because of military security, but he reiterated his desolation amid army routine, concluding:

> I look at the flowers of a wild rose which grows in the hedge of a field at the far end of the camp. There is still much for me—clouds, rain and sky, distant hills and trees, the early morning sun & the quiet twilight, red poppies & yellow daisies in a deserted corner of the camp—and on Saturday & Sunday afternoon, the wild flowers & scent and deep peace of country lanes. These things are poignant in their beauty, so exquisitely indifferent to humanity, as, perhaps, a poet must be![44]

H.D. also confided in Lowell her feelings about her husband's military experience and its affect on him and their relationship. On July 31, 1916, she wrote, "You cannot imagine how starved he is—how eager for news of people and books." In August H.D. confessed that when Aldington visited her during his weekends off, "it is hard for me to face his tragic eyes alone!"[45] On October 13, H.D. wrote, "let me thank you again for placing R.'s work for him. You can not realize what this means to him—and as my one struggle is to make him feel he is not being forgotten, is not dropping out of the world, (our world) you can hardly over-estimate my sense of gratitude to you." H.D. was more open with John Cournos about her feelings and Aldington's adjustment to the military. After a weekend visit from her husband, H.D. wrote:

> It is curious and wonderful and tragic to watch his developement [sic]. One thing is sure: he has not been hurt by all this brutal regime—only at first, it was terrible—his eagerness and his fear to speak of books, of people, of the beauty we all love. And last night was terrible—the rending, as it were, of spirit & flesh— but this morning he was calm and beautiful—and said he knew now he could come back to life—that he wouldn't lose his hold. He had hallucinations at first—I think his suffering must have been awful. But I feel I have given him hope again—and he cares so intensely, so deeply that his very love may help him to live—may bring him back. . . . I have suffered so in imagination that perhaps this agonny [sic] of mind has recalled—redeemed as it were my own sanity—Richard's beauty.[46]

H.D. and Aldington felt deep respect and affection for each other, but they also psychically seem to have identified themselves each with the other, almost sym-biotically equating their experiences and emotional and spiritual selves. For ex-ample, on August 4, 1916, H.D. wrote Cournos that she had beside her "a beautiful letter of Richards [sic] which has given me great hope"; she quoted from it at length: " 'The world, the great herd of men hates beauty; we who love beauty can but die for it, or live, if necessary. The world, our world, is beautiful, but if we are the Sampadaphoroi (tourch bearers [sic]) we must be equal to the least soldier who dies at his post. Yours is a great task . . . be strong, swift and brave; there is no hope but be strong.' " At about the same time she noted in an un-dated letter to Cournos, "It is hard for me to face this spiritual loneliness of R. alone." On August 9, she wrote:

> R. seems to grow spiritually stronger—we must be patient, very patient and tender. He is strange and even with me closed into himself—and then suddenly some curious feeling, some intense longing, some little sign of affection. He is *born*, but at times not conscious of his spirit—and he suffers when we think him indif-ferent or merely glad!— He says at first he cried, desperate tears, when he looked over toward Corfe Castle [in the town where H.D. was staying]— He is like a wounded animal:— He is like some great, beautiful, clean, sensual beast, captured galled with chains.—

In another undated letter at about the same time, H.D. wrote explicitly to Cour-nos about her relationship with Aldington: "With R. I feel older, mature, not maternal, I hope, but mature, ready to help, desirous only to obliterate myself if my help is not wanted! I feel him Greek and masculine and intellectual and strong and perhaps at times cruel. I feel him very passionate and terribly sad, and in the midst of a new growth which is tearing and causing him pain."

The Aldingtons lived these difficult months at a high emotional pitch, and their experience was intensified by their proximity and frequent visits during the summer and fall of 1916. Called up at the end of June, Aldington was sent for initial training to Wareham in Dorset. Within a few weeks, H.D. gave up Wood-land Cottage, Martinhoe, Parracombe, in north Devon, where the Aldingtons had been living since February of 1916, and in July took rooms in the town of Corfe Castle to be near her husband. She stayed in the small village in the shadow of the ruined twelfth-century fortress into the fall. Because he efficiently performed his military duties, Aldington was selected for additional training as a noncommissioned officer; he was reprieved from the trenches for a few additional weeks and so did not go to the continent in August as he had first anticipated. After the six-day leave following his basic training, which he and H.D. spent in London,[47] he went to a camp near Manchester in mid-September for further training while H.D. returned to Corfe Castle, where Aldington later also re-turned to complete his training.

H.D. analyzed at length her relationship with her husband in the letters she wrote to Cournos during the fall of 1916. This correspondence conveys clearly the tensions and intimacy of the Aldingtons' marriage. Her self-analysis is impor-tant, too, for it reveals the complex personality to which Aldington was responding in his later letters. On September 13, 1916, H.D. wrote: "I have faith in my work. What I want at times is to feel faith in my self, in my mere physical presence in the world, in my personality. I feel my work is beautiful, I have a deep faith in it, an absolute faith. But sometimes I have no faith in my own self."[48] In an undated letter written in the same month, she described her husband as "a golden, clear naked Greek," and on October 3 she stated that "Richard is the very core of my life." Yet in an undated letter in the early fall she acknowledged the tensions between them: "I am often unhappy to think that my complicated nature has led R. to think I am unhappy"; she continued, "I seem to have separated love and peace in my mind."[49] Despite the Aldingtons' love and respect for each other, H.D. felt that she was not always communicating clearly with her husband while he, in turn, was sometimes confused by her. On October 16, H.D. wrote to Cournos that she felt torn between "a sort of beautiful serenity" and "that miserable hypersensitive[,] nerve-wracked, self-centered self." During late September and October, the Aldingtons seem to have become more physically intimate. The affair with Flo Fallas appears to have subsided by mid-September after the Aldingtons' visit to London during his leave. If they had not been sleeping together at the height of the affair during the summer of 1916, it would seem that they were now sexually close to each other. It was during late September that H.D. found her husband a "naked Greek," "masculine," and "very passionate"; she wrote to Cournos with coy humor on October 16: "R. writes he can only come in the afternoon for the present—a new rule—but hopes to have the 'sleeping out' granted again later!"

As Aldington neared the end of his training as a noncommissioned officer, H.D. became briefly ill and her letters to Cournos were disjointed and visionary. On October 31, she wrote that she saw people as colors; on November 1, she stated, "I know R. will die or else something in him will die," and insisted that she had seen "his god, his Daemon." In an undated letter from this time in which she mentions her illness, she compared Aldington to Jesus Christ while simultaneously identifying herself with her husband. She mentioned considering going to America, but added, "I feel now if I leave England, something in him will break."

Once Aldington was definitely slated to go to France and H.D. had made the decision to remain in England, once she had decided to move to London, a resigned acceptance and comparative peace evidently resulted. There is a gap in her correspondence with Cournos at this point, perhaps because she was seeing him often, for he soon took an apartment above hers, but when the letters resume at the end of 1917, H.D. was no longer so open with him and no longer used her letters to him confessionally. The tone of her letters and her relationship with him had changed.

The emotional and physical instability of H.D.'s life seems at this point to have depended in large measure on Aldington's military situation, but a new stage in both their lives was about to conclude this rough period of transition. In December H.D. moved into rooms at 44 Mecklenburgh Square,[50] a flat she was to keep throughout 1917 and into the summer of 1918. By December 8 Aldington had been promoted to lance corporal[51] and on December 21 he was shipped overseas.[52] He spent the last week of 1916 in a tent at a base camp two miles from Calais. For the first half of 1917 he served in a pioneer battalion on the Lens–La Bassée front, billeted most of the time about 2,000 yards from Loos.[53]

The winter and spring of 1917 were a relatively calm period for the Aldingtons despite—or perhaps even because of—their separation from each other. The months of military training in 1916 had been particularly difficult because of a duality in the Aldingtons' lives. Understandably reluctant to give up their earlier intimacy and literary work, both Aldington and H.D. attempted to maintain two lives at once: during the week Aldington was a soldier while on duty, but in the brief free evening hours, on weekends, and during his longer leaves in the early fall and before he left for France, he tried to maintain or resume his former life. When he was called up in June, his name—now with the addition of H.D.'s—continued to appear as assistant editor on the masthead of The Egoist; not until June of 1917, long after H.D. had in fact assumed all of her husband's responsibilities on the paper, did Aldington relinquish the title. At that time, deeply involved with her own writing, H.D. was finding the task too demanding, and at Harriet Shaw Weaver's suggestion, both gave up the position to T.S. Eliot.[54]

Aldington tried to maintain old patterns as well as to begin new intellectual projects during the summer and fall of 1916, but the demands on his time and stamina were overwhelming. He found it difficult to write more than one letter a day; in an undated letter, H.D. wrote to Cournos that at camp Aldington "only gets about ten minutes to read after they are in bed." Aldington took with him to Wareham in June a volume of Heine's poetry, intending to pursue his German, the weakest of his many languages, at a time he felt ironically appropriate. The book was confiscated in suspicious horror by his commanding officer.[55] On October 1, 1916, he wrote to Amy Lowell and enclosed "several poems which register various moods of depression or otherwise," and he customarily mentioned to her their ongoing work on the last imagist anthology of this period, which appeared in 1917. H.D., too, wrote to Lowell at length about the business of the anthology, and she was working hard as well on her own poetry, which she regularly shared with her husband as she wrote. Her long poem "The Tribute," for example, was written in the early autumn of 1916.

Personally, the Aldingtons were naturally unable to establish a clear or predictable life together in late 1916. They saw old friends: Flint and his family were living that summer in Swanage on the coast near Corfe Castle; on October 1 Aldington wrote Lowell that they saw John Gould Fletcher and his wife in London during his September leave; both Aldingtons wrote affectionate letters to Cournos during this time. On October 4, H.D. also wrote Lowell that "we see

Lawrence occasionally. He seems very ill." But Aldington was concerned about H.D. and resurrected the plan of her going to America, where she would be safer and life more stable. Ironically, the plan to leave England merely further disrupted their lives. H.D. wrote to Lowell on November 3, 1916: "I may be returning to the U.S. in a few weeks. . . . I am packing etc. R. has received promotion [to corporal] + may be moved any time. He begs me to leave England—" Yet nine days later on November 12 she wrote Lowell again: "I do not know my plans from week to week. I had made all arrangements to return when R. found he would be kept on in England for a time at least. I will stay in England as long as he does though I am not able to see him as before." Their frequent visits and subsequent separations at the end of afternoons or weekends together were emotionally wrenching for them both. In December Aldington was evidently no longer in Dorset, but had been shifted for yet additional training and to wait shipment abroad. On December 8 he wrote Lowell that "H.D. won't know I've gone till I'm 'across'—I think it kinder to spare her the tedium of another parting." Yet even this plan did not work out: on December 21 H.D. wrote Lowell, "I am waiting at Waterloo to say goodbye to R. He leaves England to-night."

The atmosphere of the last half of 1916 was further intensified by the news from France. The war was not going well for the Allies. The Battle of the Somme officially began on July 1 and continued through November 18, 1916, with heavy casualties and slight gains. Trench warfare was well established and news of its horrors was reported daily. With the institution of conscription in May, the home population in Britain became even more aware of the war effort with its routine intrusion into their lives. By the beginning of 1917, it was clear that the war would last for a long time. Bread rationing began throughout the United Kingdom on February 2, while the United States did not declare war on Germany until April 6, and American troops did not actually land in France until the end of June 1917.

After Aldington's departure for the front in December of 1916, H.D. was able to settle back into a life of relative calm despite the deprivations of war. The first half of 1917 she spent in London, seeing friends (D.H. Lawrence, Cournos, Fletcher) and writing. Aldington in his turn settled into life at the front, finally adjusting somewhat to the inevitable routine and labor of the military machine. The relationship became an epistolary one, shifting of necessity into the realm of the written word, where each felt comfortable and probably more in control of their life together than during their unpredictable meetings and separations of the previous year. On January 24 H.D. wrote Lowell, "I hear from R. often." Aldington wrote to Cournos on February 9, "I go on from day to day, living spiritually on letters," and to Flint on February 22, "know that I respect *always* poems & H.D.'s letters."

Aldington also, however, managed to continue to achieve some literary work during periods when he was not actually in the trenches. In a typical month, a soldier in the British Expeditionary Forces served four days in "the front line" (the first of three parallel lines of trenches), four days in "support" (a short distance behind in the second row of trenches), eight days in "reserve" (in the third line of trenches), and the remainder in "rest" (usually at a large base camp a march of fifteen miles and a train trip of about forty miles from the trenches).[56] The Pioneer Corps, in which Aldington served in 1917, "was a relatively low-stress environment";[57] his duties involved digging and repairing trenches, preparing graves, and making the numerous crosses to put on them.[58] So while Aldington was constantly within earshot of artillery and the threat of bombardment, he enjoyed some leisure since, at least for the first months of 1917, little military action occurred in the Cambrai and La Bassée area, where he was stationed.[59] The Battle of Arras began with a British attack on April 9, and Aldington was directly involved in an area midway between La Bassée and Cambrai, but much of the fighting on the western front occurred to the south during this period, near Reims in Champagne (from April 16 through May 7) or to the north at the Third Battle of Ypres, also known as Passchendaele (between July 31 and mid-November, 1917).

Aldington wrote with some pride to Flint about his literary work on November 19, 1916: "I've written 12 poems & 3 essays [in the five months] since I've been in the army." H.D. comments on his mood and his writing in a letter to Lowell on March 4, 1917: "He is quite happy in a philosophical way and doing more work than he has had for some time"; on March 29 H.D. wrote that she was working on putting together a volume of Aldington's poems and assured Lowell that "R. is cheerful + managing to do a little writing between guns. He is seeing a good deal of the terrible side of things, but keeps his head and is very fine about it all." Aldington's letters to Cournos during the first half of 1917 frequently concern literary matters; on February 2 he writes that "there is only one's work & one's friends as a consolation in these worse than dark ages!" On February 14, he wrote Cournos again in the same vein: "I rather welcome the idea of getting out another book myself" and encouraged Cournos and H.D. in the project to select the best of his poems from "the 3 [imagist] anthologies & all my m.s.s & stuff published in mags. &c."

The military experience, however, was grim, and Aldington endured the life of the average British Tommy with a forbearance that was a mixture of humor and resentment. The tone of protest that characterizes Aldington's retrospective treatment of the army in *Death of a Hero* and in *Life for Life's Sake* is echoed in the memoirs of many British veterans.[60] In *Death's Men: Soldiers of the Great War*, Denis Winter generalizes about the soldiers' response to the military machine, a response that Aldington certainly shared:

> Faced with the impossibility of sustaining dignity in a situation so often degrading, most accepted the official line and compensated with that sad or boisterous humor and vulgarity which pretended that such an acceptance did not matter since it did

not touch the real man and related only to a temporary and unimportant phase of the man's life-span.[61]

So long as Aldington felt that the war would indeed end within a period of months and so long as he could insist on his identity as a poet-critic through literary work and reading, he was able to maintain a relatively good-humored equilibrium. Years later Walter Lowenfels would recall this aspect of Aldington's psychology, remarking that "he was brave enough never to tout [sic] ammunition in his gun at the front in World War I, refusing (he once told me in Paris, 1930) to participate in that massacre—a secret he never shared with his fellow officers, being there, as he was, when he was one of the pre-war Imagist poets, part of the ever-young avant garde movement of his youth."[62] Aldington's first months in France in 1917 reveal this phase of his response.

The experience of military life was indeed degrading. Clothing in the line was worn at least a week at a time, and "food supplies were too little, erratic, dull and unbalanced."[63] The soldier was also regularly exposed to the weather: bitter cold in winter, deep mud during the seasonal changes, heat and dust in summer. Soldiers were reduced to occupying themselves with elementary and life-sustaining chores, seeking animal comforts when possible and writing home. Aldington scraped and burned lice from the seams of his uniform; ate the cold tinned beef, occasional warm stew, and bread and jam that were the soldier's staple fare; shaved in cold and dirty water shared with others in his area of the trenches; avoided the latrines whenever possible as locations the Germans soon discovered and frequently aimed at. He suffered the digestive ailments of his diet and the standard intestinal and influenza infections rampant at the front. Amid the other odors of the trenches, mustard gas was difficult to detect and, with the stronger chlorine and phosgene gases, was a constant threat. The bronchial difficulties from which Aldington suffered for the rest of his life are surely attributable to his frequent encounters with gas, though he was never incapacitated by a gas attack just as he was never wounded. Like other soldiers, Aldington discovered that the quickest and the most immediately effective response to a gas attack was often not the gas mask but a piece of clothing (a glove, a vest) soaked with urine and pressed to one's face.

The literary work and reading Aldington was able to do while in France boosted his spirits in early 1917, and despite months in the army, he was still a fresh combatant for whom military experience at the front was somewhat new. The efficient British postal system kept him in close contact with H.D. and the few friends he had time to write. Denis Winter notes the impressive operation of the mails: "Letters and parcels from home were received with equal regularity. Nothing ever took longer than four days, even though name and regiment were the only permitted addresses. . . . mail was delivered punctually even in the very front line, where it would come up on top of the ration sandbag."[64]

Aldington's comparative good humor was bolstered by the possibility of a commission as well. By May 8 he wrote Cournos that he had completed all the necessary paperwork involved in the application and was eagerly awaiting orders to return to England for officers' training. Many infantry soldiers put in as much as a year at the front without home leave; Aldington would depart for England in early July, after six months in France, for an extensive period of training, followed by a long leave and additional training before he returned to the front in the spring of 1918.

H.D. remained Aldington's primary concern and intimate correspondent throughout the first half of 1917. About to leave for France on December 20, 1916, Aldington wrote to Cournos, "Please look after H.D. in my absence. Try to cheer her up." On the same day he wrote to Flint, "Look after H.D. won't you?" Well aware that he might be killed at the front, he masked the seriousness of his situation with jocularity in a letter to Lowell on January 4, 1917: "If I get flipped, you'll give an eye to H.D. won't you? She is my chief concern & if it were not for her I should enjoy this experience immensely." In contrast, Aldington also fantasized about a time after the war when he and H.D. could again travel to Italy together in sensual escape. He shared this idea with Flint on January 29, 1917, imagining wandering about Rome "with H.D. whose gusto for antiquities fits in gloriously with mine." H.D. was writing poems for a second volume of verse and busy with *Egoist* work, but Aldington was concerned that she not feel too keenly his absence, which might become permanent. On January 22 he wrote to Flint to amplify what he had meant earlier in asking his friend to look after his wife:

> For the Lord's sake don't interrupt H.D. if she is having a good time with anyone— when I said "Look after H.D." I meant help her to have a good time & not bother about me. I didn't want to make you a kind of Argus! Take H.D. out if you can, to theatres, & get her to meet new & amusing people. And if you can devise any sort of "affaire" pour passer le temps, so much the better.

Aldington missed H.D. deeply, yet felt impotent in the relationship from the imposed distance and deprivation; the sums she received as a soldier's dependent seemed embarrassingly small to him, and he regularly sent her additional money from his own pay. He felt that she needed him financially, emotionally, intellectually, and sexually, and that he could not in his present situation satisfy her needs. He tried to encourage others, vague and specific, to fulfill his former roles, and simultaneously felt an exclusive and intense connection with her. On May 3, 1917, he wrote Cournos about his anticipated homecoming for officers' training:

> I want you to break this tactfully to H.D., so she can make all due preparations for the event. I had an idea that I'd just stroll into 44 & say "Hullo," but it occurs to me that the shock might be too horrible even for the most affectionate spouse.

. . . I would like to see you and H.D. when we arrive. . . . Please don't tell *anyone* but H.D. I don't want to see *anyone* for a couple of days. . . . tell H.D. as quietly as possible, so as not to over-excite her. . . .

When Aldington returned from the front in early July, 1917, he was sent immediately to a camp at Lichfield near Birmingham for a short period of reassignment before several weeks' leave. While he was eager to come "home" to 44 Mecklenburgh Square, he was also eager for time alone with H.D., and she joined him for a few weeks, taking a room at Brocton, a village about twelve miles northwest of Lichfield. This was an idyllic time for them both: a reprieve from anxiety about the physical dangers of war, an escape from London and the impinging acquaintances of the city's literary life, an interlude between the trenches and the next phase of their relationship. Ironically, the calm on the western front that had characterized the first half of 1917 abruptly ended soon after Aldington left France, and news of the "big push" of the Third Battle of Ypres began at the end of July and continued through late October when, amid appalling carnage, British troops reached Passchendaele, and into mid-November, when the battle finally concluded. The atmosphere of Aldington's leave and training period in England was one of brief escape, limited reprieve from devastation. Aldington and H.D. both knew that he would return to the front, but unlike their anticipation of the previous summer, now they also knew from direct experience what this return would mean for them, and the knowledge threatened and unsettled them both.

By late July Aldington had left Lichfield for a few weeks' leave, which he spent with H.D. in London. He looked after some matters of literary business, writing on July 21 to Edmund R. Brown of the Four Seas Company in Boston, which eventually published two collections of his war poetry in 1919 and 1921, and on July 29 and August 4 to Martyn Johnson, editor of *The Dial*, which began to publish his series of six articles, entitled "Letters to Unknown Women" on March 14, 1918. Aldington and H.D. attended a party given by "Ezra Pound and his satellites"[65] and saw T.S. Eliot, who appeared to H.D. "very nice—very quiet + not at all the sort E.P. usually gets hold of."[66] Yet these busy summer weeks in town seemed awkward to the Aldingtons.

Like most men back from the front, Aldington felt disconnected from civilian life, oddly different from other people not directly involved in the war, somewhat resentful of their ongoing ordinary life, the continuity and apparent independence of their experience while his own was disrupted and at the mercy of the military. H.D., too, identifying herself with her husband, was consciously distancing herself from the literary life she had known. On August 10, she wrote Amy Lowell that imagism was essentially over and the poets who once called themselves "Imagists" were developing in different directions; of her own verse she wrote, "I, too, am going through a transition." On September 19 she wrote to Lowell that she had earlier been discouraged about her writing, "but with R. back again + you still keeping my memory green, I am tempted to have another fling!" She continued to try to define their separation from London and their former friends: "We are rather out of touch with things in London." She objected that Pound "seems untouched by all the realities that are torturing us all." She noted their separation from *The Egoist* now that they were no longer editors, insisting that "we are on quite friendly terms with all these people but think it best to lie fallow a bit." On November 14 she confided in Lowell: "I don't *really* feel friendly with E.P. nor does R.—he just does not matter." While Aldington enjoyed the conviviality of old friends in London in July, H.D. continued, "we don't really care— and, in sober mood, on our return to town, do not expect to see that gang at all."

Aldington left London in late July for the camp at Lichfield to begin his officers' training course. H.D. soon took rooms off the market square in the nearby town, where she remained except for occasional visits to London until he was commissioned on November 28. This period of rural retreat was in many ways restorative to both of them. H.D. returned to her poetry with renewed energy, spending the weeks peacefully alone and welcoming her husband each weekend. Aldington enjoyed this time of predictable routine, and wrote in relative good humor to Amy Lowell on November 18, 1917: "All my time is taken up at the Officers' Training School, and the week-end, when I do get away, is too delightfully lazy for me to spoil with writing." But this concern about his creative work was a problem for Aldington that would persist throughout the war, and he discussed it at length with Lowell here:

All writing is distasteful if one is without leisure—for one must have time to live. . . . I cannot write as I could once, though I have captured a certain stern ideality, have regained a serenity by leaving any kind of journalism or publicity for the anonimity [*sic*] of my present life. After all in the general futility of things it matters very little whether I use my superfluous energies to write poems or to make stories and tales & jokes for the soldiers ("rough men" as The Little Review in its daintiness calls them) who are my companions.

But don't think that I haven't ambition or the desire to make beautiful things. I have lost a great deal, I am handicapped in ways you cannot imagine, but this abrupt withdrawal from the rapid current of my life into something alien & painful may, perhaps, be as salutary for me as prison for the author of De Profundis! One sees the importance of the "literary life" and the supreme importance of literature, the one imperishable record of the human soul, the means of multiplying personality, the expression of destiny.

Most of the things I thought about poetry two years ago I still think; but in the present pause in my intellectual life I am not sure whether it is the final pause or a period preceding intense creation. In any case I do not complain. . . .

Aldington in officer's uniform, probably taken in
London in late 1917 or early 1918.

In the same important letter, Aldington recounted biographical information Lowell had requested and concluded with a reaffirmation of his intimacy and identi-
fication with H.D.: "Hueffer, Yeats & Lawrence have all taught me something,
but apart from any personal feelings, H.D.'s poetry is the only modern English
poetry I really care for. Its austerity, its aloofness, its profound passion for that
beauty which only Platonists know, make it precisely the kind of work I would
like to do myself, had I the talent."

The war's power to damage Aldington's creativity drove him closer to H.D.
and encouraged him to emphasize her spiritual and artistic sensibilities, the elements of her nature which seemed to him to transcend his traumatic and reduc-
tive experiences in the military. Her art, as evidenced in his letter to Lowell,
became particularly precious to him as he turned more and more to translation in

the last year of the war. Aldington was also to a degree suffering from the shell shock which would make him especially emotionally sensitive after demobilization in 1919. He wrote to Flint on September 7, 1917, sharing his pleasure that H.D. was staying in Lichfield "only 3 miles from here. She has a room in the Place de la Ville overlooking the statues of Boswell & Johnson. . . . Each weekend I get a sleeping out pass. . . ." He qualified his joy, however: "I think I shall just lie down and sob if I get into another artillery barrage." For all these reasons, the Aldingtons seem to have been particularly close during these months away from London. In March of 1917 D.H. Lawrence had written to Amy Lowell that he found H.D. "very sad and suppressed" in her letters to him;[67] the calm and restraint of the first half of 1917 was replaced in Lichfield with healthy if serious reflection and some joy. The period probably fulfilled H.D.'s expectations when she wrote to Flint at the end of August that she was looking forward to moving to Lichfield. She was gathering books to take with her and wrote that her husband was "doing very well—but I am sick of single blessedness!"[68]

While away with Aldington in the Midlands, H.D. had kept her apartment in Mecklenburgh Square, but it had not been vacant. Dorothy Yorke (known to her close friends as "Arabella"), an American woman whom John Cournos had courted unsuccessfully in the United States before the war, had arrived in London in the late summer of 1917. She and her mother had been touring in France, living in Paris, were compelled to leave because of hostilities, and now were casting about for lodgings in England.[69] The city was flooded with war workers and country people seeking employment because with millions of men missing, dead, or fighting at the front, maintaining the family farm or local shop was sometimes impossible; accommodations were naturally in short supply. When H.D. left for Lichfield she wrote Flint that "a beautiful lady has my room."[70] Throughout September Cournos, still in the upper apartment at Number 44, resumed his courtship, but in early October he left London as a translator and journalist with the Anglo-Russian Commission to Petrograd. Although the intimate relationship with Yorke which he sought had evidently not been realized, he left with the apparent understanding that H.D. would watch over his friend in his absence. In late October D.H. and Frieda Lawrence moved into H.D.'s large room and Yorke moved into Cournos's smaller one upstairs.

The Lawrences, like the Aldingtons in 1916, had been seeking refuge in the country during the war. Living in Cornwall since March of 1916, in October of 1917 they were staying in a cottage at Zennor near St. Ives. A friend of theirs, the young London music critic Cecil Gray, had taken a neighboring cottage, Bosigran, and joined them in Cornwall in the summer of 1917. They saw a good deal of one another, and after singing German songs one night with a light shining from their window, the Lawrences were compelled by the local police to leave the coastal area under suspicion as spies. When the Lawrences arrived precipitously in London, they moved temporarily into Mecklenburgh Square.[71]

When the Aldingtons returned to London at the end of November, the Lawrences moved in with Cecil Gray's mother at 13b Earl's Court Square, where they
stayed until December 18; they then moved on to Berkshire, where by January
they had settled into a cottage at Hermitage owned by Lawrence's friend, Dollie
Radford.[72]

Aldington had a month's leave before he was sent first to a camp at New
Haven, then to Tunbridge Wells where he was stationed until he finally left for
France in mid-April of 1918. He had several "short leaves" in the first months of
the new year and spent them in London. This period was a tumultuous one.
Immediately after he left London on December 28, 1917, Aldington wrote to
Flint and reflected on his changes in attitude since entering the army:

> I didn't say much when you told me that you had to go into the army, but,
> believe me, I felt & feel it very much. There are many things I'd like to say to
> you, but don't know how. I wish I could save you many inevitable pangs, some of
> which you cannot foresee. Yet, in a strange way, I believe the miseries and depri-
> vations and melancholies you will undergo, will benefit you as they have benefitted
> me.
>
> Dear boy, you are sensitive and quickly wounded, proud and a poet—do you
> need any further composition for misery? I know you will feel most bitterly the
> separation from those who are dear to you. They will not understand your isolation
> & your pain, & it will seem to you as if your friends have forgotten you. Time,
> which passes so cruelly & monotonously for the soldier, passes swiftly for them.
> But you will have compensations. You will feel the implacability of destiny, the
> hard reality of war—wh. no civilian can know—you will have the spiritual gain of
> suffering, of a disruption of your life, of severed affections, of lost leisure. You will
> realise then how much you now enjoy. And also you will come to hate and perhaps
> to love men, as never before. With death imminent & threatening you will find
> courage to support terror, & in the gaps of liberty allowed you to grasp at life with
> a zest you never before had. Rosy, not legal life, will tempt you!
>
> Perhaps, things will be very different for you. Certainly your psychology will
> not immediately & exactly follow mine, as I have sketched it for you. But, when
> you do go, remember, if you feel lonely and betrayed by life, that I shall under-
> stand, as perhaps no one else, & can sympathise.

H.D. wrote Cournos on December 28, 1917, that she felt quite unsettled: "I
cannot work these days. . . . R.'s very fine—but so broken at going away—"
Aldington was also concerned about H.D.'s attitude toward her work and wrote
Amy Lowell on January 2, 1918, that

> unfortunately she has burned some most poignant lyrics and a long poem of about
> 10,000 words. I can't forgive her for it, but she said she thought them inadequate!
> The long poem—such as I saw of it—had beautiful passages. But she is so relentless.
> I think she has grown very much spiritually. Everything she writes has now that

sure touch which seems to me immortal—the arrangement of simple poignant words in an absolutely original way yet perfectly inevitable, so that one wonders why one has not thought of it oneself. But she is frightfully reserved—I had to beseech her for hours to prevent her burning a lot more!

The atmosphere at Mecklenburgh Square during that December in London was extremely tense. Aldington met Arabella and immediately responded to her sexually, beginning an affair with H.D.'s knowledge that was consummated not only in Cournos's former flat but in the Aldingtons' own bed curtained off at one end of H.D.'s large room. As with Aldington's affair with Flo Fallas in 1916, H.D. seems to have been initially accepting, then upset: depressed, exasperated, and anxious. Her destruction of poetry on which she had been working for months and her husband's pleading with her at length to preserve it suggest H.D.'s self-doubt and frustration as well as Aldington's guilt and powerlessness. The Christmas season did not calm the turbulent climate but rather intensified the pain of Aldington's imminent departure: the irony of holiday celebration seemed at best ridiculous, at worst pathetic. The Lawrences and Cecil Gray were frequent visitors and did little to assuage the rising tensions. Lawrence quarreled with his wife, sometimes affectionately, often pointedly. Gray and Frieda Lawrence were sexually attracted to each other, but the height of their passion had evidently passed and Gray shifted his attentions to H.D. Lawrence and H.D. felt an artistic bond with one another as fellow artists who responded instinctively to spiritual aspects of experience, but despite H.D.'s sense of erotic chemistry between them, Lawrence's personal reserve prevented any sexual consummation of the relationship.[73]

Additionally, both H.D. and Aldington knew that their good friend John Cournos would be angry with them, as indeed he was, when he returned from Petrograd in early April of 1918. H.D. suggested the persistent tensions at Mecklenburgh Square when she wrote to Cournos on January 25, 1918:

> Things are strange here . . . Dorothy is *quite* well & happy & working. You need not fear for her. . . . R. has not yet had orders—is waiting in England. But far from London.
>
> I may go to Cornwall for a little while. But will return the moment you write you may come back.

She did not tell him about her husband's ongoing affair with Dorothy Yorke, nor any details of the visit to Cornwall that she was considering. A week later she reiterated her intentions and reassurances, but was no more specific: on February 2, she wrote, "I want to go to Cornwall & live very, very quietly for some time. I feel I can *work* there. . . . D. is quite well—is busy & seems happy."[74]

With her husband's lover living upstairs; with Miss Elinor James, the landlady, quite displeased with the goings on in her house; with Aldington occasionally home on short leaves and weekends; and with Gray urging her to come away with him, H.D. was unable to work in London. Her capacity to work productively was always a barometer of her emotional state, as was her capacity to love, to be in love, to express love emotionally and sexually; just as Freud would assert in his own writing and she would affirm in her own relationship with him in the thirties, the healthy individual was characterized by her ability to love and work ("lieben und arbeiten"). However, H.D. wavered in her inclination to go off with Gray. Periods in the country had regularly assuaged for her the difficulties of war-torn London (in 1916 in Devon, in 1917 in Lichfield), and now the idea of spring and summer in Cornwall seemed to promise her a period of quiet in which she could write and perhaps also love. But she did not love Cecil Gray, and there was something retaliative that was not attractive to her in beginning her own affair in response to her husband's.

Aldington was acutely aware of H.D.'s continuing unrest and its affect on her work worried him. Still in England, he wrote to Amy Lowell on March 3, 1918: "Hilda has done a certain amount of work, but naturally feels unsettled through my being away for so long—two years now. She needs tranquility for her work & the raids in town, though comparatively harmless, are rather noisy & disturbing to a person with fragile nerves. She will probably go to the country when I leave." More open with Lowell than was H.D., still Aldington was seldom intimate and here conceals much of the cause of his wife's distress.

In fact, much remained unsettled, inconclusive, and unclear in the Aldingtons' lives on the brink of his return to France and the beginning of the surviving correspondence between them. Cournos's imminent return was somewhat unnerving: both Aldingtons were about to lose an intimate friend who had also been a frequent correspondent. H.D.'s hesitation about the trip to Cornwall was about to be resolved, but her relationship with Gray was no clearer to her and rather than consciously asserting her own will, she seems to have been reacting to the atmosphere at Number 44 and to Gray's own pleadings. Gray wrote to her from his room in West Hampstead on a Monday evening probably in early March:

Dear gray eyed One,

I was rather depressed and sad at not seeing you today, though perhaps it was really very wise of you all the same. But I think I rather resent, or fear, this cold, abstract, impersonal kind of wisdom of yours. It makes me feel that I have no hold over you—that at any moment you might simply cease to have any feeling for me— that I might no longer exist for you. But this is possibly only the exaggerated expression of my fear of losing you which is always very strong when I am away from you. You must try and dissipate this mistrust and apprehension. If only I could feel sure of you—as you put it yourself—"secure."

Forgive this rather maudlin exhibition, and do not think I am reproaching you. One of the things I love most about you is your detestation of any kind of falsity or deception in our relations. You do not pretend to love me any more than you do. That is something, at any rate, but it is not enough to keep me from being unhappy now and then. Why are you so elusive, so unapproachable? It is to a certain extent true of you what Lawrence and White in that ridiculous poem seem to imply—you refuse to give anything, you will only receive. Others must pledge themselves—you alone have the privilege of withdrawal, of non-committal.

Do not think that because I say these things I love you any the less, you crafty, subtle, perfidious Argive—that unfortunately is something over which I have no control. Hence my fury. My dear, my dear, I love you so. Never mind what I say, it really doesn't matter much.

A rivederci
Cecil

I shall come along tomorrow between 4 and 5.[75]

Such an insistent, petulant and rather possessive lover provided a stark contrast to Aldington, but certainly did not seem to H.D. to be clearly what she wanted. From Gray's letter, she appears to have been reluctant to respond to him as fully as he wished: willing to have him love her, but unsure whether or how much to respond to him; trying to assert some control over herself and her life.[76]

Yet she did eventually decide to go off to Cornwall, and Gray left London on March 11 with the clear hope that she would soon follow. In an undated letter postmarked March 12, 1918, Gray wrote her from Bosigran:

Dear Person,

I arrived last night at Penzance about 6 and drove out in a trap, getting here about 7:30. A very boring journey it was, and by the time I got to the house I was in a dreadful state of depression which continued to increase with the wind as the evening wore on. I do not know whether the wind or I howled the loudest.

The food problem is a very acute one here and I am thinking of shifting over to Tregerthan after my year's lease runs out here—ie. in May; but that can be decided when you come down.

And how are things with you. Are you also feeling grisly? And did you go away with Brigit? But I suppose you are writing me all this.

I have not yet made up my mind as to your status in my household, so have not yet broached the subject to the fisher. The only decided thing is that you must come, whether you want to or not, because I need you very, very much. It doesn't matter how soon you come; we can manage all right about beds and things like that. Nothing really matters very much.

My piano is in a dreadful state—can't touch it until the tuner has come. That adds considerably to my woes.

Forgive me if I can't write a more amusing or interesting letter, but I am still bouleversé, as I always am after a deracination; and cannot collect myself. Shall be better tomorrow.

much love, in fact all my love.
Cecil

P.S. Letters take two days to London from here so don't scold me for not writing earlier.

Gray's moodiness, depression and general pessimism here do not seem attractive qualities, nor does his arch authority in commanding H.D. to join him, whether she wants to or not. Nevertheless, H.D. did join Gray in Cornwall before the end of March, and Aldington addressed his initial letter to her there.

The Aldingtons' relationship with Cournos also figures in the immediate background as the correspondence from Aldington to H.D. begins. On April 6, 1918, Aldington responded to an angry letter from Cournos which reached him at Tunbridge Wells. Aldington declared brashly and sincerely: "I am not ashamed of anything I have done; I regret nothing. . . . there are events which are stronger than we are; there seems a kind of fatality about it, a bitter irony. . . . I am not excusing myself. . . . We fell in love with each other, that is all. . . . I accept full responsibility." Aldington insists at once here on his own responsibility and on an ironic fate determining his life; about to leave for France once more, he asserts that he is in control of his actions while acknowledging his powerlessness in the face of forces beyond his control.

In this psychological context, his relationship with Arabella appears understandable as an emotional response to his impending departure for the front, experience of which he knows and dreads. In the affair, Aldington managed to escape—under the illusion of a free assertion of his will (his own "responsibility")—the emotional demands of an intensely erotic and poetic life with H.D., a life which the dehumanizing life of the trenches was about to deprive him of anyway, perhaps permanently. It is as if Aldington were committing a kind of suicide rather than allowing the military to kill him either in body or in spirit. Certainly this is the kind of destructive self-assertion that appears in the character of George Winterbourne, who commits suicide in France at the end of *Death of a Hero*. It is also possible to see his affair with Arabella as an unconscious attempt to make a mess of his marriage, to create in himself a guilt commensurate with the responsibility he insisted upon, a guilt which in turn would give purpose to the suffering his return to France would cause. Throughout his life Aldington was a vigorously independent man, and his struggle to assert some control over his experience, even (or particularly) at the cost of threatening relationships very dear to him, seems a characteristic reaction to the extreme pressure he was currently enduring.

H.D. was confused, frightened, hurt, and sympathetic in response to Aldington's actions and state of mind. When Cournos discovered the affair on his return from Russia, he wrote her as he had immediately written Aldington. She responded and shared with him her conflicting and complicated feelings:

> I was very anxious— Yet, as you say, there was nothing to be said! They *are* to be pitied—O, it was so terrible—you can't imagine. Though I was of it—still I felt detached. I don't know what will happen.
>
> . . . I am not able to think of myself as a *person* now. I must move, act, & do as it is *moved* upon me to do & act. . . . I am cut off from everyone in the old

world. . . . Lawrence seems not to exist and R. seems far & far. I do not even write—poor boy—I suffered so for him. I think him very strange & unbalanced now—his actions were quite unaccountable. I pray for him—indeed they both need our pity—[77]

Neither H.D. nor Aldington, however, was ever able to regain their intimacy with Cournos, and it is against the backdrop of H.D.'s relationship with Gray and Aldington's with Yorke that the story of the letters unfolds.

NOTES

1. Letter from Alister Kershaw to the author, 1 February 1988.

2. H.D., *Bid Me to Live* (1960), Redding Ridge, Connecticut: Black Swan Books, 1983, 27.

3. Norman Holmes Pearson's notes toward a never-written biography of H.D. (BL).

4. Taped interview by David Wilkinson with Mrs. Gertrude Hilda Brown Cotterell, 10 December 1981, shared personally with me. The ellipses in the quotation indicate the omission of Wilkinson's questions and of the comments of Mr. Brown, who was attempting to clarify his wife's responses; she had recently suffered a stroke and her statements were not always clearly articulated.

5. Sir Alec Randall, a reminiscence in *Richard Aldington: An Intimate Portrait*, ed. Alister Kershaw and Frédéric-Jacques Temple, Carbondale: Southern Illinois University Press, 1965, 119.

6. Unpublished letters from Richard Aldington to Glenn Hughes, 31 August 1928 through 1 March 1929 (HRC), chronicle the events of this period and Aldington's efforts to move his possessions out of his Berkshire cottage while he was in Italy and France.

7. Unpublished letter from Albert Aldington to St. Loe Strachey, 7 July 1910, quoted by permission of Alister Kershaw and the British Library.

8. Anne de Lenclos (1620–1705) was well known for her liaisons with some of the most distinguished men of her time. She was also famous for her charm, intelligence, and good sense. She had a salon in Paris, befriended writers, and was portrayed as Clarisse in the novel *Clélie* (1644–60), by Madelaine Scudéry, known as "Sapho," who (like H.D. in her novella "Hipparchia," 1926) portrayed people she knew as characters in Greek and Roman settings (in H.D.'s work, Aldington appears as Marius Decius, H.D. as Hipparchia). When Lenclos's lover left for the army, he requested from her a written promise of fidelity, but she was soon unfaithful. See *The Oxford Companion to French Literature*, comp. and ed. Sir Paul Harvey and J.E. Hazeltine, Oxford: Oxford University Press, 1959, 407–408, 667.

9. "Confessions," in *The Little Review*, Vol. 12, Spring (May), 1929, 11.

10. Penny Smith, in her perceptive article "Hilda Doolittle and Frances Gregg" (*Powys Review*, Vol. 8, No. 22, 1988, 46–51), quotes a letter from Frances Gregg to her mother, Julia Gregg, on 18 August 1913. This letter further suggests the unfulfilled passion in H.D.'s relationship with Pound. Gregg commented on the " 'expression of veiled resent-

ment with which Hilda used so much to look at Ezra,—that resentment that is based in unsatisfied sexual desire' " (48). I am grateful to Louis Silverstein for bringing this article to my attention.

11. In an intimate correspondence with Eunice Black Gluckman, Aldington reflected on his own sexual past and on the sexual experiences of women he had known. He is discreet in these unpublished letters, writing that "As a rule, I never speak about one woman to another" (August 8, 1960) and reminding her that "I always follow the rule of the Officers Mess, and never mention a woman's name nor drop any hints" (August 4, 1958). Reflecting on homosexuality in both women and men, Aldington noted: "I think women are quite often bi-sexual, having affairs with women without in the least losing their pleasure in men; and some of the women I've been with longest have gone to be with other women quite frankly, and with no disturbance. Both my wives did it . . ." (November 11, 1960). Explicitly discussing oral sex, Aldington commented on what appeared to him its apparent universality, reflecting that all the women he had known had experienced orgasm through cunnilingus before their sexual experiences with him: "I have never had any wife or mistress who had not already experienced it" (August 7, 1961). In the apparent absence of another candidate for H.D.'s affections, and from Frances Gregg's remarks on H.D.'s unsatisfactory sexual relationship with Pound and Aldington's remarks to Gluckman here, it seems probable that H.D. and Gregg did indeed engage in physical and fulfilling sexual activity during the most intense period of their friendship in 1910 and 1911. I quote from Aldington's letters to Gluckman by permission of Alister Kershaw and the Beinecke Rare Book and Manuscript Library at Yale.

12. Aldington recalled this early affair in letters to Brigit Patmore in 1928 at the beginning of their second, eight-year affair. In a letter dated merely "Tues.," and likely written in late December 1928, Aldington wrote to her as "you who first held my body." In a letter dated merely "Thurs.," and likely written early in 1929, he recalled their first "honeymoon" as "the good old days," then referred to their renewed intimacy at Port Cros in October 1928, as a second honeymoon, finally stating explicitly "seventeen years ago I loved you" (HRC).

13. I discuss this poem at greater length and publish the sonnet in its entirety in my article "H.D. and R.A.: Early Love and the Exclusion of Ezra Pound," in H.D. Newsletter, Vol. 3, No. 1, 26–34.

14. All the quotations in this paragraph are taken from H.D.'s unpublished 1912 diary (BL).

15. In The Poetry of Richard Aldington: A Critical Evaluation and an Anthology of Uncollected Poems (University Park, Pennsylvania: Pennsylvania State University Press, 1974), Norman Gates reprints Aldington's "Song of Freedom," first published in the newspaper Justice, 29 October 1910, 5 (Gates, 227–228). Gates notes that "this poem, written when Aldington was eighteen, is the earliest published poem" he has discovered (228). Gates reprints other early verse: "In Memoriam: Arthur Chapman" (Union Magazine, Vol. 5, No. 3, December 1911, 254; in Gates, 228–229), "Chanson of Winter" (Evening Standard, 6 February 1912, 3; in Gates, 229), and "Villanelle" (Evening Standard, 8 February 1912, 3; in Gates, 230) are typical examples. Aldington continued to publish verse in the Evening Standard, the Pall Mall Gazette, and the Westminster Gazette during the spring and summer of 1912 before the appearance of his "Imagiste" works in Poetry in November 1912. Publication of H.D.'s early work has yet to be so specifically chronicled, but in

autobiographical notes she made for Norman Holmes Pearson, H.D. stated that she first published work in New York syndicated papers in 1910 (BL). Such work was probably poetry; her cousin, Francis Wolle, in his memoir, *A Moravian Heritage* (Boulder, Colorado: Empire Reproduction and Printing Company, 1972), notes that during the autumn of 1910 H.D. lived for several months in Greenwich Village so that she could "work at her poetry" (56).

16. This information and all subsequent details about this trip unless otherwise noted are drawn from the unpublished 1912–13 travel diary of Helen Wolle Doolittle, H.D.'s mother (BL).

17. Unpublished letter from Margaret Snively Pratt to Bryher, 6 December 1968 (BL).

18. Pound found them "disconsolate on the piazza [in Venice] yesterday afternoon & spent the evening consoling them for the absence of their offspring" (Ezra Pound to Dorothy Shakespear, May 1913, *Ezra Pound and Dorothy Shakespear, Their Letters; 1909–1914*, ed. Omar Pound and A. Walton Litz, New York: New Directions, 1984, 220). In her autobiographical notes, H.D. recalled the period in Venice particularly: "Ezra was there; general feeling of disapproval." Her fragmentary comments on this trip suggest that it was essentially full and happy, however, despite the tensions she also remembers: "Rebellion, stay on in Florence, go Venice, cheap third class, no food. Ezra takes on mother and dad" (BL). Phyllis Bottome (in her memoir *The Challenge*, New York: Harcourt, Brace and Co., 1953, 381–385) found Aldington's and particularly H.D.'s relationship with the Doolittles unconventional. Drawn more to Aldington than to H.D. but interested in both of them as "highly stimulating companions," in Rome in late 1912 Bottome was still "violently shocked at their unkind treatment of H.D.'s simple and kindly parents" (381). Certainly H.D. was rebelling against her childhood and much that the Doolittles represented. By the time they arrived in Rome the dynamics of her relationship with her parents must have been complex; to an outside observer it is not surprising that her behavior would have appeared "shocking." I am grateful to Louis Silverstein for drawing Bottome's comments to my attention.

19. Pound wrote to Dorothy Shakespear on 8 May 1913 that H.D.'s "family distresses her & seems to drive her more fawn-wards" (that is, toward Aldington, nicknamed "Faun" by both Pound and H.D.; *Ezra Pound and Dorothy Shakespear*, 224).

20. Pound wrote to Dorothy Shakespear on 21 April 1913 that he expected to be amused by Aldington and H.D. together in Venice. On 29 April, Pound sent Dorothy a first version of "The Faun" (published in revised form in *Poetry and Drama*, 2, in March, 1914). In this poem he addresses Aldington as the faun, accusing him of "sniffling and snoozling about among my flowers," but finally the speaker, conceding defeat, states, "But take it, I leave you the garden" (*Ezra Pound and Dorothy Shakespear*, 207, 213).

21. Pound to Dorothy Shakespear, 8 and 9 May 1913, *Ezra Pound and Dorothy Shakespear*, 224, 226.

22. For example, in H.D.'s unpublished letters to Isabel Pound, Pound's mother, 5 and 30 December 1912 (BL).

23. Aldington sent twenty-one postcards to his father and his sisters between 12 December 1912 and 25 June 1913 (TU).

24. Richard Aldington, *Life for Life's Sake: A Book of Reminiscences*, New York: Viking Press, 1941, 121.

25. *Life for Life's Sake*, 122.

26. In *Life for Life's Sake*, Aldington notes that Pound invited "each of us" to the now famous tea and there "informed us that we were Imagists" (135). On 7 August 1928 Aldington wrote Pound that he, Aldington, and H.D. should agree that officially "The 'movement' was decided upon by the three of us, in a Kensington tea-shop, to launch H.D." (SIU). In a late letter to H.D. on 2 November 1955, he recalled imagism as " 'une affaire de famille' between us three [H.D., himself, and Pound], mainly to boost your poems and to a less extent mine" (BL).

27. *Life for Life's Sake*, 134.

28. H.D., *End to Torment: A Memoir of Ezra Pound*, New York: New Directions, 1979, 5.

29. Unpublished letter from Richard Aldington to Amy Lowell, 21 September 1914; all letters from Aldington to Lowell are at HU.

30. *Life for Life's Sake*, 139.

31. Aldington's and H.D.'s correspondence with Amy Lowell during these years makes clear that Aldington with H.D.'s help spent a good deal of time and effort soliciting poems for these anthologies, encouraging contributors to make alternative selections and to revise or expand the number of their submissions. It seems clear that Lowell was responsible for contracting with their American publisher and through her influence publicizing the volumes on her side of the ocean; however, Aldington—who was in England until late 1916 at a time when transatlantic mail was unpredictable and who thus had more direct and dependable contact with contributors and with their English publisher, Constable and Company—seems in fact to have done most of the actual work the anthologies entailed. A letter from Aldington to Lowell on 7 December 1914 is typical: he begins with three and a half single-spaced typed pages of numbered points which offer Lowell discussion and advice about matters of publication (HU).

32. Richard Aldington, *Very Heaven*, New York: Doubleday, Doran and Company, 1937, 224–225.

33. For example, Aldington discussed a plan for both Aldingtons to go to America for the duration in a letter to Amy Lowell on 28 December 1915; H.D. wrote to Lowell on 20 January 1916 that the plan would need to be postponed.

34. Aldington described his efforts either to avoid conscription altogether or at least to get into officers' training in a letter to Amy Lowell dated 5 January 1916, concluding, "My father assures me that nothing can be done." He further detailed his father's efforts on his behalf in another letter to Lowell on 6 May 1916 (HU).

35. Aldington discusses these legal details at some length in a letter to Amy Lowell on 6 May 1916 (HU).

36. Aldington's and H.D.'s letters to Amy Lowell in 1915 and 1916 recount this ongoing debate as the Aldingtons struggled to plan for the future.

37. Frank Flint detailed the reasons that he felt H.D. should remain in England and chance forced labor in a letter to Aldington on 23 November 1916 (HRC). Flint indicated that the decision to stay was finally H.D.'s, but that she discussed the matter at length with Alec Randall and with Flint himself and his wife Violet. I am grateful to John Wardrop for transcribing this letter for me from Flint's shorthand.

38. Unpublished and undated letter from H.D. to Amy Lowell, February 1916.

39. *Life for Life's Sake*, 177.

40. Unpublished letter from Richard Aldington to Frank Stewart Flint, 27 March 1916.

41. Undated letter from H.D. to John Cournos, probably written 8 September 1916, in Donna Hollenberg, "Art and Ardor in World War One: Selected Letters from H.D. to John Cournos," *Iowa Review*, Vol. 16, No. 3, Fall 1986, 134.

42. Unpublished letter from Richard Aldington to Frank Flint, 6 July 1916.

43. Unpublished, undated letter from Richard Aldington to John Cournos.

44. The heading of this letter has been cut off, evidently by military censors, but it is dated August 1916 in Lowell's hand.

45. Undated letter, dated in Lowell's hand August 1916.

46. Unpublished letter from H.D. to John Cournos, dated "Sunday evening" and probably written in July 1916.

47. Unpublished letter from H.D. to Amy Lowell, 13 October 1916.

48. Hollenberg, 136.

49. Hollenberg, 136, 137.

50. Unpublished letter from H.D. to Amy Lowell, 1 December 1916.

51. Unpublished letter from H.D. to Amy Lowell, 8 December 1916.

52. Unpublished letter from H.D. to Amy Lowell, 21 December 1916.

53. Richard Aldington, "Books in the Line," *The Sphere*, 12 April 1919, 26.

54. Letter from H.D. to Harriet Shaw Weaver, May 1917, quoted in Jane Lidderdale and Mary Nicholson, *Dear Miss Weaver: Harriet Shaw Weaver, 1876–1961*, New York: Viking Press, 1970, 138.

55. *Life for Life's Sake*, 182–183.

56. Denis Winter, *Death's Men: Soldiers of the Great War*, London: Penguin 1978, 81.

57. Winter, 130.

58. Malcolm Brown, *Tommy Goes to War*, London: J.M. Dent, 1978, 147.

59. Winter, 213.

60. Winter, 42.

61. Winter, 43.

62. Walter Lowenfels, "A Letter to Angela" (unpublished manuscript), quoted in Selwyn Kittredge, "The Literary Career of Richard Aldington," Ph.D. dissertation, New York University, 1976, 573.

63. Winter, 148.

64. Winter, 164–165.

65. Unpublished letter from H.D. to Amy Lowell, 19 September 1917.

66. Unpublished letter from H.D. to Amy Lowell, 14 November 1917.

67. D.H. Lawrence to Amy Lowell, 23 March 1917, in *The Letters of D.H. Lawrence*, Vol. 3, ed. James T. Boulton and Andrew Robinson, Cambridge: Cambridge University Press, 1984, 104.

68. H.D. to Frank Flint, 30 August 1917, in "Selected Letters from H.D. to F.S. Flint: A Commentary on the Imagist Period," ed. Cyrena N. Pondrom, *Contemporary Literature*, Vol. 10, Autumn, 1969, 584.

69. John Cournos, in his *Autobiography* (New York: G.P. Putnam's Sons, 1935), details his relationship with Yorke at great length. I am drawing on his account here as well as on information revealed in a taped interview with Yorke conducted by Walter and Lillian Lowenfels on 25 October 1964. I am grateful to Fred Crawford for sharing with me his typed copy of Miriam J. Benkovitz's transcription of this interview.

70. H.D. to Frank Flint, 30 August 1917, in "Selected Letters," 584.

71. H.D. went down from Lichfield to London briefly to see that the Lawrences were settled in her flat (Autobiographical Notes, BL), but she remained "off in the country still," as she wrote to Lowell on 14 November 1917, seeing her husband regularly on the weekends until his training ended and he received his commission on November 28.

72. Keith Sagar's A. D.H. Lawrence Handbook (Manchester: Manchester University Press, 1985) is an invaluable resource for determining Lawrence's precise whereabouts, and I have drawn on his work here.

73. H.D.'s novel Bid Me to Live, probably begun as early as the summer of 1918, chronicles the events of December 1917 and the first months of 1918 in great autobiographical detail. While I have attempted as much as possible here to rely on letters and other primary sources in my account, it is this novel itself which most explicitly conveys the experience of the group's interaction. Specifically, I am relying heavily here on H.D.'s account of her relationship with Yorke, Gray, and Frieda and D.H. Lawrence, although Aldington, in D.H. Lawrence: Portrait of a Genius But . . . (1950; New York: Collier Books, 1961), gives his own brief, more general, and rather detached account of the Lawrences' departure from Number 44 (192–194). Yet throughout his biography Aldington clearly indicates Lawrence's attitude toward women, which H.D. examines at length in her novel and which I draw on here. Aldington writes: "there can be no doubt that he had a great attraction for many women, all the more so since his innate puritanism kept them at a distance. . . . yet he considered his own marriage inviolable, and noli me tangere [don't touch me] in a snarl was about all that the others ever got" (103). It is this same characteristic recoiling that H.D. attributes to the Lawrence character in Bid Me to Live (81–82), even quoting his own expression, also cited by Aldington: "noli me tangere" (82).

74. Hollenberg, 141.

75. This and the following letter from Cecil Gray to H.D. are at BL.

76. D.H. Lawrence satirized H.D.'s vacillation here in his fictional portrait of Julia Cunningham, who hesitates to go off with Cyril Scott (the Cecil Gray character) to his "house in Dorset" (Aaron's Rod [1922], New York: Viking Press, 1961, 43). Despite Lawrence's unsympathetic treatment, Julia's concerns ("compromising herself" in the eyes of others; her concern for her husband, Robert; her reluctance or inability to consider her own feelings and to make her own decisions [44–47]) do indeed seem to be H.D.'s in her relationship with Gray.

77. Hollenberg, 144. This letter is merely dated "Monday" and seems to me probably to have been written 7 April 1918, not sometime in 1919 as Hollenberg suggests.

The Letters

1

[Letterhead:] E.F.C. Officers Rest House and Mess.[1]
April 19, 1918

Dearest Dooley/[2]

Arrived here[3] last evening after a stormy passage, though I am happy to say I was not sea-sick! Some ways it is good to be back with the B.E.F.[4] though it looks as if most of us are in for a hot time. I guess there's not really much chance of coming through this time, yet I feel very calm about it all, kind of indifferent you know!

I am at an I.B.D.[5] waiting to go up the line, which I presume will be pretty soon. Only address is: 9th Royal Sussex, J. Depot, 32nd I.B.D., B.E.F. France. I shall be 9th Royal Sussex all the time now; I know their Division quite well—they were next to us last year at Loos.[6] It is a pukka[7] infantry batt.—no pioneer business[8] this trip!

Have just heard a rumour that we are going up the line[9] to-morrow. Don't know if it's true, but I must run along & see if it's true. There are one or two things I want to buy.

I hope C.G.[10] is all right & that he'll be left undisturbed.[11]

Love from
Richard.

1. Aldington is writing from the officers' area of an Expeditionary Forces Canteen.
2. One of Aldington's pet names for H.D.
3. France.
4. The British Expeditionary Forces.
5. Infantry Base Depot. All base camps in France were composed of such depots, where men were sent for training and for re-allocation to units fighting in France.
6. Before returning to England for officers' training in July of 1917, Aldington was stationed for six months near Loos in the Cambrai–La Bassée region of the western front.
7. Genuine; the term is Anglo-Indian and is often used, here, derisively. It indicates as well the acme of gentlemanliness.
8. For the first half of 1917, Aldington served as a lance corporal in a pioneer battalion. Pioneer battalions were intended to perform as manual or infantry units whenever the occasion arose, and were accordingly trained in both functions. In their manual capacity they worked with the Royal Engineers field companies and were responsible for building and repairing trenches and dugouts and maintaining roads, railways, and tramways, work often undertaken in forward areas under heavy fire. In their infantry capacity they were used to consolidate captured positions and were often involved in defending these positions against enemy attack. Aldington's duties had also included making wooden crosses and digging graves.
9. Aldington is at a base camp from which he will go "up the line" to the trenches.
10. Cecil Gray, the young British musician and music critic who was H.D.'s lover; see Biographical Appendix.
11. Gray's draft category at this time exempted him from military service.

2

April 23, 1918

Dearest Dooley/

This is just to let you know that I got to the battalion on Sunday afternoon.[1] So far we are on rest,[2] several kilos behind the line, but are expecting to go up in a day or so.

There is plenty of work here, so I've had no time to write at all. In fact I've only written to you & A.[3] since I've been out here. Life is much better this time than before. Yet I'm hoping for something in the shape of a blighty one[4] at the earliest possible moment!

How are you? I hope to hear from you soon. My address is "D" Coy, 9th Royal Sussex, B.E.F. How is Gray? Still free I hope.

Will write more when I get a chance.

Love from

Richard.

1. April 21.
2. The Ninth Royal Sussex Battalion was in training behind the lines at La Comte from April 19 through April 29.
3. Dorothy ("Arabella") Yorke, the American woman who was Aldington's lover; see Biographical Appendix.
4. "Blighty" is England or home; a "blighty one" is World War I slang for a wound which will cause one to be shipped home, a lucky wound.

3

May 6, 1918

Dearest Dooley/

I am O.K.[1] Hope you and Cecil[2] are all right. Are you still happy in Cornwall?[3]

I am right in the line in temporary command[4] of a company, which means a lot of work & responsibility. However, that helps to pass the time.

When I have done my 10 days trip up[5] (5 of wh: has passed) I am going to the base[6] for a course, which lasts until June 15! I am not really pleased as I was hoping to get wounded. I saw in the paper yesterday that Carl Fallas[7] is wounded. Lucky little pig!

There is no time for more. So, au revoir.

I love you—too much.

Richard.

I haven't had a letter from you yet.[8]

1. Throughout his correspondence with H.D., Aldington is careful to shelter her from his deep frustration and despair with the war and military life. His letters to others during the war years often provide a stark contrast to the sometimes jaunty and restrained tone of his letters to H.D. For example, he writes to Alec Randall on 2 May 1918:

> You see I am still alive though horribly fed-up. It is not within the compass of any language to express to you how fed-up I am with a Gargantuan disgust at this démodé folly. Sometimes when I wake up from my somewhat rare slumbers I am more than surprised to find what pestilential surroundings I have.
>
> But really this life is brutish & tries my patience almost beyond endurance. The horrible thing is that one has nothing, absolutely nothing to live for. (HL)

2. Cecil Gray.

3. In mid-March of 1918 H.D. left London to join Cecil Gray at Bosigran Cottage near St. Ives in Cornwall.

4. Aldington received his commission as a second lieutenant in the infantry on November 28, 1917.

5. Aldington is writing from the trenches.

6. Probably Étaples or another large base camp near Calais.

7. A friend of the Aldingtons with whom Aldington enlisted in the eleventh Battalion, the Devonshire Regiment, in late May 1916. See Biographical Appendix.

8. The extreme tensions of the months immediately preceding this correspondence (see Introduction) evidently made H.D. resolve not to write to her husband despite his letters to her since the end of his last long leave in late December 1917. They often saw each other until H.D.'s departure for Cornwall in mid-March, but she clearly decided not to write for a time. In an undated letter to John Cournos, probably written in early April 1918, H.D. writes that she feels distant from Aldington: "I do not even write—"

4

May 11, 1918

[On this date Aldington sent a field postcard similar to the one reproduced as letter 12, indicating that he had received a letter from H.D.]

5

May 17, 1918

Dearest Dooley/

My exquisite one—can you know how cool & lovely the memory of you is to me? Recently I have been very close to the place where I wrote "Reverie"[1] and I remembered, I remembered many things.

No doubt things seem very tragic & bitter to you, but what seems to me the great bitterness is my own apathy. Back here once more everything goes; I ask myself often what am I living for? Why do I trouble to hide from a shell or bullets? Only the mere weakness of the flesh. There really isn't anything or anybody I care for. My loneliness is complete. But it is not a beautiful loneliness. It is a loneliness haunted with horror and regret.

I suppose in a way I care for Arabella, & in a way I care most terribly for you. But nothing is real; there is nothing I really want. Isn't that rather sad?

O my dear Dooley, I would so like to be gay & witty, contemptuous of "ordinary" people—how I envy Gray his contempt—but there are too many dead men, too much misery. I am choked and stifled not so much by my own misery as by the unending misery of all these thousands. Who shall make amends for it?

How silly all this is! But you are silly to think that our love would ever be broken. Don't I long sometimes to throw myself at your knees & call passionately to you?

But what will happen who can tell? And I do not want anything any more, except perhaps sleep.

> Sleep, what have the gods to give but sleep
> After warring & after loving?
> The closed eyelids shall forget to weep
> And the heart its roving.[2]

Or some such nonsense.

Yesterday I found some lilac in a ruined garden and its beauty was too poignant. Isn't it the uttermost cruelty of the gods to sprinkle flowers in hell—some gainless glimpse of Proserpine's veiled head?

I am glad you have the beauty of those Cornish hills & the tranquility & comfort of a pleasant house—you must think of yourself as Fred's "Friend of Paul"[3] in his house in Spain, meditating on Lucretius & the vanity of things.

Really, Dooley, I want to come back to you very much. Someday perhaps we will run away together—some unsuspected isle in the far seas. But now you are more unreal than the memory of the shadow of Narcissus in a pool. I *belong* no more to the life that is in tranquil places, but just to this odd distorted existence.

Yes, work at Greek[4] if it helps you—I nearly said "what is Greek"!

I should like very much to kiss you.

Your
Richard.

[In the margin of page 1: I have been 18 days in the trenches[5] & am wearied out.]

1. Aldington's poem was first published in *Reverie: A Little Book of Poems for H.D.* (Cleveland: Clerk's Press, 1917). The poem conveys poignantly his feelings about both love and war:

It is very hot in the chalk trench
With its rusty iron pickets
And shell-smashed crumbling traverses,
Very hot and choking and full of evil smells
So that my head and eyes ache
And I am glad to crawl away
And lie in the little shed I call mine.
And because I want to be alone
They keep coming to me and asking:
"How many billets have we in such a trench?"
Or, "Do you know the way to such a redoubt?"

But these things pass over, beyond and away from me,
The voices of the men fade into silence
For I am burned with a sweet madness,
Soothed also by the fire that burns me,
Exalted and made happy in misery
By love, by an unfaltering love.
If I could tell you of this love—
But I can tell only lovers,
Only irresponsible imprudent lovers
Who give and have given and will give
All for love's sake,
All just to kiss her hand, her frail hand.

I will not tell you how long it is
Since I kissed and touched her hand
And was happy looking at her,
Yet every day and every night
She seems to be with me, beside me,
And there is great love between us
Although we are so far apart.

And although the hot sun burns in the white trench
And the shells go shrilling overhead
And I am harassed by stupid questions,
I do not forget her,
I do not forget to build dreams of her
That are only less beautiful than she is.

For there are some who love God,
And some their country and some gain,
Some are happy to exact obedience
And some to obey for the sake of a cause—
But I am indifferent to all these things

Since it was for her sake only I was born
So that I should love her.

Perhaps I shall be killed and never see her again,
Perhaps it will be but a wreck of me that returns to her,
Perhaps I shall kiss her hand once more,
But I am quite happy about Fate,
For this is love's beauty
That it does not die with lovers
But lives on, like a flower born from a god's blood,
Long after the lovers are dead.

Reason has pleaded in my brain
And Despair has whispered in my heart
That we die and vanish utterly;
I have seen dead men lying on the earth
Or carried slowly in stretchers,
And the chilled blood leaped in my heart
Saying: "This is the end, there is no escape."

But for love's sake I brush all this away
For, since I do not know why love is
Nor whence it comes, nor for what end,
It may very well be that I am wrong about death,
And that among the dead also there are lovers.

Would that we were dead, we two,
Dead centuries upon centuries,
Forgotten, even our race and tongue forgotten,
Would that we had been dead so long
That no memory of this fret of life
Could ever trouble us.

We would be together, always together
Always in a land of many flowers,
And bright sunlight and cool shade;
We should not even need to kiss
Or join our hands;
It would be enough to be together.

She would stoop and gather a flower,
A pale, sweet-scented, fragile flower
(A flower whose name I will not tell,
The symbol of all love to us).

And I would watch her smile
And see the fair flowers of her breast
As the soft-coloured garment opened from her throat.

I would not speak, I would not speak one word
Though many ages of the world's time passed—
She would be bending by the flower's face
And I would stand beside and look and love.

Not far away as I now write
The guns are beating madly upon the still air
With sudden rapid blows of sound,
And men die with the quiet sun above them
And horror and pain and noise upon earth.

To-morrow, maybe, I shall be one of them,
One in a vast field of dead men,
Unburied, or buried hastily, callously.
But for ever and for ever
In the fair land I have built up
From the dreams of my love,
We two are together, she bending by the pale flower
And I beside her:
We two together in a land of quiet
Inviolable behind the walls of death.

2. Unidentified. It is possible that these lines are a part of a poem Aldington never finished or published.

3. In Frederic Manning's philosophic tale "The Friend of Paul," which appeared in *Scenes and Portraits* (1909), the central character, Serenus, has retreated to his country house after the death of his wife and child; there he tells visiting friends of his near conversion by Paul at Corinth and his abiding affection for the holy man.

4. It seems that H.D. has finally written to Aldington and that letter 5 is in some measure a response to the particulars she has written him of her work on Greek translation as well as details about her situation in Cornwall.

5. On May 1 Aldington's battalion was stationed near St. Maroc; D Company, in which he served, was in "Chalk Pit Alley." The battalion was in the trenches near Loos until May 19 when the Ninth Royal Sussex moved into rest at Brébis.

6

May 20, 1918

It is more difficult not to love you when I am away from you than when I am with you. Really, it is true that one has many lovers but only one love.[1] And I gave you everything, so that I have only desire and consideration to give to others. But I wonder if I was your love or just one of your lovers?

To-day I have looked at whole trees all green with spring and fields and I have seen an old French woman[2] I used to know out here who nearly wept over me & gave me tea & cognac!

But still, though things are kind, I am terribly indifferent. The truth is: I love you & I desire—l'autre.[3] Really I can never be happy without you; and very often it seems I couldn't be happy without her. Folly to talk of happiness when this horror goes on. But on remâche ses idées[4] in the long nights of watching. The stars are very powerful instillers of truth. Somehow, Dooley, I have made a great mess of my life. But I would have been content if I hadn't made you suffer so much. And then, and then, I must look after A. C'est de la démence.[5] I find it hard to write to her. Do you realise what that means? It is a psychological point which gives me distress.

Out here I really don't know what one lives for. I don't pretend it is all misery and horror; there are moments of rest, compensation, gaiety even. But there is constant wear—& having lost somehow the pearl & essence of life there seems no point in keeping on. Je vis en bête.[6] Do you think there is any point in keeping on? Twice last week I tried to get killed[7]—and was unlucky or lucky, whichever you like.

Isn't this folly? Do be happy with Cecil. I shall get over this someday.

R.

1. Aldington is ascribing here to the then current romantic theory that despite other sexual liaisons, two people may be destined for one another and have an inviolable union which transcends their actual behavior or the vicissitudes of the times.

2. Probably the owner of the bookshop at Grenay whom Aldington writes about in "The Bookshop at Grenay" in *The Sphere*, April 19, 1919, 54. When Aldington returned to the section of the front where he now is after an absence of over a year, he recalls in his article that "Madame" greeted him with joyous surprise and invited him into her kitchen as if he were a relative. An excerpt from this sketch is reprinted as a part of my article "Richard Aldington in Transition: His Pieces for *The Sphere* in 1919," *Twentieth Century Literature*, Vol. 34, No. 4, Winter 1988, 498.

3. The other; that is, Arabella Yorke.

4. One broods over one's ideas.

5. That is the pure folly of it.

6. I live instinctively.

7. Aldington's attempted suicide here anticipates George Winterbourne's successful effort when he stands up in the trenches at the end of Aldington's popular war novel, *Death of a Hero* (1929).

7

May 28, 1918

Dearest Dooley/

I often think of you in the hours about dawn and hope you are happily sleeping. It is a great comfort to know that you are safe and well and not too unhappy. It seems a long time since I heard from you, but of course time does drag in the front line; so perhaps it is not so long as I think. Have done ⅔ of our time up here—I shan't be sorry when we are relieved.

Have you any news of Yeats & White[1] over this Irish business?[2] I do hope Yeats has managed to steer clear. I notice Mrs. Gonne[3] is under arrest. Some people have odd ideas of happiness. Mine is to be let alone—an impossible ideal.

I suppose where you are there is sea & a clean wind & flowers, and inside books & white linen and more flowers. And I suppose you don't really feel happy—

I mean that you are probably a little bored sometimes, not enjoying every hour? I feel that I wouldn't ever want to "grouse" if I could be clean and quiet and undisturbed again. One goes over & over things—what am I living for? What do I hope? And then even if the war did end & I got out how could I live? I'm too [old] to learn a trade or profession now & I don't feel like writing any more. Even if I did it wouldn't amount to much.

Well, I am a grouser, Dooley, don't you think? Anyhow you mustn't think I'm nothing but a grouser, for I keep pretty cheerful. We all had our photographs taken in tin hats the other day—I'm going to send you a copy as soon as some arrive. That will be in about a fortnight I expect.

Do hope you are well & happy. Remember me to Hulun[4] when you write.

Richard.

1. William Butler Yeats (1865–1939), the Irish poet, and James Robert White (1879–1946), who helped to organize the Irish Citizen Army during the transport workers' strike in Dublin in 1913. Both men were acquaintances of the Aldingtons.
2. In late May of 1918, a bill to establish an Irish parliament and executive was being hotly debated, and Aldington is probably referring to the discovery of a German intrigue in Ireland on May 16. On May 18, a proclamation was issued to apprehend those allegedly involved; 150 Sinn Feiners were arrested in Dublin and interned under the Defense of the Realm Act.
3. Maud Gonne MacBride (1866–1953) was arrested in Dublin on May 22, 1918, for complicity in the Irish-German plot and interned in Holloway Jail for six months for revolutionary activity.
4. A private nickname for Gilbert Doolittle, H.D.'s older brother; see Biographical Appendix.

8

May 31, 1918

Dearest Dooley/

This is just a short note to tell you that I am quite all right. I thought possibly you might be wondering as there is another offensive beginning.[1]

I am not in the very front line, but about 1000 yards back.[2] Soon we should go out for six days rest & if all is well I shall probably not go in[3] with the battalion next trip. This will take me almost to the end of June. So you see things are not too bad.

I have one or two French books up here which I manage to read for half an hour at a time. In a fit of optimism I nearly wrote to Crès[4] & the Mercure[5] for their list, but it hardly seems worth while. "Patience & endurance"[6] are all that is really necessary.

Cornwall must be very lovely[7] now if the days are as full of sunlight there as they are here. Extraordinarily pitiless and ironic these bright days are here, but get more physically comfortable—no mud, & nights are warm. We have no blankets,—just a trench coat. Yet I sleep very well.

Remember me to Cecil.

Your
Richard.

P.S. I had my photograph[8] taken about 10 days ago—I am sending you a copy.

1. The Germans reached the Marne on May 27, 1918, and by June 4 the Allies had mounted a counterattack at Château-Thierry.

2. That is, in the third line of trenches.

3. Aldington is anticipating a period of additional training which would keep him at base camp for the first two weeks of June; his training actually lasted from early June through mid-July.

4. Georges Crès of *La Nouvelle Revue Français;* founded in 1909, the influential French review of literature and the arts also had a publishing house.

5. *Le Mercure de France* (1890–1965) was a famous literary and artistic monthly which featured original work by writers of all schools and nationalities. Aldington's friend Remy de Gourmont was an editor from 1895 until his death in 1915.

6. Unidentified.

7. Aldington tended to identify himself almost symbiotically with H.D. and frequently paralleled his experience with hers.

8. Several times Aldington sent H.D. photographs from the front, but it is not clear exactly which one he is referring to here.

9

June 1, 1918
11 pm

Darling

Just a word to you to-night, in a hurry to catch the ration limber.[1]

Your letter melted much bitterness of heart. I thought you did not write[2] because you did not care. And I wanted you to care so much.

It is horrible here[3]—you probably know where I am. But yet I have not forgotten to love you. You write sweetly & I pardon your reserve. If only I had more than myself to give.

My sweet, you seem so beautiful and tranquil—any flower makes me think of you.

No more time. To-morrow.

Richard.

1. A limber is an articulated two-wheeled cart which can be joined to other similar carts. The ration limber brought warm food to the lines, but it also transported mail.

2. Aldington apparently received a brief note from H.D. on May 11 (see letter 5), but it is not until now that H.D. responds to his letters with personal and detailed letters of her own.

3. Aldington is in the line north of Loos. Although his battalion commander char-

acterized the period from May 25 through June 1, 1918, as "a fairly quiet tour" in the line, he also noted on May 31 that "about 400 gas projectors [were] fired on to Battalion" and that "casualties were rather heavy" (the war diaries of the Ninth Royal Sussex Regiment, PRO).

10

Dearest Dooley/

I have just sent you a little note saying how glad your letter made me; I wanted to get if off at once in case anything should happen[1] to prevent my writing to you later.

Ah yes, I do think of our days together. What strange, despised creatures we were & yet what a treasure we had. At times I think of some statue we looked at together or remember some book we both cared for. How could there ever be anyone but you?

Maupin.[2] It was in London, I think, that we read it. But how far, far away that time is. In such a way people spoke of The Golden Age.[3] I wonder what is gained through this deprivation & suffering? After all we have scarcely known each other for two years.[4] It is a lot.

"Friends"[5] you say. Not verse now, only prose?[6] Once when I threw myself at your feet I felt your heart beat so wildly I was frightened. Friends—I would like you to kiss me passionately just for one night, to realise once with you, my Beatrice, the great frisson[7] with the woman I love best.

Oh, I know the world is a queer place, & those who love each other best hurt each other most. Perhaps it will be only "friends," but I cannot bear to think it yet; I shall think "lovers" until you tell me "no" with your own lips. But, as I told you I have changed, through misery, through routine, through the strain of things. Perhaps I may get back equilibrium, some sort of life, even write again, but "never glad confident morning again."[8] One acquiesces in the death of a flower but it is hard to admit that the flower of one's unique life dies as surely & nearly as quickly as the summer lilac.

Isn't it strange. I know the date & what time it is; but none of us knows which day of the week it is. All days are alike. I think it is Friday or Saturday.[9] But, really now, aren't days of the week a superfluity?

Do you get enough money,[10] enough to eat & buy clothes & books? Won't you let me give you "of my scant pittance"?[11] (you can see, can't you, how hard I'm trying to make up to you!) Ah, but I'm nearly crying as I write, my wife, my Dooley. I am so proud that you have my name—please, please won't you keep it,[12] whatever happens, in memoriam as it were?

I shall go on writing until dawn if I don't stop. For a while thinking of you I forget the horror.

I never forget you.

Richard.

1. Aldington is aware of the possibility of his imminent death, but tends to refer to it euphemistically throughout his correspondence with H.D.

2. *Mademoiselle de Maupin* (1835), a novel by Théophile Gautier, explores in detail the subject of physical beauty and contains much erotic description. The preface was one of the first declarations of "art for art's sake."

3. Aldington is using the term loosely here to mean the best of all possible times, as the period before the war quickly came to appear after August of 1914.

4. Aldington is referring to the time since he entered the army on June 24, 1916. Not since then have he and H.D. lived together the life he is idealizing here.

5. H.D. has evidently suggested in her letter that she and Aldington exclude the sexual from their relationship and think of their marriage as merely a partnership between "friends."

6. In late 1917 H.D. had destroyed the poetry on which she had been working for some time (see Introduction) and is now, it would seem, beginning to write the autobiographical novel which will eventually become *Bid Me to Live* (1961). She writes to John Cournos on July 17, 1918: "I have begun really seriously on a novel."

7. Shudder.

8. Robert Browning, "The Lost Leader" (1845), line 28. In this poem Browning laments the "leader's" betrayal of literature for material wealth and earthly glory. The "leader" is specifically Wordsworth, who had accepted a Civil List pension in 1842 and become poet laureate in 1843, but the identity of the "leader" is intentionally ambiguous, and Aldington's quotation is in the spirit of the poem: the experience of the war has destroyed his confidence in the transcendent power of both his marriage and literature.

9. June 1, 1918, was a Saturday.

10. In addition to a small allowance from her parents, H.D. received a small sum as a soldier's dependent and a few pounds sporadically in royalties from her own *Sea Garden* (1916), from Aldington's *Images* (1915) and from the various imagist anthologies.

11. In "Meditation," which appeared in *Images of Desire* in 1919, Aldington echoes this phrase, referring to the "scanty pittance" he felt capable of earning as a poet (*The Complete Poems of Richard Aldington*, London: Allan Wingate, 1948, 146).

12. H.D. did keep Aldington's name; throughout her life she was known personally as Mrs. Aldington or Hilda Aldington.

11

June 2, 1918

My dear Dooley/

I hope you don't mind my writing to you so often. You must tell me if it causes any difficulty in your new ménage[1] and I will then abridge my correspondence. But I shan't stop writing until you tell me that you don't want to hear— & perhaps not even then!

On the day after to-morrow I am being sent down the line[2] for a five weeks course. It may not last anything like that time as I should be sent for if reinforcements were badly needed. But at least for a little I shall be back of the line. Better keep the same address if you write—letters will be sent after me.[3] I don't particularly want to go—I'm more or less at home now with this battalion, but as it's an order I can't refuse. It makes a change anyhow, though I am more or less indifferent.

I think of you perhaps too much and wonder if I shall ever see you again. Arabella sends me very kind letters & seems genuinely grieved to have me gone. But I can't tell. In any event I don't really care, but sometimes I would give everything just to touch your little finger as I did that first day at Brigit's.[4] It's queer to be living in memories so early in life.

I can't quite give up the idea that we shall be together again. There is of course the complication of Cecil and Arabella, but they seem—to me at least—to fade into the arrière-plan[5] when we two are concerned. Ah, Dooley, we have not been as happy as we might—somehow I have failed. Of course it makes no difference that we have had other lovers—though sometimes it hurts, hurts. But out of this present utter darkness of mine, this confusion & complete lack of direction & interest, there is one thing that seems to matter—you.

The little less & what miles away! Why didn't you love me passionately *before* Arabella & not after?[6] Don't you know that it's you, you I wanted & want life, everything with? The bitter irony of it! Like St. Augustine I repeat to myself bitterly: "too late have I loved thee O pulcritudinem antiquam!"[7]

Infinite problems circle about us, but, dear Dooley, let us at least keep a certain tolerance, a certain tenderness for each other. Here I am in this wretched dug-out & there you are in Cornwall. What the next year will do for us, god knows. Perhaps it is very wrong of me to write you love-letters—perhaps I ought not to disturb you. You are very reticent—you do not tell me if you are happy with Gray. It is a great consolation to me to know that there is someone to look after you now[8] & in the future, if by chance I should not be able to do so.

How one wanders in words—half expressing half one's thoughts. I write rather my meditations than a letter—chiefly writing because for a time I concentrate on the memory of you, all I seem to possess now. Why should one agonise with hope? I won't ask anything of you, anything of some things I was going to ask. I'll just finish & go up & listen to the guns a bit.

Richard.

1. H.D.'s relationship with Cecil Gray in Cornwall.
2. To base camp near Calais where Aldington received additional training.
3. Letters to a soldier at the front needed only his rank and regiment to reach him.
4. Aldington is recalling the day they met at a party at Brigit Patmore's house in early 1912.
5. Background.
6. The Aldingtons' sexual life together was not always one of equal or mutual passion; see Introduction.
7. "Pulcritudinem antiquam" literally means "beauty of long ago," but here Aldington clearly intends "my first and true love." It is likely that the quotation comes from Augustine's *Confessions*.
8. This was one of Aldington's constant concerns.

12

June 9, 1918

Form postcard indicating that Aldington has received a letter from H.D. dated May 31, 1918. At critical times, when a movement was occurring that needed at all costs to be kept secret, no correspondence was allowed except for field postcards such as this one, in which a soldier crossed out sentences he did not want.

13

Voici[1] presque deux années, mon amie, que je subis cette vie immonde de soldat. Pendant tout ce temps nous ne nous sommes pas vus que par bribes de temps. J'avais vingt-trois ans quand je te quittait; or dans un mois j'aurais vingt-six. A-tu [sic] bien compris ce que cela veut dire? C'est que le temps passe, ma chère, et nous sommes toujours plus loin.

Je veux bien un peu te gronder. Ta lettre m'a l'air un peu malhereuse [sic]. Mais qu'est-ce que tu as de t'affliger ainsi? Tu es libre, tu as un amant sy[m]pathetique, tu as—à ce qu'il paraît—une bonne maison, des fleurs, des livres, de quoi manger, des livres, de la musique—enfin, tout ce qu'on peut souhaiter. Or, je crains que la Destinée ne te prépare quelque sale coup pour te faire regretter ces temps. Ah, je sais bien que tu es de celles pour qui le bonheur n'existe pas. Sais-tu pour quoi? To exiges de la vie plus que la vie ne peut te donner. Vraiment, ton ardeur de perfection te fait bien malheureuse, pauvre petite.

Mais j'ai l'air assez prêtre [sic] de te sermoner ainsi. Chère enfant—car, somme tout, avec tout ton beauté et sensibilité tu n'est [sic] qu'une enfante—combien je te plains. Combien je voudrais te faire douce la vie! Tu te sens déracinée. Mais lequel de nous n'est pas déraciné? Il faut bien se trouver quelque but dans la vie ou l'existence n'est qu'un sinistre farce. Je te conseille les livres de Renan; je ne sais pas de livres qui sont aussi confortants [sic] pour un esprit sensitif. Mais je sais bien que tu ne te fiches pas mal de la philosophie.

Je divague. Vraiment, je ne sais pas au juste ce qu'il faut dire à toi. Je t'ai déjà un peu expliqué mes sentiments à ton égard. Je me trouve toujours au même point—je t'aime, je vais t'aimer pendant tout ma vie, mais, mais, tu l'as très bien dit—mon corps avait faim d'une femme qui fusse de la terre comme moi. Et toi aussi tu avais besoin d'une spiritualité moins grossière que la mienne. Mais, je te previeu que tu ne peux jamais rompre le lien qui te jouis [sic] à moi. Je n'entends pas le lien tout legale et vulgaire de la marriage—je veux dire celui de l'amour que nous avons eu chacun pour l'autre. Notre union qui était parfait en beaucoup de choses manquait à certains égards—comme tous les unions à ce qu'il paraît. Je sait parfaitment que presque tous les torts sont à moi. C'est vrai que je t'ai traitée fort mal. Mais, que veux-tu, les hommes sont cuistres. Je crois que je t'ai moins fait de la pèine que n'importe quel bourgeois auquel tu aurais pu très bien te lier. Est-ce que je me flatte?

Le temps coule très doucement ici. Puisque nous sommes à trente kilos de la ligne nous nous moquons les Boches, bien que la position de Paris ne semble pas des plus gais à ce moment. Mais nous avons tout un mois à vivre—c'est beaucoup. Il y a tant de choses qu'on peut voir dans un mois, surtout quand il fait beau temps. J'ai des livres et un lit de fer dans un pavillion. Je travaille de sept heures du matin à cinq heures du soir. Je lis, j'écris, je regarde pousser l'herbe et les feuilles de cinq à dix, ou onze. Je sommeil [sic] de onze à six. C'est parfait. Le dimanche j'assiste au service de L'Eglise Angleterre et je prends un vif plaisir à constater la bêtise de tout cela. J'ai tout l'après-midi de Samedi et Dimanche à moi. C'est beaucoup. Mais je ne m'ennuis pas du tout.

Enfin, je dois me taire. J'ai trop bavardé. Mais si on est tranquil—je ne dis pas heureux—on prend l'habitude de trop parler. Puissse-tu te trouver de la tranquillité!

Pardons à ton vieux amant tous ses torts et tous ses petitesses et ne te souviens que de cette partie de lui que tu as aimé autrefois—Atthis!

Bonne chance. Mes amités à G.

Richard.

P.S. Quand tu écris à un soldat du B.E.F. tu n'as qu'à mettre un timbre de 1 penny, comme auparavant.

[Translation]

It's almost two years,[2] my girl, that I have endured this foul soldiers' life. During all this time we have seen each other for only scraps of time. I was twenty-three when I left you; and in a month I will be twenty-six.[3] Do you understand what that means? It means that time is passing, my dear, and we are always further apart.

I really want to scold you a little. Your letter seems to me a bit unhappy. But why on earth do you worry about things so? You are free, you have an amiable lover, you have—or so it would appear—a nice house, flowers, books, something to eat, more books, music—in sum, everything you need to make you happy. But I'm afraid lest Destiny is preparing you some dirty trick to make you miss these times. Ah, I well know that you are among those people for whom happiness does not exist. Do you know why? You ask of life more than life can give you. Really, your ardour for perfection is making you very unhappy, poor girl.

But I seem like a priest to preach thus to you. My child—for, above all, with all your beauty and sensitivity, you are only a child—how much I pity you. How I would like to make life sweet for you! You feel yourself uprooted. But which of us is not uprooted? One really needs to find some purpose in life or existence is nothing but a sinister farce. I recommend Renan's books[4] to you. I do not know any other books which are so comforting for a sensitive spirit. But I well know that you don't give a damn about philosophy.

I digress. Really, I don't rightly know what to say to you. I have already somewhat explained my feelings with regard to you. I always find myself at the same place—I love you, I am going to love you for my whole life, but, but, you have already said it well—my body hungered for a woman who was earthy like me. And you, too, needed a spirituality less gross than mine. But, I warn you that you will never be able to break the bond that joins you to me. I don't mean the utterly legal and common bond of marriage—I mean rather that of the love we each have had for the other. Our union which was perfect in so many ways was lacking in certain respects—as all unions are it would appear. I know perfectly that almost all the wrongs are mine. It's true that I have treated you very badly. But, what do you want, men are absurd. I think that I have given you less pain than any other bloke you could have hooked up with. Do I flatter myself?

The weather is very mild here. Since we are thirty kilometers away from the line, we mock the Boches, although the position of Paris[5] does not seem very gay at this moment. But we have a whole month to live[6]—that's a lot. There are so many things one can see in a month, especially when the weather is good. I have books and an iron bed in a house. I work from seven in the morning until five at night. I read, I write, I watch the grass and the leaves grow from five till ten, or eleven. I sleep from eleven to six. It's perfect. On Sundays I attend an Anglican Church service and I take a lively enjoyment in observing the foolishness of all this. I have the whole of Saturday and Sunday afternoon to myself. That's a lot. But I don't get bored at all.

Finally, I must stop writing. I have prattled on too long. But if one is at peace—I don't say happy—one gets into the habit of talking too much. I wish you could find peace!

Let's pardon your old lover all his faults and all his pettiness and remember only that part of him that you used to love—Atthis![7]

Good luck. My regards to G.[8]

Richard.

P.S. When you write to a soldier of the B.E.F. you only have to put on a 1 penny stamp, just as before.

1. Aldington routinely wrote in French to his good friend Frank Flint as an academic exercise and as a way of privileging intimate information. Writing in French seems to serve both purposes here as well as two additional ends: the effort it requires apparently assuages somewhat the boredom and dislocation Aldington felt at the front while simultaneously restraining his real irritation with H.D.'s most recent letter. Later letters to her in French seem to function similarly.

2. Since June 24, 1916.

3. Aldington's birthday is July 8.

4. Ernest Renan (1823–92) was a French historian, Hebrew scholar, philologist, and critic. He published his well-known *Vie de Jésus* in 1863, the first volume of *Les Origines du Christianisme* (1863–83), in which he treats the Christian tradition critically, eschewing exegesis and dogma for a psychological and biographical approach. Renan was very attractive to intellectuals at the end of the nineteenth century because of his admiration for scientific progress and romantic spiritualism.

5. Paris was constantly threatened, though never occupied, by the Germans in 1914–18.

6. Aldington is away from the trenches at base camp for additional training until mid-July.

7. In a poem by Sappho, of which five stanzas and parts of two more survive, she

writes of Arignota, now married to a man in Sardis, who remembers with affection her former lover, Atthis, who has deserted her for the awkward and less sophisticated Andromeda. Aldington's own poem, "To Atthis," after Sappho's, appeared first in *Glebe*, Vol. 1, No. 5 (1914), 19, then in *Des Imagistes* (1914), and bears reprinting here:

> To Atthis
> (After the Manuscript of Sappho now in Berlin)
>
> Atthis, far from me and dear Mnasidika,
> Dwells in Sardis;
> Many times she was near us
> So that we lived life well
> Like the far-famed goddess
> Whom above all things music delighted.
>
> And now she is first among the Lydian women
> As the mighty sun, the rose-fingered moon,
> Beside the great stars.
>
> And the light fades from the bitter sea
> And in like manner from the rich-blossoming earth;
> And the dew is shed upon the flowers,
> Rose and soft meadow-sweet
> And many-coloured melilote.
>
> Many things told are remembered of sterile Atthis.
>
> I yearn to behold thy delicate soul
> To satiate my desire. . . .
> . . . .

8. Cecil Gray.

14

June 13, 1918

Dearest Dooley/

Yes, I was interested to get Hulun's letter. I have written to Gilbert[1] "toot sweet" to say how-do. No doubt he's fearfully pleased at being in France—I wonder how long it will last? There are umpteen Yanks in these back areas[2] so I may just possibly run across him. He has—or will have—my address, anyhow.

It must be charming for you to know so many of your family are here or on the way. Specially nice, too, if they get wounded & come down to Cornwall to convalesce!

Thank you for the card of Newlyn.[3] It used to be a very "arty" place, where R.A.s.[4] instructed their pupils in the obviously picturesque. There is a man who does pictures of naked boys in boats—they always suggest Newlyn to me.

Ah, it was so sweet of you to write to me. And to send me your love & speak of Italy[5]—I kiss your hand, dear, and cannot tell you how happy I am to know you think of me a little.

There is a most mysterious ruined castle[6] in this village, an immense thing on a great mound—rather like Corfe[7]—with a 50 foot moat still damp with water. All the approaches are overgrown with tall grass, shrubs & trees, so that one has to force a way through like the prince in the "Sleeping Beauty." Inside the front courtyard which is now a tiny field of grass & shrubs there is an immense peace and a deep solitude. The tower of the donjon is vast—twice as broad & thrice as high as those at Corfe & immutable as time itself. I don't think I have ever felt so deep a sensation of mystery and seclusion as I got from this place.

Time is slipping by only too quickly. Already it is a week since I came[8] & there is only a month now. How I shall hate going up the line again! But—as the Tommies[9] say—"we've done it before." Really, I've been awfully lucky, for these courses are supposed to be for officers who are "tired" after many months of hard fighting. And I still haven't hit a German. Every morning in the line I used to watch through glasses for Boches & then shoot at them & dodge down when they shot back. But all was wasted—neither side scored a hit!

By the way I am sending you 3 more of my photographs—one for Hulun, one for Amy[10] & one for the Four Seas Coy.[11] Do you mind sending them on? I don't think they will be stopped by the censor puisqu'il s'agit d'un militaire.[12] Also, there is no harm in letting Hulun know my address—the censor can cut it out if he damn well likes. One mustn't respect these beastly officials too much. I have Samain's "Contes"[13] which I am going to send you when I am through. They remind me a little of Imaginary Portraits,[14] though they haven't the same "maestria."[15] Here is something will please you: "Oui, tout tend vers la Beauté, tout lutte, tout s'efforce, tout s'épuise pour la réaliser; mais comme elle est infinie, ceux-la seuls s'en approchent le plus qui doivent le plus à la Douleur."[16] And there is a wonderful description, more Wilde than Wilde, of an aesthetic Renaissance duke, qui "avait développé jusqu'à l'acuité son aptitude originelle à s'émouvoir de la beauté des choses, et à cet effet il rassemblait sans cesse autour de lui les éléments des plus délicates jouissances."[17] And there is a story of a sad faun[18] which will make the Dryad cry.

Au revoir, chère belle fantôme, souviens-toi un peu de moi.[19]

Love from

Richard.

1. "Hulun" is a nickname for Gilbert Doolittle (1884–1918), H.D.'s brother, who had just arrived in France as an officer serving as an engineer in the United States Army.

2. In the area of the large base camps near Calais, Boulogne, and Rouen about forty miles from the actual front.

3. A town much frequented by landscape artists, just west of Penzance on the southern coast of Cornwall.

4. Members of the Royal Academy.

5. Throughout the war and after, Italy and the time Aldington spent there with H.D. on their "honeymoon" in 1912 and 1913 would represent to him, and to a lesser degree to her, escape, freedom, art, the past, and an ideal time in their relationship before the war. In this vein Aldington recalls Italy, both real and idealized, in "Theocritus in Capri," an essay collected in *Literary Studies and Reviews* (London: George Allen and Unwin, 1924):

> We all have a few nooks of enchantment in our memories to turn back to for consolation and pleasure. In the creation of them perhaps more depended upon the inner man than upon outward events; the determination to find beauty and at least momentary happiness will find some satisfaction almost everywhere. Youth, spring in a Mediterranean island, Greek poetry, idleness—those were the simple factors of an enchantment whose memory will only end with life. It was of no importance that youth was qualified by penury, that the spring was a mere phenomenon, the result of sidereal motions, that the island was the tourist-ridden Capri and the Greek poet— Theocritus—had never attempted to describe it. Such contingencies have no effect upon a happily constituted mind. . . .
>
>   . . . the mood did not vanish nor the happiness fail. It was an enchantment, a plentitude of beauty sufficient to sweeten much bitterness, though, like all enchantment and all beauty, it faded too soon into the past. (241, 245)

6. The Château de Fressin near the village of Azincourt. Aldington writes about visiting this castle in his article for *The Sphere*, "The Château de Fressin" (September 3, 1919, 260), and invests the experience with a good deal of mystic emotion: "It was like Beaudelaire's [sic] dream of order and luxury—the order of natural life untroubled by the poisonous activities of stupid men, the luxury of silence. I will not say it made me in love with death, but it reconciled me in a quarrel with life."

7. Corfe Castle, the ruined twelfth-century fortress which towers above the village of Corfe Castle in which H.D. lived for several months in the summer and early fall of 1916 when Aldington was in basic training in nearby Worget Camp in Wareham, Dorset.

8. Aldington has been in base camp for additional training since June 6, 1918.

9. Ordinary British soldiers.

10. Amy Lowell, the American poet and critic whom the Aldingtons had come to know in the early days of imagism. See Biographical Appendix.

11. An American firm in Boston which published Aldington's first book of poems, *Images (1910–1915)*, in 1916. The volume had appeared the year before in England. In 1919 Four Seas published *War and Love (1915–1918)*, a combination of two books (*Images of War* and *Images of Desire*) that appeared separately in England in the same year. In 1921 Four Seas published *Images of War* in a single volume edition.

12. Since it is a picture of a soldier.

13. Albert Samain (1858–1900), the French poet who helped to found the *Mercure de France* in 1891, was influenced by the symbolists and by Greek sources. He wrote several tales published posthumously in *Contes* in 1903. Amy Lowell devoted a chapter to his work in *Six French Poets: Studies in Contemporary Literature* (1915).

14. Walter Pater's *Imaginary Portraits* (1887). Aldington included several essays from this collection in his edition, *Walter Pater: Selected Works* (London: Heinemann, 1948).

15. Italian; mastery, skill, proficiency.

16. "Yes, everything tends toward Beauty, all fights, struggles, exhausts itself to realize it; but as it is infinite, those solitary ones approach closest to it who owe the most to Sadness." Aldington is quoting from "Rovère et Angisèle" (see *Oeuvres de Albert Samain*, Vol. 3, Paris: Mercure de France, 1920, 157).

17. Who "had developed to the point of acuity his original aptitude for exciting himself with the beauty of things, and to that end he assembled around him ceaselessly the elements of the most delicate enjoyments." Aldington is quoting a description of Rovère, the son of the Duke of Spoleto, in "Rovère et Angisèle" (see *Oeuvres de Albert Samain*, Vol. 3, 113–114).

18. Probably "Hyalis le petit faune aux yeux bleus," although a faun also figures as a character in "Xanthus ou la vitrine sentimentale."

19. Goodbye, my beautiful phantom, think a little bit of me.

15

June 18, 1918

Ma chère femme,

Je me porte très bien. Je suis ni blessé ni malade (malheureusement) et voici quelques jours que je n'ai pas reçu de tes nouvelles.

Mes jours se rassemblent tellement que je ne crois pas qu'il y a grand chose à ajouter à ce que je t'ai déjà dit. Mais ici on a la paix—ce qui est beaucoup. On regrette sa liberté quelquefois, mais somme tout on s'y habitue à la fin.

C'est aujord'hui [sic] l'anniversaire de Waterloo. Je parie que tu ne l'avais pas rapellé—dis? Il y a precisément cent trois ans que La Vieille Garde faisait sa suprême attaque—tiens, je devient heroique genre Victor Hugo. Espérons du moins que cela ira mieux pour les français aujourd'hui.

Je ne sais pas au juste pourquoi j'écris puisque j'ai l'esprit tellement vide qu'il ne me reste rien à dire. Alors, faut bien dire au revoir, n'est-ce pas?

Richard.

[Translation]

My dear wife,

I am very well. I am neither wounded nor sick (unfortunately) and for some days now I have not heard from you.

My days are such that I don't think that there is anything of great moment to add to what I have already told you. But here we have peace—which is a lot. One misses one's freedom sometimes, but over all one finally becomes accustomed to it.

Today is the anniversary of Waterloo.[1] I wager you didn't remember it—tell me? It is precisely one hundred and three years since The Old Garde launched its final attack—goodness, I am becoming heroic in the style of Victor Hugo. Let's hope at least that this present situation will go better for the French.

I don't know exactly why I write since I have a spirit so empty that there is nothing left for me to say. So, it's best to say goodbye, isn't it?

Richard.

1. The famous battle in which the Duke of Wellington defeated Napoleon in 1805. Aldington's interest in this battle eventually led to his biography *The Duke: Being an Account of the Life & Achievements of Arthur Wellesley, 1st Duke of Wellington* (New York: Viking, 1943).

16

June 20, 1918

Dear Dooley/

All your letters seem to be coming backwards! Last night I had the one saying you didn't want to write any more and to-night I have your "third installment." The others will come on later from the batt'n,[1] so I shall be able to piece them together. I am very interested in the little girl[2] in the garden & the German conversation seems very thrilling to me—someday I must learn German.[3] Really it is very kind of you to send me these letters—like of [sic] sort of realistic fairy tale "to be continued in our next," though I hope I shan't be here for 1001 days.[4]

Amy's lecture[5] is dreadful, but I am very touched by it—the poor old thing was really trying to please me & to help me. It isn't her fault that she can't see how very foolish she is—"vanity of vanities" blinds her. The whole "lecture" is laughable—my chief concern is to conceal it now I've got it!

I don't like my article on Sappho[6] at all—it's bad prose & contains not one original idea. Je m'en fiche.[7]

These days I am learning to write all over again. My method may amuse you. I write on a sheet of paper a line of French prose upon which I "meditate" until out of the confusion of my sensations & thoughts & emotions something definite frames itself. This I translate as briefly & clearly as possible in two or three prose paragraphs, upon which I work at odd minutes and half hours during a week or so. I've done 8 so far, 6 of wh: I sent to Flint[8] with the remark that he might pass them on to you. I am trying to avoid 1. All complaint & self-pity, 2. All excessive depression, 3. Any lack of candour with myself, 4. Everything that is not at least abstractly true. I am rather proud of this paragraph: "There, lingering for a while beside the marble head of some shattered Hermes it (the soul) shall strew the violets of regret for a lost loveliness as transient as itself. Or, perhaps, by some Homeric sea it shall watch the crisp foam from a straight wind & gather sea-flowers exquisite in their acrid restraint of colour & austere sparseness of petal."

Richard.

Please *note*: Correspondence for soldiers of H.M. Forces needs *only one penny stamp*.

1. Battalion headquarters.
2. H.D. did not routinely keep her early manuscripts and the stories which she is sending to Aldington here were never published and apparently have not survived.

3. Aldington was never so comfortable with German as H.D. was (she had studied German throughout her years at Friends' Central School, from 1901 through 1905), but he was not the ignoramus he implies here. In *Life for Life's Sake*, Aldington notes that when in training in Dorset in the summer of 1916 he took with him a copy of Heinrich Heine's *Buch der Lieder*, which he planned to read to "brush up" on his German (182).

4. An allusion to the continuing fairy tales in *1001 Arabian Nights*.

5. I have been unable to determine whether Aldington is referring here to something Amy Lowell has recently published or to something she has written in a recent letter to one or the other or both of the Aldingtons.

6. As part two of a series of six articles entitled "Letters to Unknown Women," which appeared in *The Dial* between March 14, 1918, and May 17, 1919, Aldington's essay "To Sappho" appeared in the May 9, 1918, issue (No. 766, 430–431).

7. I don't care.

8. Frank Flint, fellow imagist poet and translator. See Biographical Appendix.

17

Dear Dooley/

The first "installment"[1] has come to join the third which arrived yesterday. I am expecting the second tomorrow to make the sequence complete. I am very glad you are sending them especially if it is any help or pleasure to you to write them. Certainly it gives me pleasure to hear from you.

I think I like the third better than the first. Yes, the third is charming and touching and somehow the little German conversation makes it quaint and like a fairy-tale. The first one is—shall we say—un peu cinglant.[2] But it's astonishing what a thick, thick skin one grows—dodging whizz-bangs,[3] I suppose, helps one to this indifference.

Harriet's[4] letter & the extract from Poetry are, I suppose, some sort of a belated "tribute"—can't you see them unctiously quoting Choricos[5] if I happened to stop a whole one! I am genuinely pleased, though, that some American lad has found even a rhetorical consolation in my words. But I don't really believe he thought of anything *but* shells when shells were falling. Perhaps I am mistaken.

I can't see you writing a "Deirdre"[6]—no, no, sharp edges not mist. Yet it is perhaps good that you should add the stimulus of music to your great gifts—yes, excellent, you will do beautiful things. Why not assassinate H.D.[7] since Amy has mangled her? The combinations of the alphabet are quite numerous. Or a name—something Anglo-Boche?

Ah, well; time passes. Will you post the enclosed[8] to Harriet, please?

With love from
Richard.

On second thoughts I'm going to ask you to type the enclosed—for old acquaintance sake?—and to send them to Harriet for me. Will you, please?

1. An "installment" of prose H.D. has recently begun; see letter 16.
2. Rather bitter.
3. German flat trajectory bombs whose detonation was preceded by an audible "whizz."
4. Harriet Monroe, editor of *Poetry*; see Biographical and Periodical Appendix. Monroe sent him with her letter a copy of her review of Aldington's *Reverie: A Little Book of Poems for H.D.* (Cleveland: Clerk's Press, 1917), which appeared in *Poetry*, Vol. 12, No. 1, April 1918, 44–45:

> An American soldier now in France writes, in acknowledging a copy of the new *Poetry:*
>
>> Certain poems, like the *Choricos* of Aldington, have shuddered with me along night roads, and through their bold beauty have saved me from terror at moments when one of the great shocks—the explosion of an enemy shell, the sudden presence of pain or awful agony, the nearness of death—fell without preface upon me.
>>
>> I remember once particularly, in the drab of light of a cloudy dawning, when I saw near the edge of a road a poilu quietly lying. I should have fainted, I think, from the sheer tragedy of the incident, had I not heard, singing in my head, Aldington's invocation to death.
>
> Such a letter proves, more sharply than any review, the value of a poet's work. No later lyric by Aldington can ever dim the Greek-marble-like beauty of *Choricos*, but neither can that poem dim the more tender and human beauty of *Reverie*. The contrast of moods in the two poems bridges the gulf between youth and manhood. *Choricos*, which was first printed over five years ago in the second number of POETRY, was written while the poet was still in his teens. It presents the feeling of adolescence, that high and impersonal exaltation not uncommon when noble youth confronts the thought of death:
>
>> Thou art the silence of beauty,
>> And we look no more for the morning;
>> We yearn no more for the sun,
>> Since with thy white hands,
>> Death,
>> Thou crownest us with the pallid chaplets,
>> The slim colorless poppies
>> Which in thy garden alone
>> Softly thou gatherest.
>
> Since writing it, the poet has experienced love and war—love at its highest, war at its most terrible. He has compassed life, from extreme to extreme, and after that there is no longer question of youth or age—life moves in the larger rhythms of eternity.
>
>> All men love for a flash, a day,
>> As I love now,
>> But all men do not always love so long
>> Nor find in love the excuse for life,
>> The sanction for the bitterness of death.
>> Not far away as I now write
>> The guns are beating madly upon the still air
>> With sudden rapid blows of sound,

And men die with the quiet sun above them
And horror and pain and noise upon earth.

To-morrow, maybe, I shall be one of them,
One in a vast field of dead men,
Unburied, or buried hastily, callously.
But for ever and for ever.
In the fair land I have built up
From the dreams of my love,
We two are together, she bending by the pale flower
And I beside her:
We two together in a land of quiet
Inviolable behind the walls of death.

This tiny book of nine brief poems contains "no murmur against Fate."
The poet accepts war, as he might accept a cyclone, in anguish and bitterness
of spirit but without revolt. He feels no élan, no conviction of war's necessity
or righteousness, but he takes his place in the ranks and does his part with a
grim and resolute stoicism. And out of his despair, out of his hunger for
beauty, comes a lyric note clearer and richer than anything we have heard
from him since those earliest poems, and an exaltation of spirit as noble and
impassioned, and perhaps more humane.

> We are of those that Dante saw
> Glad, for love's sake, among the flames of hell,
> Outdating with a kiss all-powerful wrath;
> For we have passed athwart a fiercer hell,
> Through gloomier, more desperate circles
> Than ever Dante dreamed:
> And yet love kept up glad.

H.M.

5. First printed in *Poetry* in November 1912 (Vol. 1, No. 2, 39–40), "Choricos" 's
title appeared in Greek, "XOPIKOS":

> The ancient songs
> Pass deathward mournfully.
>
> Cold lips that sing no more, and withered wreaths,
> Regretful eyes, and drooping breasts and wings—
> Symbols of ancient songs,
> Mournfully passing
> Down to the great white surges,
> Watched of none
> Save the frail sea-birds
> And the lithe pale girls,
> Daughters of Oceanus.
>
> And the songs pass from the green land
> Which lies upon the waves as a leaf
> On the flowers of hyacinths.
> And they pass from the waters,

The manifold winds and the dim moon,
And they come
Silently winging through soft Cimmerian dusk,
To the quiet level lands
That she keeps for us all,
That she wrought for us all for sleep
In the silver days of the earth's dawning—
Proserpina, daughter of Zeus.

And we turn from the Cyprian's breasts,
And we turn from thee,
Phoebus Apollo,
And we turn from the music of old,
And the hills that we loved and the meads,
And we turn from the fiery day,
And the lips that were over-sweet;
For silently
Brushing the fields with red-shod feet,
With purple robe
Searing the grass as with a sudden flame,
Death,
Thou hast come upon us.
And of all the ancient songs
Passing to the swallow-blue halls
By the dark streams of Persephone,
This only remains—
That in the end we turn to thee,
Death,
We turn to thee, singing
One last song.

O death,
Thou art an healing wind
That blowest over white flowers
A-tremble with dew;
Thou art a wind flowing
Over far leagues of lonely sea;
Thou art the dusk and the fragrance;
Thou art the lips of love mournfully smiling;
Thou art the sad peace of one
Satiate with old desires;
Thou art the silence of beauty,
And we look no more for the morning,
We yearn no more for the sun
Since with thy white hands,
Death,
Thou crownest us with the pallid chaplets,
The slim colourless poppies
Which in thy garden alone
Softly thou gatherest.

And silently;
And with slow feet approaching—
And with bowed head and unlit eyes,
We kneel before thee;
And thou, leaning towards us,
Caressingly layest upon us
Flowers from thy thin cold hands,
And, smiling as a chaste woman
Knowing love in her heart,
Thou seelest our eyes
And the illimitable quietude
Comes gently upon us.

6. Yeats's play "Deirdre" (1917), which was based on the Irish myth of Deirdre of the Sorrows.

7. Aldington suggests that H.D. abandon the persona which Amy Lowell has now misrepresented; see letter 16. H.D. herself often had reservations about her pen name, using others from time to time (*Nights* appeared under the pseudonym "John Helforth" in 1935, and "Delia Alton" was a pseudonym H.D. seriously considered when she was preparing *Bid Me to Live* for publication in 1960). She wrote to Lowell about her name as a literary identity on March 5, 1917: "My signature is 'H.D.' for poetic purposes. *Please* let it be *just* that. I have always wanted to keep R's and my literary personalities absolutely distinct. . . . I must keep *H.D.* clear from R.A. R. has his career + it is best for him not to have me as an appendage."

8. Aldington probably enclosed "Prayers and Fantasies I-VIII," dated "France, 1918," which appeared in *Poetry* in November 1918 (Vol. 13, No. 2, 67–71):

I

To have passed so close to annihilation, and (which is worse) to have become
stained so inalterably with the ideas and habits of masses—this leaves me
immeasurably discouraged, out of love with myself.
Now I am good only to mimic inferior masters. My thoughts are stifling—
heavy grey dust from a scorched road.
For me silence; or if speech, then some humble poem in prose. Indeed I am
too conscientious—or shall we say too impotent?—to dare the cool rhythm
of prose, the sharp edges of poetry.
Nymphes de Parnasse! Encore un Pégasse raté!

II

Touch once again with the lips of thought the fair rigid limbs of goddesses
men imagined beside the inland sea. Give the life of our blood to one
among them, and worship in her oval of tremulous gold the beauty of that
body whose embrace would murder us with ecstasy.
Recall from Orcus the Foam-born, lady of many names; make for her a broid-
ered throne among the dusky colonnades of the soul.
Death, a fierce exaltation, sweeps from the lips of the conqueror; but from
hers, gently, a frail kiss, breathes a savor of life.

III

Slowly, too slowly, the night, with its noise and its fear and its murder, yields
to the dawn. One by one the guns cease. Quicker, O dawn, quicker—
dazzle the hateful stars, lighten for us the weight of the shadows.

The last rat scuttles away; the first lark thrills with a beating of wings and
song. The light is soft; deliberately, consciously, the young dawn moves.
My unclean flesh is penetrated with her sweetness and she does not disdain even me.

Out of the East as from a temple comes a procession of girls and young men,
smiling, brave, candid, ignorant of grief.

Few know the full bitterness of night, but they alone will know the full beauty
of dawn—if dawn ever comes.

IV

Life has deceived us. The thoughts we found so vivid and fresh were dull and
crass as the prayers muttered to a worn rosary by an infidel priest.

The joy we felt in beauty, our sense of discovery at the touch of some age-
green bronze; even the sick horror at some battlefield where the flesh had
not quite fallen from the shattered bones—all this was old, a thousand
times felt and forgotten.

And is the kiss of your mouth then but the reflection of dead kisses, the gleam
of your breast a common thing? Was the touch of your hand but a worn
memory of hands crumbled into cool dust?

V

And in the end one comes to love flowers as women, and women as flowers.
Beauty recoils from excess. Imitate the wise Easterns, and let a few sprays
of blossom decorate the empty chamber of the soul and spread their fragrance through its recesses.

Ah! To retain this fragrance, to make permanent this most precious of es-
sences, this mingling of suave and acrid perfumes—something wild and
tender and perverse and immortal!

I will make for myself, from tempered silver, an Aphrodite with narrow hips
and small pointed breasts, and wide brow above gay, subtle eyes; and in
her hand shall be a perfume ball sweet with this divine fragrance.

VI

Escape, let the soul escape from this insanity, this insult to God, from this
ruined landscape, these murdered fields, this bitterness, this agony, from
this harsh death and disastrous mutilation, from this filth and labor, this
stench of dead bodies and unwashed living bodies—escape, let the soul
escape!

Let the soul escape and move with emotion along ilex walks under a quiet
sky. There, lingering for a while beside the marble head of some shattered
Hermes, it strews the violets of regret for a lost loveliness as transient as
itself. Or perhaps, by some Homeric sea, watching the crisp foam blown

by a straight wind, it gathers sea-flowers, exquisite in their acrid restraint of color and austere sparseness of petal.

There, perhaps, among flowers, at twilight, under the glimmer of the first stars, it will find a sensation of a quiet, almost kindly universe, indifferent to this festering activity.

VII

The gods have ceased to be truth, they have become poetry. Now only simple pure hearts and those who are weary of doubt believe. Why not pray to the gods, any god? Perhaps even from the immensity of space will come a gently ironic echo.

"Dionysios, lord of life and laughter, from whom come twin gifts of ecstasy, hear me.

I pray the noble Iacchos of reverent mien and wide tolerant eyes, to look mildly upon me and to show me the mystery of beauty, the mystery of vineyards, the mystery of death.

And I pray the young Dionysios, the bearer of the fawn-skin, the charioteer of leopards, the lover of white breasts, to show me the mystery of love.

And grant that nothing ignoble may render me base to myself; let desire be always fresh and keen; let me never love or be loved through ennui, through pity or through lassitude."

VIII

The moon high-seated above the ridge, fills the ruined village with tranquil light and black broken shadows—ruined walls, shattered timbers, piles of rubbish, torn-up ground, almost beautiful in this radiance, in this quiet June air. Lush grass in the tangled gardens sways very softly, and white moths dart over the bending sprays.

Somehow to-night the air blows clearer, sweeter—the chemistry of earth is slowly purifying the corrupting bodies, the waste and garbage of armies. Sweetness, darkness, clean peace—the marble rock of some Greek island, piercing its sparse garment of lavenders and mints like a naked nymph among rustling leaves.

Heavy-scented the air to-night—new-mown hay?—a pungent exotic odor— ah! phosgene. . . .

And to-morrow there will be huddled corpses with blue horrible faces and foam on their writhed mouths.

18

June 23, 1918

My dear Dooley/

This letter will be written in rather a hurry as I feel I'm sickening for "pyrexia"[1] wh: will put me to bed for a couple of days. I daresay you've heard of it, this new mysterious disease which is going over Europe, especially the armies, like the old plagues. Fortunately it is quite harmless & only lasts a few days—one has a dreadful head & back ache, legs like lead, a high temperature & a rapid pulse. Then it goes as suddenly as it came. I'm one of the last to get it here & I guess I shan't have it badly.

I am very happy to get your letters and to live with them either your child's or girl's life or something we lived together. That scene in Paris. I had almost forgotten it, but now I remember it all so clearly, so plainly. Perhaps I exaggerated a little the odd sensation of Margaret's regret.[2] Yet it was there, and she was there or seemed to be. One's nerves play these games, induce these hallucinations. Just as to-day any over-weary Frenchman, struggling on, battling long after all strength has gone, may see Joan of Arc on her white horse in the barrage-smoke. These eidola have no existence in themselves, but are real because of the emotion that creates them. (Am I writing dreadful nonsense? I feel so damn queer—it wouldn't surprise me now if the war ended!)

I think, rather against you, that Death does settle nearly everything. Somewhere back in my mind is a memory of some stately prose Elizabethan discourse on death.[3] I cannot remember the words but this is how I should write them: "O kingly, O pontifical death, at whose touch, Midas-like yet priestly, all the vain efforts of man crumble into the golden dust of oblivion; Death, that receivest into thy great Commonwealth not only the stately dames & great lords of history but the most humble, the most childish, the weakest and most despised of mankind. By thy graves, O Death, all must bend in sorrow, & in thy sepulcres all must at last rest. Thou art that Basanos[4] whereby we may test the vanity of all flesh & prove what fools' baubles be those crowns, those lands, that honour, those riches, that lust, that beauty, those busy affairs wherein the jewish race of man doth so agitate & afflict him. Over all thou triumphest, O Death, for whatever be the play thou speakest the funereal prologue & all our histories & pomps are summed up by thine inevitable 'Hic Jacet.' "[5]

Isn't that Sir Thomas Browne[6] with the genius cut out? Yet it is true and I for one am "too timid, too frail in hope"[7] to deceive myself (as I think) with any talk of Islands of the Blessed.[8] "Dust hath closed Helen's eyes,"[9] and not all Homer's rhetoric nor all the tears that have been shed for her will ever make that dust pure red & white again or give that heart one thrill of the many kisses of the young prince.[10]

Ah, well one can go on for pages enwinding the sadness of one's heart in more or less picturesque rhetoric. I'm going along to the Doc. now & shall find out if I'm in for a slight or a serious do. It feels very slight to me.

Au revoir—I will go on writing something each day when possible.

Richard.

1. Known to doctors as P.U.O. ("pyrexia of unknown origin") and to soldiers as "trench fever," pyrexia was a virus carried by lice and characterized by chills and fever. In Aldington's battalion between June 11 and June 23, 1918, five officers and 250 men of

other ranks were hospitalized because of an outbreak of influenza (the war diaries of the Ninth Royal Sussex Regiment, PRO).

2. Margaret Lanier Cravens (1881–1912) was a young American pianist whom the Aldingtons met in Paris through Ezra Pound in the spring of 1912. H.D., Aldington, and Pound were shocked when she committed suicide in June 1912 in response to her friend Walter Rummel's sudden engagement to Thérèse Chaigneau. Robert Spoo's edition of the Pound-Cravens correspondence (*Ezra Pound and Margaret Cravens: A Tragic Friendship, 1910–1912*, Durham: Duke University Press, 1988) discusses the impact of Cravens's suicide on Aldington and particularly on H.D., who chronicled her response at the time in two sonnets to "M.L.C." written in the summer of 1912 and published in Spoo's book.

3. Unidentified.

4. A transliteration from the Greek word meaning "a touchstone."

5. Here lies.

6. Sir Thomas Browne (1605–82) was a British physician and miscellaneous writer, an antiquarian known for rhetorical elegance in the grand style.

7. Unidentified.

8. Imaginary islands in the west thought proverbially to be the home of good people after death.

9. A line from Thomas Nashe's "In Time of Pestilence":

> Brightness falls from the air;
> Queens have died young and fair;
> Dust hath closed Helen's eye.
> I am sick, I must die.
> Lord have mercy on us.

10. Paris.

19

June 24, 1918

Just to say that I'm all right & that the little fever is progressing normally. Have to stay in bed a couple of days, that's all; which, as you can imagine, I don't mind in the least!

Will write more to-morrow.

Richard.

P.S. Have you heard anything from the Dial[1] about paying for those articles?[2] I must write to them.

R

1. The American periodical edited by Martyn Johnson; see Periodical Appendix.

2. *The Dial* accepted six articles from Aldington, which appeared under the title "Letters to Unknown Women": "To the Slave in 'Cleon' " appeared March 14, 1918 (226–

227); "To Sappho" appeared May 9, 1918 (430–431); "To Helen" appeared June 6, 1918 (525–526). Aldington is probably awaiting payment for these three. The other articles in the series appeared after this time: "Heliodora," December 28, 1918 (598); "To the Amaryllis of Theocritus," February 22, 1919 (183); and "To La Gross Margot," May 17, 1919 (510).

20

June 26, 1918

Well I've got over my little fever fit and am walking about again, rather slowly as my head feels a little queer still & my legs shake a bit. But I'm better, much better; very terribly tired of the war though & rather tending towards discouragement. There is just the hillside & its trees & the white bend in the road that one seems to cling on to frantically as the man in Notre Dame[1] clung to the bending lead gargoyle. In the end of course one must let go but for the time being . . .

Your letter of the 20th came to-day with its virginal mood, pellucid & wistful. A little convalescent in texture, perhaps, and so rather fitting in with my present state. Of course as always the heart of another is a dark forest; I cannot "place" you, especially at this distance. I mean have you, at last, really found out something of what you want or are you just wrapping in Attic parables an almost legitimate repulsion to me? You liken me to Antinous,[2] to Meleager[3]—ah, but I am very far from that now—a kind of mixture of Le Feu of Barbusse[4] & Remy's Diomède,[5] blood & fire annihilating that elusive, perhaps imaginary, freshness.

But I'm not in a proper state to write coherently to-day—very little things irritate me & entirely divert my thoughts. Someone spoke to me & I've quite forgotten all I was going to write. So it must just go—do you know how easy that renouncing things becomes? (You say "Keep young"; you say, "we must not meet for years."[6] Then, lady, say how be young away from the fountain of all youth—your eyes?)

Presently I shall go for a little walk down the village street and come back for tea, speak outworn trivialities, & so gradually to bed. They say the Italians have beaten the Austrians—what does it matter? A few Sou [?] thousand more widows and "loverless"—nothing, a mere nothing.

I haven't heard from Gilbert, but I think I know where he is, a good way from here, in a very charming place. No chance of our meeting I think.

Please go on writing. I like to get your angle of vision.

Richard.

1. Quasimodo, the hunchback who loved Esmeralda in Victor Hugo's novel, *Notre Dame de Paris* (1831).
2. The shameless leader of Penelope's suitors in *The Odyssey*, killed by Odysseus on his return to Ithaca.

3. The first century B.C.E. Greek poet and philosopher who is known for his erotic verse and as the first editor of the Greek Anthology.

4. A realistic novel published in 1916 by Henri Barbusse (1874–1935), *Le Feu: Journal d'une Esconade* was one of the most widely read works of the First World War. It detailed the soldier's experience in the trenches, behind the lines, and on leave.

5. *Les Chevaux de Diomède* (1897), a novel by Remy de Gourmont, which appeared in installments in *The Egoist* in 1914.

6. In her most recent letter H.D. has evidently suggested that their relationship continue as merely an epistolary one.

21

June 29, 1918

I'm glad you got those two books but they were sent off a long time ago—before I left the line in fact.[1] Gyp[2] is not much—one gets tired of her in no time. She is the Frenchwoman comme il faut[3]—a horrible type.

I never hear from Mrs. Shakespeare[4]—is she ill or something.

Frank[5] didn't mean any ill by his question. Clearly, someone has made the suggestion to him—Hutton,[6] I fancy. But he hasn't replied to my letter—perhaps the gods have put him in the army as a punishment.

Sanity, yes that is worth having. What exactly does it mean? Giving things & people & ideas that correct relative importance. That is why a sane man always looks a little mad to other people. But if Gray can give you sanity from that marmoreal calm of his, then indeed he is not one who gives nothing. You must beware, though, of staying too long in Cornwall. Don't you think an occasional "bout" in town would be good, or are you utterly fed up with London? μηδὲν ἄγαν [nothing in excess] you know. You have been quite fourteen weeks in Cornwall now.[7]

My flu left me very spiritless & unpoised, & I am only just getting back that sense of self-satisfaction so necessary to comfort. I have written nothing for a week & have no desire to; à quoi bon noircir du bon papier blanc?[8]

The woods here are still lovely, but "lack a somewhat"[9] as friend Pound would have remarked in his exquisite classic English.

Au revoir
Richard.

1. Aldington left the trenches on June 4 for additional training at the base camp where he now is.

2. Pseudonym of Marie-Antoinette de Riguetti de Mirabeau (1850–1932). Her light and witty books include *Petit Bob* (1868), *Autour de Marriage* (1883), *Mademoiselle Loulon* (1888), and *Le Marriage de Chiffon* (1894).

3. A proper lady.

4. Olivia Shakespear (1864–1938) was the mother of Dorothy Shakespear, Ezra Pound's wife. She had many literary friends and Aldington had met her through Pound in 1912.

5. Frank Stewart (F.S.) Flint (1885–1960) was Aldington's closest male friend and a fellow imagist; see Biographical Appendix. Aldington wrote to Flint often during this time. He had just entered the army and evidently wrote Aldington in late May asking if the Aldingtons had parted ways. Aldington wrote back on June 2, 1918: "I knew of course that there would be "facheux bruits" [angry noises, gossip] about H.D. and myself. We are "parted" to the extent that I am in France and she in Cornwall. But we are not "parted" in any other sense. We write to each other comme toujours. You—et le monde—are very blind if you think anything could ever part us two."

6. Edward Hutton; see Biographical Appendix.

7. If Aldington is being precise, H.D. arrived in Cornwall on March 23, 1918.

8. To what good purpose blacken good white paper?

9. Aldington is here making fun of Ezra Pound's idiosyncratic locutions. Aldington early perceived that Pound's witty and sometimes bizarre phrasing was a result, conscious or not, of a mistranslation of a foreign phrase into English (as in *Des Imagistes*), of an amusing mishearing (as in Pound's later reference to New Directions as "Nude Erections"), of peculiar orthography, cryptic shorthand, or coded elision (as in Hamadryad for H.D. or H.D. for Hilda Doolittle), or even of mistyping or gross typographical error, which Aldington in the late twenties generously attributed to Pound's typewriter itself, which by some fluke of circumstance Aldington inherited, probably when Pound left England for Italy in 1920.

22

July 1, 1918

Where was I in my discourse?[1] Somewhere about "life," I fancy. Once at 44[2] I tried to get at what was moving in me, by talking about "keeping in touch with common humanity." That is not quite what I meant, but it is somewhere near it. The attitude I am getting at is very hard to define. One acts & yet at the same time one reflects on action: one does the ordinary things that quite common people do, simply because one is convinced that what happens to humanity happens to oneself, that the things which quite stupid poor men do are the real things of life. The man who sows the wheat, the man who grinds the grain, the man who kneads & bakes the bread—just to take one instance—these people are exceedingly important. One's art must take note of them, be at least sympathetic towards them. Why is it Ezra, for instance, seems to us so utterly dead? Just because he has cut himself off from this common humanity—which is fundamentally the same which Christ walked with and Plato talked with & Villon[3] played the scoundrel with. Don't mistake me; I am a thousand miles from the philanthropic man, the man who wants to reform the world, the democrate. No, and I would by no means be blind to all the misery & treachery & petty lusts & cruelties of this "common humanity." But I think one should realise one's own clay, be part of the drab or golden pageant, be at ease with common men as well as with exceptional men. That is very hard for such as we, yet we cannot but gain by it. For that is the true romance, that the great living truth which makes vital our love of beauty, our knowledge of dead worlds—here, I mean, on this earth.

Aldington enclosed this photograph with his letter of July 1, 1918.

I seem always to be describing loops about my subject, always shooting à peu près;[4] but I think perhaps you will get me. For myself I see clearly that I want to avoid the dead-egotism of Pound, the very foolish paltryness of Chelsea,[5] the ridiculous splurging of Chicago,[6] the diseased strength of the Cubists,[7] and the mere belly-worship of the bourgeois, the mere struggle with poverty of the poor. What is left then? Why just that full consciousness of life I speak of, that almost fanatical sincerity I am seeking. Oh, yes, books are good and it is good to know all about Gothic churches & the philosophy of Lucretius[8]—but it is good too to know how a soldier puts together his marching order, how a blacksmith shoes a horse & why we do not grow as much wheat in the west of England as in the east. And beyond all this knowledge one should be sincerely interested in common lives, realise I mean what these people do. They are the salt of the earth; we, I don't quite know what we are, not "unacknowledged legislators"[9] certainly! We are, perhaps, a kind of unauthorised priesthood, the go-betweens of the spirit & the flesh. We interpret humanity to itself, & ourselves. It doesn't matter at all whether anyone ever reads what we write. The great point is to think rightly & clearly—and all these things shall be added unto you.[10]

Thus, I now know that Alexander the Great was an imbecile; but he was a very brilliant imbecile. He did things which were perhaps not worth doing; but if anyone thinks the handling of armies an easy thing let him take charge of a company for a week. What I mean is this: that Alexander was not a great man— he added nothing to the world—but he cannot have been a fool. One must understand even Alexander, just as one must understand the scrub-woman.

At once, you will see that there is a tremendous lot to be learned. One knows nothing of these things. Could you make a pair of shoes? Can you hoe a row of turnips? Do you understand, say, the difference between municipal government in the United States & in Italy? Oh _not_ dull, because these are people's lives & we live in this world, not in Sirius,[11] certainly not in "Chelsea." The problem of expressing these things is infinitely difficult—much more than, say, the record of one's ecstacy before an "old garden"![12] I am trying to approach it obliquely, through little prose poems,[13] feeling my way & waiting for the illumination which may or may not come.

But there I am. We have before us the warning of certain futile personalities and I feel it is better to do nothing & seek something than to do something & seek nothing. What is James Whitall[14] seeking, what Ezra Pound? Lewis,[15] Joyce, Lawrence are all seeking something—wrongly, because haughtily, with a "what a great man I am" gesture—but they are seeking; they are not dead.

So it is up to me, isn't it? But, yes, life first.

Richard.

1. Aldington is talking to himself in this letter as much as to H.D., although he does touch on the idea of "sanity" that he refers to in the previous letter (see letter 21). He is here trying to make sense of his military ("common") experience, yet he does not identify himself with the ordinary Tommy; by his values he distinguishes himself from the soldier. A letter such as this one makes H.D.'s later fictional treatment of Aldington as the quintessential military man seem particularly unfair: Aldington appears as Marius Decius in "Hipparchia" and as Captain Rafton in "Secret Name," both sections of *Palimpsest* (1926).

2. The Mecklenburgh Square flat H.D. had rented since December 1, 1916. She gave up the apartment at the end of July, 1918.

3. The French poet François Villon (1431–?). In his first known poem, the *Lais* or *Petit Testament* (1456), he suggests that he is driven from Paris not because of theft (as

was in fact the case) but because of his betrayal by the woman he loved. His longer autobiographical poem, *Testament* (1461), recounts his disappointments in love, his poverty, and his periods of imprisonment. Both words include witty bequests to a variety of friends and acquaintances.

4. Near the mark.

5. A district in the southwest of London which flourished as a bohemian community of artists at its height in the generation before the Aldingtons'.

6. Aldington associates Chicago with *Poetry* and its editor, Harriet Monroe (see Periodical and Biographical Appendices). Monroe's philosophy included a Whitmanesque belief in the democracy of art that Aldington is clearly rejecting here. Despite his emphasis on the importance of the artist's awareness of common humanity, Aldington's position shares a great deal with Pound's insistence on art as aristocratic in the latter's "Editorial" in *The Little Review* in May 1917; Aldington is, however, rejecting in large measure Pound's conclusion that "there is no misanthropy in a thorough contempt for the mob" (Vol. 4, No. 1, 6).

7. For Aldington, the cubists emphasized form at the cost of content; their work had a modernist power without meaning, and thus was ultimately ridiculous.

8. T. Lucretius Carus (c. 99–55 B.C.E.), Latin author of the calmly reasoned *De Rerum Natura.*

9. In *A Defense of Poetry* (1840), Percy Bysshe Shelley states that "poets are the unacknowledged legislators of the world."

10. This is not a direct quote, but is sufficiently biblical in phrasing to suggest divine justice or retribution.

11. Literally the dog star, in Egyptian mythology identified with Isis.

12. One of Aldington's earliest poems was the relatively simple "Au Vieux Jardin" which first appeared in the second issue of *Poetry* in November 1912. It later appeared in *Des Imagistes* in 1914 as "In the Old Garden."

13. On January 1, 1919, Aldington enclosed in a letter to Bryher (see Biographical Appendix) a prose poem dated June 1918 and entitled "ESCAPE"; the brackets are Aldington's:

> Escape, escape! From the monstrous sin of this insanity, from the chains of restraint, from this ruined landscape, these murdered fields, these fetid striations across the body of earth, from this insult to God, this murder & bitterness & agony, from this harsh metallic death & more disastrous mutilation, from this filth & this labour, this stench of unmasked bodies, this resentment & trickery & slavishness—escape, escape!
>
> Let the soul escape & move with emotion along ilex walks in the company of lyric women, with tenderness, with delicacy. There, lingering for a while beside the marble head of some shattered Hermes it strews the violets of regret for a lost loveliness as transient as itself. There, perhaps, by some Homeric sea it watches the crisp foam of a straight wind & gathers sea flowers exquisite in their acrid restraint of colour & austere sparseness of petal.
>
> There, remote from turbulence, it lies at twilight among flowers that simulate the drooping asphodel and at the first glimmer of frail stars it catches for a moment some [inkling] of harmony, a sensation of a quiet, almost kindly universe, indifferent to [the festering] activity [of perverted intelligence.]

Yes, the escape is perfect & complete; the spirit moves more easily from the flesh, hoping eagerly for some complete separation which will render it all liberty & return to it that tranquility which formerly it enjoyed as a right.

14. A wealthy American from Philadelphia whom the Aldingtons met before the war; see Biographical Appendix. Whitall was aware of his conventional sympathies and his literary limitations, which he acknowledged in his discussion of his friendship with the Aldingtons in his memoir *English Years* (New York: Harcourt Brace, 1935, 54–59).

15. Percy Wyndham Lewis (1882–1957), writer and artist; see Biographical Appendix.

23

July 4, 1918

Recently I have been reading Zarathustra.[1] Not with very much pleasure, though. Nietzsche is a kind of epigramatic Carlyle. He tries to be apocalyptic & often only achieves apoplexy. I suspect all thought which needs such tumultuous obscurity. Emotion may be difficult in expression (Mallarmé,[2] Dante) but pure thought must be clear (Renan,[3] Plato). What is well thought is well expressed; but what is well thought can only be clear. Somehow I feel that obscurity always masks a weakness—in Mallarmé, for instance, a fundamental sterility; in Dante (who is not often obscure except in the Paradiso) an ignorance of psychology. (& *you* might add "of astronomy!")[4] But then one has to find a hair line to divide the mystic from the obscure. I get lost here & have to fall back on Renan and France and the Greeks.

Yet after all obscurity is a vice. No man writes obscure advertisements; few, except intentionally through calculation, write obscure love letters. So if a man writes confusedly, dear Dooley, surely we are not unjust if we say he has been thinking confusedly? Surely that gives one a line on which to approach the moderns—doesn't the obscurity of, say, a Marinetti,[5] just mask the nullity of ideas, the void of talent? I had an idea of analysing James Joyce's new prose, but refrained in view of the ultimate futility of all things. (So that is why I work these things off on you!) Where Joyce thinks clearly he is really marvellous. That scene by the sea-shore in "Ulysses" has amazing passages—& amazing rot too.[6] But like all of us he lacks a guiding principle. He doesn't really believe in anything except himself; & that is fatal. Scepticism is of its essence sterile—one sees it in Remy de Gourmont,[7] where a nature abnormally rich is reduced to comparative poverty by the vice of cynicism. Joyce tries instinctively to make up this void with an astonishing *verbal* energy. His sentences are like spectres, grotesque, phosphorescent, clanking rusty chains of phrases from their boneless limbs. He has a little of Job, a good deal of Blake & even something of Leautréamont[8] in him. And Flaubert! [in margin] He is incredibly selfish but not confident. He is, I think, more interesting (yet more repellent) than any of "us youth." Perhaps he has escaped the blight of Dostoievski which has consumed Mackenzie[9] & is consuming Lawrence & will consume Lewis. Melodrama masked as intensity, rhetoric walking as thought, & eloquence (shades of Slonimski!)[10] posing as energy.

There are moments when I doubt even the Greeks; clearly Aristotle ruined the poetry of the 17th and 18th centuries (in France especially) but perhaps that was only because the poets misunderstood the "Poetics." On the whole, Racine is more boring than Hugo, but less repulsive because more sincere. Yes, I suppose the "Greeks" are our norm, the inventors of our criticism, the dictators of our taste. For us Europeans I mean. Perhaps future Americans working from the East[11] instead of the West may escape this tyranny; but we cannot or if we do we fall into the grotesque, the obscure, the flatulant.

For, after all, the Greeks alone of European nations, succeeded in solving the great problem—they coincided life & art, so that the prose which Pericles talked to the mob is really the best Greek prose, & the poetry which Sophocles wrote for the mob is the best poetry. But since then the arts have abandoned life, or, when touching her, have been making prostitutes of themselves. Can the theory of the intellectual élite really stand? Granted Plato did not talk to slaves; but with his 40,000 free Athenians &, say, 50,000 colonials, he had the largest intellectual audience any man ever had. You remember Remy over calculated that the audience of a French intellectual was about 4000, of whom more than half were foreigners—Germans, Russians, Spaniards, Americans & English. And the little Greek states offered more than 20 times that number!

But why continue in this strain? I feel sure you've had more than enough, & I'm only sowing discouragement before one of the few authentic children of the Muse now living.[12] Your cuckoo song[13] had charm & certain of your inevitable vivid phrases; but it has not the virtú,[14] the sublime essence, of your best work. (True, French critics now recognise "quintessentialism"[15] as a literary vice, but I think our literature needs it.) But you, how are you going on? Are you in a cul-de-sac? You have gathered your garland of sea-flowers,[16] exquisite, unique; but another such garland, however exquisite, will have lost something, the novelty which is a condition of beauty. You destroyed your work of a year[17] & perhaps rightly, I don't know. You had some poems which were fine & vivid & inevitable, though bitter. But how are you going on now? Prose? No![18] You have so precise, so wonderful an instrument—why abandon it to fashion another perhaps less perfect? You have, I think, either to choose pure song or else drama or else Mallarméan subtlety. Which will you choose? I am anxious to know. Perhaps you will send me a copy of anything you write. I shall seize on your tendencies with how avid a critical "goût"![19]

Richard

This is now the 8th Corps. Letters should be so addressed until the 13th, when they should go to 9th R. Sx. again. Always put regiment on.[20]

1. Nietzsche's *Also Sprach Zarathustra* (1883–92), in which the author posits his idea of the "superman" who will survive the loss of transcendental illusions.

2. Stéphane Mallarmé (1842–98) was an influential French symbolist poet who wrote among other works *Après-midi d'un Faune* (1876), an eclogue which inspired Debussy's prelude. His poetry was characterized by obscurity resulting from elaborate symbols and metaphors and experimental syntax and rhythm. He attempted to evoke an ideal beauty based on an emotional and mystical apprehension of reality. Despite or perhaps in part because of his obscurity and certainly because of his compression of ideas and language, he appealed to the imagists.

3. See letter 13, note 4.

4. Aldington recalls that H.D.'s father, Charles Leander Doolittle (1843–1919), was a professor of astronomy at the University of Pennsylvania and first director of the Flower Observatory.

5. Filippo Marinetti (1876–1944), Italian futurist writer and artist. Aldington reviewed Marinetti's lectures in London in *The New Freewoman* as early as December 1, 1913 (Vol. 1, No. 2, 226) and once brought him to Yeats's flat for a poetry reading (*Life for Life's Sake*, 108). Marinetti's bombast and passionate rejection of the past seemed ridiculous to Aldington, whose reverence for history and practical nature were antithetical to Marinetti's modernism.

6. The Proteus episode of Joyce's *Ulysses* (1922), which appeared in *The Little Review* in May 1918.

7. French writer whose work Aldington championed; see Biographical Appendix.

8. Comte de Lautréamont, the pseudonym of the French writer Isidore Ducasse (1846–70). The hallucinatory quality of his prose anticipated French surrealism and impressed Remy de Gourmont.

9. Compton Mackenzie (1883–1972) was a prolific British writer of both poetry and novels.

10. The Polish-American philosopher Henry Slonimski (1884–1970). The Aldingtons met Slonimski in London in early 1912 and again in Paris later the same year. In *Life for Life's Sake* Aldington recalls the impression Slonimski made:

> Slonimski talks books better than most people write them, but though you listen spell-bound and enchanted by his grave elegant voice and marvelous gift of finding the right phrase, the brilliant image, the books vanish with the sound of his voice. In another age he would have been appreciated. . . .
>
> . . . He made philosophy as attractive as a Persian tale. He had wide literary culture and a sensitive aesthetic appreciation. He presented philosophical ideas so poetically that what for me was the dark forest of abstractions became temporarily real and living; and he talked of poetry so profoundly that it took on fresh significance. (118–119)

11. Aldington refers here to Pound's lovely free "translations" from the Chinese in *Cathy* (1915). Other Americans (James Whitall, Amy Lowell) were also interested in the Eastern literary tradition, as was the English writer Allen Upward (whose translations from the Chinese often appeared in *The New Freewoman* and *The Egoist*). Aldington tended to find English enthusiasm for the East, as evidenced in English enthusiasm for Rabindranath Tagore, fatuous and insincere, and he satirized such attitudes freely (see *Life for Life's Sake*, 108–109).

12. Aldington always had the highest esteem for H.D.'s work and responded throughout their lives with encouragement and praise for her literary gifts.

13. H.D.'s "Cuckoo Song" was published in *Hymen* (1921):

Ah, bird,
our love is never spent
with your clear note,
nor satiate our soul;
not song, not wail, not hurt,
but just a call summons us
with its simple top-note
and soft fall;

not to some rarer heaven
of lilies over-tall,
nor tuberose set against
some sun-lit wall,
but to a gracious
cedar-palace hall;

not marble set with purple
hung with roses and tall
sweet lilies—such
as the nightingale
would summon for us
with her wail—

(surely only unhappiness
could thrill
such a rich madrigal!)
not she, the nightingale
can fill our souls
with such a wistful joy as this;

nor, bird, so sweet
was ever a swallow note—
not hers, so perfect
with the wing of lazuli
and bright breast—
nor yet the oriole
filling with melody
from her fiery throat
some island-orchard
in a purple sea.

Ah dear, ah gentle bird,
you spread warm length
of crimson wool
and tinted woven stuff

for us to rest upon,
nor numb with ecstasy
nor drown with death:

only you soothe, make still
the throbbing of our brain:
so through her forest trees,
when all her hope was gone
and all her pain,
Calypso heard your call—
across the gathering drift
of burning cedar-wood,
across the low-set bed
of wandering parsley and violet,
when all her hope was dead.

14. Moral excellence.

15. Aldington calls himself a "quintessentialist" in a letter to Amy Lowell on February 1, 1915. In a letter to Lowell on January 24, 1915, Frank Flint implies that Lowell thought of renaming the imagists as "Quintessentialists," evidently in anticipation of the imagist anthology of 1915. The term may simply describe imagism after Pound left the movement.

16. H.D.'s first volume of poems, *Sea Garden,* appeared in the fall of 1916.

17. Aldington regrets this destruction in a letter to Amy Lowell on January 2, 1918; see Introduction.

18. Aldington's antipathy to prose shifted dramatically by 1920. His early espousal of free verse depended in part on a rejection of prose. His own preference for poetry over prose in the hierarchy of art was a conviction held by many writers in the years before the war. He developed this early position in "Free Verse in England" in *The Egoist,* September 15, 1914 (351–352). He clarifies his increasing sympathy with prose as art and its relative relation to verse in "The Art of Poetry" in *The Dial* in 1920 (August, LXIX, 168) and in an exchange with T.S. Eliot, "Prose and Verse," in *The Chapbook* in 1921 (April, No. 22, 21). Aldington's attitudes toward the relative merits of poetry and prose depend on a wealth of fine distinctions and definitions, but his reservations about H.D.'s interest in writing prose is not personal here. It is worth noting, too, that like H.D., Aldington would soon draw on his experiences during the war years both in poetry and in his prose fiction.

19. Appetite.

20. H.D.'s tendency to be inaccurate in practical details is frustrating to Aldington: he is eager to receive her letters without delay and her impracticality is antithetical to his pragmatic nature. His letters abound in reminders such as this one.

24

July 7, 1918

Dearest Dooley/

Yesterday I didn't write you because I wanted to write you a love-letter and I felt somehow that it would make you unhappy, would infringe the bounds of your compromise,[1] and insult that sovereign pride & modesty behind which you en-trench yourself. So you see not being able to feign moods there was nothing left for me but silence.

Your last letter was delightful, but the little pencil note scribbled on the back made me happy. No, I haven't really been ill at all—only a couple of days in bed with "Spanish influenza"[2]—but it is so good to know that your dear loyal heart responded when you thought I was ill. You must be careful not to get this Spanish influenza—it affects one queerly & leaves one weak & terribly depressed. It is a sort of physical expression of our war lassitude.

You will be pleased to hear that Beaumont[3] is printing my war poems (just the war poems) under the title of "Images of War." Paul Nash[4] is illustrating the book which will be a kind of edition de luxe—just 200 copies, 50 of which will be coloured by Nash himself. Nash has done illustrations for Bombardment, Barrage, Dawn & Fatigues & in each case has interpreted the "image" rather well I think. I gather from Beaumont that others are being done.[5]

I haven't heard from Brown[6] & don't particularly care what happens in America, now that I can thus publicly register my denunciation of the machine-made war.

If you have used the Dial money,[7] please don't trouble to send it. I will be delighted for you to have it; I only wanted to be certain that they had paid, since these distant editors are a little apt to swindle one. Did you acknowledge cheque? And what do you mean by cheque returned from Nutt[8] wrongly endorsed? Please let me know at once—if a cheque of mine is not honoured I run the risk of a court martial.[9] I can't understand at all what it is—Nutt has said nothing to me &, so far as I know, all my self cheques have been paid by Cox.[10]

Thank you for doing the typing of my "proses";[11] will you tell Harriet[12] to pay up "toot sweet," for these be parlous times[13] & I rather like to enjoy anything I earn while I'm still alive to do it!

To-morrow is my birthday.[14] I think my 21st & 25th birthdays have been my happiest—last year at Brocton you know.[15] Mysterious girl! You didn't want to come, do you remember? What was the counter-attraction?

I had a long letter from Flint, very apologetic &c. He means well & you know there is a certain gain in his having written to me thus clumsily—he will—with his naïveté—immediately contradict anything that may be said.[16] The greatest danger is Cournos[17] who is going about London in that damned Jew way of his,[18] hinting here & hinting there & implying that I have committed some deed of revolting treachery. Alec,[19] Flint & Mr. Whitall[20] all wrote in one week asking what Cournos & I had quarrelled about. Now, I really don't mind whether John speaks well or ill of me, but I do think he might at least say that we've quarrelled about art or the Bolsheviks or any old thing instead of being such a bloody fool. Selah![21]

I am so glad to know that you are writing poetry again. As they said in the 18th century: "I am consumed with impatience to peruse your works, Miss Biron."[22] Do let me have them at once, before I go up the line again, so that I can read them in the comparative tranquility of this place.[23]

Paul Nash, illustration accompanying the poem "Bombardment,"
p. 30, *Images of War.*

Paul Nash, illustration accompanying the poem "Fatigues,"
p. 13, *Images of War.*

Have you read Stendhal's "de l'Amour"?[24] It is extremely thoughtful & has remarks of great penetration. Speaking of America—where he'd never been—he says: "Des jeunes filles de la gaité la plus folle et la plus innocente y deviennent, en moins d'un an, les plus ennuyeuses des femmes."[25] How often you have made the same remark about American girls in America! And Stendhal adds that the Germans are the same. He says it's the climate & the Bible! Perhaps. But in America I think the population is being emancipated from the Bible by the climate. What do you think?

I have just re-read the pencil postscript to your last letter and it emboldens me to say that I am tenderly and passionately in love with you as always. I don't care whether you believe me or not; I know myself. How the most brilliant of women are the slaves of conventional ideas! C'est désespèrant![26] Never mind, I shall just go on loving you & hoping for things to "pan out." I suppose the psychology of each sex is incomprehensible to the other. My fault is really, I suppose, that I treat women as equals, instead of pretending that I consider them superior & secretly despising them.[27]

Dear Dooley! Here I am plunged in a disquisition which needs a hundred pages to bring to a clear point. And so au revoir. And I kiss your dear white hands tenderly and your mouth qui ne m'aime plus.[28]

Richard.

1. In an earlier letter H.D. has evidently outlined the terms of their current relationship. She has apparently decided that she and Aldington should maintain a correspondence about literary matters and avoid the personal. See letter 10.

2. The pyrexia Aldington refers to in letter 18. This was the common name for the virulent influenza strain that swept through Europe and America in 1918 and 1919.

3. Cyril Beaumont (1891–1976), bookseller, publisher and aficionado of the ballet, published Aldington's first collection of poems after the war, Images of War: A Book of Poems, in April of 1919.

4. Paul Nash (1889–1946) was the illustrator whose stark, stylized woodcuts accompanied Aldington's poems in Beaumont's edition of Images of War (1919). Aldington was very impressed with his work and wrote Beaumont on July 5, 1918: "Nash has very fine imagination—the drawing of the Ypres front is A1. . . . Nash's drawings are simply splendid—they give me great satisfaction & I'm quite proud to think that he has used anything I've written so admirably" (UIL). Nash later illustrated covers for Aldington's Death of a Hero (1929) and his collection of war stories, Roads to Glory (1930).

5. Beaumont's edition of Images of War was quite elegant. Only forty-six pages, it included twenty-seven poems, eleven of which were illustrated by Nash, including "Bombardment," "Barrage" and the prose poem "Fatigues"; "Dawn" was not illustrated. The colored woodcuts are particularly effective in conveying the brutality, terror, and irony of the war in various shades of blue, green, orange, yellow, brown, and gray against the black and white of the woodcuts themselves. Nash's maroon cover is also dramatic, with modernist woodcuts of slashes and crescents that suggest explosions.

6. Edmund R. Brown, editor at the Four Seas Company in Boston which published Aldington's Images Old and New (1916), War and Love (1915–1918) (1919) and War: A

Book of Poems (1921). Each of these was essentially a republication of a collection of poems published previously in England.

7. See letter 19.

8. Bookseller David Nutt, with whom Aldington had a running account in London.

9. Aldington's reaction here may seem excessive, but his experience of war made him hypersensitive to the legal consequences of even the most minute act that might involve him with civil or—in this case—military bureaucracy.

10. Cox and Company was Aldington's bank.

11. The prose poems on which Aldington has been working and which he earlier asked H.D. to type for him in letter 17.

12. Harriet Monroe, editor of *Poetry*. See Biographical Appendix.

13. In the lead article, "New Lamps for Old," in *The Dial*, March 16, 1914, William Morton Payne vehemently criticized Carl Sandburg's "Chicago" and Harriet Monroe's *Poetry*, in which the poem had appeared: "The parlous times in which we live" demanded a return to what was valuable in "the old standards" (No. 666, Vol. 56, 231). Aldington's humor depends in part on knowing that Payne wrote for *The Dial*, then edited by Waldo Browne, at a time when it was more socially conservative and less sensitive to new trends in modern literature than it would become after July 1916, under the editorship of Martyn Johnson.

14. Aldington would be 26 on July 8, 1918.

15. Aldington recalls here the time he spent with H.D. just after he returned from his first tour of duty at the front in early July 1917. He was stationed at Lichfield and H.D. had taken a room in the village of Brocton. See Introduction.

16. That is, gossip to the effect that the Aldingtons' marriage is endangered.

17. John Cournos, an intimate friend of the Aldingtons until this time. He is particularly angry with Aldington for taking Arabella as his lover. Cournos felt that he and Yorke were in love before he left with a diplomatic mission to Petrograd in October of 1917. When he returned to England in early April of 1918 he discovered that Arabella was in love with Aldington and became furious with him, and to a lesser extent with H.D. See Biographical Appendix and Introduction.

18. Aldington had many Jewish friends and his criticism of Cournos here is not so much personal as representative of the anti-Semitism of the period.

19. Alec Randall; see Biographical Appendix.

20. James Whitall; see Biographical Appendix.

21. So be it!

22. Aldington alludes here to the naughty and erotic memoirs of Armand Louis de Gontaut Biron, Duc de Lauzun (1747–94). The first edition of the memoirs appeared in 1821; Aldington described Biron as "a sort of romantic madcap" in his introduction to C.K. Scott Montcrieff's translation, *Memoirs of the Duc de Lauzun* (London: George Routledge & Sons, 1928, v).

23. The base camp at which Aldington is undergoing further training before returning to the trenches.

24. "Stendhal" was the pseudonym of Henri Beyle (1783–1842), novelist and critic. He published his well-known study *De L'Amour* in 1822, in which he divides love into four types: passion, social experience, controlled self-indulgence, and physical pleasure.

25. "Young girls of the wildest and most innocent gaiety become there, in less than a year, the most annoying of women."

26. It is disheartening.

27. In *All Men Are Enemies* (1933), Aldington expands this idea. The central character and his attractive older female cousin discuss the equality of women and men: "They had quite a long and heated argument about it, an instinctive attitude of equality clumsily and hesitatingly opposing the hereditary English contempt masquerading as chivalry—put them [women] on a pedestal and make it your footstool" (*All Men Are Enemies,* Garden City, New York: Doubleday, Doran, 1933, 38).

28. Which no longer loves me.

25

July 8, 1918

Dearest Astraea/[1]

It is strange how utterly empty one's mind becomes sometimes. To-day—by way of a birthday present from the ironic gods—I have not observed in myself a single glimmer of intelligence. Everything has been dull and indifferent. The effect of routine & the crushing heat I suppose. We have been displayed all day for the benefit of an old general whose ideas are detestable to me but whose influence on my unfortunate country is great and decisive. He has amazing gifts & great though banal eloquence. He came & preached the doctrine of action, of efficiency, of duty—everything that is contrary to us who worship thought, and freedom & reverie! I realised when I stood beside him that here for the first time since I had landed in France was a man who was my intellectual equal—and yet, malheur sur nous,[2] we are at opposite poles. C'est triste, effroyablement triste.[3]

Well, perhaps one must not worry about these things, yet that is why the war continues.

There, violet-wreathed as your own Attic hills,
And golden-sandalled as your own white isle,
Your spirit for a moment stooped to mine.

Too long had I been starved of beauty,
Too long done violence to myself,
Mocked at by the thing I held most dear,
Too long suffered the insult of authority.

But the echo of your song
Pierced me to tears & left me faint
With the misery of old memories.

I am exiled, even as you, & miserable.
But for your sake, white violet of the Muse,
Violets shall be dear to me & dear
The sparse woods sweetened with the violets' breath.[4]

R.

Just to amuse you & show I sometimes think of other things than shells & bayonets!

Your letter of 14th July to hand[5]—I can't contradict you in any way or think too much about these things now.

The Faun[6] sends kisses to his dear Dryad.[7]

[The following poem was included in the letter to H.D., July 8, 1918]

The Faun Captive

A god's strength lies
More in the fervour of his worshippers
Than in his own divinity.
Who now regards me or who twines
Red wool or threaded lilies round the brows
Of my neglected statues?
Who now seeks my aid
To add skill to the hunter's hand
Or save some pregnant bitch or ewe
Helpless in travail?
None, since that fierce autumn noon
I lay asleep under Zeus-holy oaks,
Heavy with sirupy wine & tired
With the close embraces
Of sòme sweet wearer of the leopard skin—
That noon they snared & bound me as I slept
And dragged me for their uncouth mirth
Out of my immemorial woods & crags
Down to their bastard hamlets.

Then the god's blood my father spilled
To get me upon a mortal stock, dwindled & shrank
And I was impotent, & weak
As the once desireable flesh of my human mother;
I, that should have been dreaded in wan recesses,
Worshipped in high woods, a striker of terror
To the wayfarer in lonely places,
I, a lord of golden flesh & dim music—
I a captive & coarsely derided!

Ai! I could bite the brown flesh
Of my arms & hands with shame & grief.

I am weary for the freedom of free things,
The old gay life of the half-god

Who had no dread of death or sorrow.
I am weary for the open spaces,
The long damp sands acrid with many tides,
And the infinite wistfulness of evening seas.
I am weary for wooded silences,
The nymph-rapt hours of heat,
The slow cool lapse of moonlit nights,
The solitude of the mysterious stars
Pearlwise scattered upon the domed breast
Wherewith the Great Mother suckles the earth;
Ah, weary for my brown clean streams
And cold petals of woodland flowers
Scented with dew & delicate as a kiss.

Here they grow careless, thinking me a coward
But soon I shall break these thongs
And kill, kill, kill in sharp revenge;
Then out of doors by the lush pastures
To the heath, the foot-hills & the hills,
To the wild-rose kisses of the deathless girls
Who laugh & flash between the sombre trees,
Out to the unpeopled lands no foot oppresses,
The lands that are free, being free of man.[8]

1. Aldington's pet name for H.D., Astraea (the starry maid), is another name for the constellation Virgo, the zodiacal sign under which H.D. was born. Astraea is associated with Justice, who used to live among people in the Golden Age, retired to the Mountains in the Silver Age, and fled to the heavens during the wickedness of the Bronze Age, where she may yet be seen on starry nights. Ovid gives a brief account of her in his *Metamorphoses*, I, 149–150.

2. Unhappily for us.

3. It's sad, dreadfully sad.

4. Aldington never published this poem. I discuss this work as well as "We are those . . ." (see letter 32) in my article "Two Poems for H.D.," *Journal of Modern Literature*, Vol. 16, No. 1, Winter 1989.

5. Aldington must mean "14th June." H.D. appears to be writing to Aldington regularly at this point, and it would seem that her letters are attempting to shift and redefine the grounds of their relationship. Aldington's response is reactive and generally accepting.

6. Aldington was called "Faun" by H.D. and Pound.

7. "Dryad" is a pet name for H.D. used by Pound and Aldington, recalling her association with trees as early as 1905–1907, when Pound included "The Tree" in a series of early poems written for H.D. and bound together as "Hilda's Book." The collection is included at the end of *End to Torment: A Memoir of Ezra Pound by H.D.*, ed. Norman Holmes Pearson and Michael King, New York: New Directions, 1979, 67–84.

8. This poem, with some revision, was finally included in *Images*, second and revised edition, London: The Egoist Press, 1919, a volume later reissued by Allen and Unwin. In

the published version, "pregnant bitch or ewe" in line 9 becomes "pregnant ewe or bitch"; the comma is omitted after "impotent" in line 22; the break between lines 28 and 29 is omitted; in line 41 "the domed breast" becomes "the domed breast of The Great Mother"; line 42 is omitted; "Ah" in line 43 becomes "oh"; "cold" in line 44 becomes "wet"; "soon" in line 47 becomes "one night"; in line 50 "and" is inserted after the comma; in line 52 "between" becomes "among"; and in line 53 "unpeopled" becomes "unploughed." The poem first appeared as "The Captive Faun" in *The Nation* on May 31, 1919 (Vol. 25, No. 9, 265).

26

July 9, 1918[1]

"A spirit beyond all tyranny."[2] That is a spirited phrase and would be a fine epitaph for the William Wallaces[3] & George Washingtons of the world—but how few deserve it. They say Madame de Staël[4] was the only person who ever dared to tell the Emperor Napoleon to his face that he was a tyrant. Anyway I am sure I do not deserve it. But it was "like your gracious ways"[5] to think of saying that.

One has above all things to guard against vanity, the besetting sin of the French as hypocrisy is that of the English. Pride, I suppose, is legitimate, though it is not amiable in the successful but only in the unfortunate. The difference is, I think, between Rouchfoucald's "amour propre"[6] & the determination of Shelley's Prometheus.[7]

It is curious, one talks of the possessive instinct of men for women but I believe it is stronger in women. I don't mean that I agree with the rather vulgar viewpoint of Shaw;[8] but to some extent the history of an impulsive or erotic man is simply that of successive enslavements & exceedingly painful emancipations from different women. Unfortunately, it seems as if another woman is the only means of escape.[9] . . . Of course I see with astonishing clearness (astonishing because I ought to be blind to it) that Arabella is trying hard—let us be genial I say also "unwittingly"—to enslave me completely.[10] I see perhaps the working of her instinct more clearly than she herself and I am appalled, yes positively appalled, at the degree of subjugation she intends for me. Mind you I don't condemn her in the least; it is just what the majority of women—who live merely instinctively & sensually—try to do & usually succeed. One thinks of Flint[11] and Lawrence[12] with a shudder. Ford too, by Jove.[13] You are right; one must possess oneself. But that is exceedingly difficult, because one cannot be "reasonably" in love—it would be tedious & bourgeois—and any "amour-passion"[14] at once betrays one into a state of abject submission. Therefore, one must live entirely apart from women—which is absurd—or else engage in this perpetual warfare of passion versus freedom. I cannot compass the cynicism of Diomède[15]—who, himself, got into a horrible mess by falling in love with one of his mistresses—nor can I aspire to Petrarchan heights.[16] Life is that way. One must be like England—muddle through somehow.

I daresay this sounds devilish blunt—in any case, most of it doesn't apply to you—but I merely reciprocate.[17]

The case of Brigit[18] is rather curious. She has now entirely dropped me. Why? Clearly because it was you she cared for.[19] Therefore, as long as she thought I belonged to you she was charming & flirted most graciously—arguing, I suppose, that this prevented a more dangerous concurrance. Now, there is no point in being charming—as she believes—she shows her complete indifference. I don't say it's a great grief to me but in a way it is a grief to lose so old and so sweet a friend. Wounded vanity, eh? No doubt I seem unjust, but I believe I have caught the nuance of psychology here just as with Arabella. (Of course Brigit must now be getting into a ghastly state because of that ill-advised operation.[20] You may remember Ellis' remarks[21] on the matter—I think in an appendix to one of his volumes.)

You will see that the problem from the male point of view is thorny with difficulties. Though it simplifies itself eventually into the ancient problem of eating one's cake & having it. Perhaps Euclid[22] might be of assistance—& perhaps not.

My dear, you saw, possibly earlier than I, the terrific possessive instinct which A. has. You have exercised extraordinary restraint in not mentioning it; though I've been aware of it for some considerable time. Me voici prévenu en tout cas.[23] But—forgive, if you can, this ultimate irony—I smile to think of you watching with so delicately aesthetic & appraising an eye the physical loveliness of *your* Cecil! Tu quoque, Brute?[24] Is it the "yours" or the "loveliness"? A problem to be meditated.

I forsee that you are going to hate me very much for this letter. Even with the best & greatest of human beings we should employ a certain amount of humbug. But we agreed to cut it out, didn't we? Dangerous, most dangerous. I wonder if even our love can endure perfect frankness? From "color che sanno"[25] I gather that is impossible. How does it seem from your angle of the triangle—or perhaps one should say acute-angled rectangle?

Well, my dear, in about a week[26] I shall be trotting up the same old line to the same old tinny tune of M.G.'s[27] & whizz-bangs. One gains, if not philosophy, a sort of resignation. Certain pretentions to the good things of life have to be abandoned—& one "accepts whatever comes with equal mind" (Landor?)[28]

With my love—that tempestuous monosyllable—

Your

Richard

1. This letter was enclosed with letter 27 on July 10.
2. H.D. has evidently written Aldington that he has such a spirit.
3. William Wallace (1844–97), Scottish philosopher who was professor of moral philosophy at Oxford from 1882 until his death. He specialized in German philosophy, particularly Hegel, whose work he translated.
4. Anne-Louise-Germaine Necker (1766–1817). Her Paris salon was both an intellectual and political meeting place for those who shared her antipathy to Napoleon, who exiled her three times, in 1803, 1806, and 1810.
5. Aldington is quoting from Coventry Patmore's "Departure," stanza viii:

It was not like your good and gracious ways!
Do you, that have nought other to lament,
Never, my love, repent
Of how, that July afternoon,
You went
With sudden, unintelligible phrase,
And frighten'd eye,
Upon your journey of so many days,
Without a single kiss, or a good-bye?

6. The French moralist François, Duc de la Rochefoucauld (1613–80). His famous *Maximes* was published in 1665. "Amour propre" is self-esteem.

7. In Percy Bysshe Shelley's *Prometheus Unbound* (1820).

8. George Bernard Shaw (1856–1950).

9. Ironically, in Aldington's own life, falling in love with another woman tended to become his way of concluding for whatever reason an ongoing relationship.

10. Evidently Dorothy Yorke (Arabella) wanted an exclusive relationship; she wanted to marry Aldington and to have a child with him.

11. F.S. Flint married early and in 1918 had two children; see Biographical Appendix.

12. D.H. Lawrence fell in love with Frieda von Richthofen while she was married to Ernest Weekly. Lawrence insisted immediately upon marrying her, so she felt compelled to leave her husband and three children and to secure a divorce. See Biographical Appendix.

13. Ford Maddox (Hueffer) Ford (1873–1939) fell in love with Violet Hunt and, after a long affair, travelled with her to Germany. On their return to England he encouraged the rumor that he had there assumed German citizenship and married Hunt, an act with complicated political consequences. See Biographical Appendix.

14. Sexual love.

15. Aldington recalls Remy de Gourmont's treatment of Diomedes. See Biographical Appendix.

16. That is, move from sexual to Platonic love, as Petrarch (1304–74) does in his sonnets to Laura.

17. H.D. has evidently written in her last letter about her relationship with Cecil Gray, whom she is beginning to find petty and possessive.

18. Brigit Patmore, a friend of both Aldingtons and one of Aldington's first lovers; see Introduction and Biographical Appendix.

19. Patmore was clearly in love with H.D., as evidenced in H.D.'s fictional treatment of her as Morgan in *Bid Me to Live* and in Patmore's own autobiographical fiction (*This Impassioned On-Looker* [1926] and *No Tomorrow* [1929]) and in her memoir, *My Friends When Young* (1968). It seems unlikely that Patmore's relationship with H.D. was ever sexually consummated, in large measure because H.D. was not particularly sexually responsive to her overtures.

20. Patmore has evidently recently had an abortion or Aldington may be referring to an abortion she had several years earlier. In autobiographical notes made for Norman Holmes Pearson, H.D. recalled that at the time of the Aldingtons' wedding, "Brigit is having operation" (BL).

21. Havelock Ellis (1859–1939); exactly which of Ellis's works Aldington has in mind is unclear.

22. Greek mathematician (fl. c. 300 B.C.E.) whose geometrical theories and calculations Aldington sardonically surmises may help him and H.D. out of their two triangles.

23. I have been forewarned in any case.

24. You, too, Brutus? These are Julius Caesar's words to his friend Brutus when Caesar saw him among his murderers.

25. Those who know. In Dante's *Inferno*, Canto 4, 1. 131, Aristotle is the master of "those who know."

26. Aldington is nearing the end of his six weeks of additional training at base camp.

27. Machine guns.

28. Aldington is not quoting Landor, but recalling line 883 of Book 3 of John Dryden's *Palamon and Arcite*: "With equal mind, what happens, let us bear."

27

July 10, 1918

I wrote the enclosed[1] yesterday, kept it until to-day, thought very seriously of destroying it & then felt that it would be a pity as I had said several things I wanted to say as well as others it was unnecessary & perhaps unworthy to say. Cynicism, as our friend Oscar[2] remarks, is the bank-holiday of sentimentality. Keeping that profound truth in your mind you will be able to gauge fairly nearly the mood of the letter. The remark about Gray is rather unforgiveable, but since it was once written it seemed a lack of candour to erase it. Of course if you can interpret it you will observe the profound compliment[3] underlying it, but I don't know whether you take the trouble to find out the *implied* sense of words & acts as well as their direct sense. Do you? One needs a certain tranquility, and perhaps a little indifference as well as intuition.

And, you see, the discussion of most of these points is really rather academic. I mean I shouldn't look at the position quite so whimsically and carelessly if I thought there was a great chance of my ever having to face again the whole problem. That gives me a certain advantage and I can deal with the situation in a peculiar way which I can only describe as "ante-post-mortem." Pater's detachment, you know.

I am enjoying these last days here[4] immensely—six weeks of summer in wartime is a generous gift of the gods. In the line, you know, one has no pleasure in these things; it is either hot or cold, wet or dry; beauty of earth there can be none; even the beauty of the sky becomes a sinister, sneering sort of thing. But here one recognises the great plan, the alternation of seedtime & harvest, the spirit of the earth. I say to myself that I do not envy you your Cornwall, your books, your sea, your leisure, your lover. For if life to me is often horrible and wearing & terrifying & exhausting, it has also moments of respite, poignant in their intensity. After a long period of revolt and depression I have reached "un bel indifférance";[5] I take no more than the barest necessary interest in army work and am, as it were, preparing myself for something different & eternal. One gets to a certain point when any misfortune or discomfort or loss comes more or less naturally & is borne tranquilly. Perhaps it is because one gets purged of the necessity for unessentials. Of course it is much pleasanter to have money and books & friends & someone to love and an art; but one can do without all these things. Latterly I do not bother to write down my poems—I just think them sitting quietly in my tent. It is perhaps in this way that one should love—carefully discriminating between "l'amour passion" and "l'amour physique." (You should read Stendhal "de l'Amour.")[6]

In the books I sent you I think you will like Samain's tales[7] and possibly Gide's book[8]—the latter seemed a little forced to me. The Renan[9] has charming passages. I advise you not to bother with his correspondence with his seminary friend—it is tedious, parsonic & lowers one's estimation of Renan's character. Renan is a kind of artistic protestant—too obsessed with logic to be happy in Catholic sophisms, too refined in senses to fall into the ridiculous self-mutilating Calvin point of view. He interests me exceedingly, though the lack of force & determination is his great weakness.

I have placed Nietzsche at last. He is not a modern but a 19th century Romantic, the last of the bunch. His tedious superman is no other than our friend Jean Valjean[10] elevated to the intellectual plane. The sense of uneasiness one gets in reading Zarathustra is not because Nietzsche was mad or amazingly egotistic, but simply because he is out of date. He preaches the individualism of 1840 to the communism of 1920—useless. We don't need a doctrine of violence, but a doctrine of common-sense. I would like to conduct friend Nietzsche through, let us say, the town of Loos[11] as it now is. He would find that his violent effort towards more life had merely utterly annihilated it. And there are dozens, scores of such villages given over to the rats & the lice, sole benefactors of the superman ideal. No, let us get back to the sanity of Voltaire[12] & plant each his own cabbages in his own garden. We do not need all to do the same thing. (God forbid that the majority of mankind should become artists.) Let us amuse ourselves tranquilly and try to refrain from assassinating our neighbors. I do not think the world at present is capable of any higher ideal.

Of course, when one looks coldly at the present state of affairs, one sees pretty clearly that this turmoil is very far from being appeased. Actual hostilities will not cease in this decade & the next will be a mass of tumult. It is possible that there will be a re-shuffle of the belligerants—Germany, Russia & Japan uniting against the Latin-Anglo-Saxon menace. It is, of course, a contest of jackals for the lion's skin.

So you must organise your life at least with the forethought that the present state of affairs will continue for some years.[13] When people tell you that the war will be over soon it's simply a case of the wish being father to the thought.

Au revoir.

With love

Richard.

1. Letter 26.
2. Oscar Wilde.

3. Aldington suggests that his comments on Gray reveal his own jealousy, which is an indication of his love for H.D.

4. His last days of training before returning to the trenches.

5. A beautiful indifference. H.D. evidently shared Aldington's feelings here at this time. Describing her physical situation in Cornwall, she wrote to John Cournos on July 17, 1918: "The country is lovely—much finer than Devon. There is a pool below the house where I bathe almost daily now and I get nice food and have so much time to work. I am really awfully fortunate. Only I feel so detached, I really sometimes wonder where I am. I have never lived so completely in the imagination. And nothing much matters" (HU).

6. See letter 24, note 24.

7. See letter 14, note 13.

8. André Gide (1869–1951), French essayist, critic, novelist, and dramatist. His early work was influenced by the symbolist movement. He founded the *Nouvelle Revue Française* in 1908. Gide was a strong influence on the literary avant-garde and rebelled against convention and inhibition. Exactly which of his many works Aldington sent to H.D. I have been unable to determine.

9. See letter 13, note 4.

10. The admirable peasant hero of Victor Hugo's novel *Les Misérables* (1862), who tries repeatedly to escape his past of petty crime by assuming various identities.

11. The French town near which Aldington was stationed during the first half of 1917 and where he fought in the spring of 1918.

12. François-Marie Arouet Voltaire (1694–1778), French poet, historian and philosopher, who argued deistically for religious tolerance and a transformation of political thought through rational criticism in the name of social justice.

13. Aldington, like many other soldiers, was convinced that the war would last at least until 1920.

28

July 12, 1918

I am very glad that you see it is no solution of life merely to perpetuate one's species. Thinking of my mother[1] & her narrow maternal instinct I once said—I think to you: "Many women think they have solved the problem of life when they have gotten someone else to face it." A little "smarty" perhaps, but on the whole surprisingly true.

For, whatever may be the gift of parenthood it has ghastly pitfalls—the fruited individual forgetting, unlike the fruited tree, that it must blossom again. The danger, too, of living for & in one's child. "I have not found happiness—I will see my child does; I have failed in life—my child shall succeed; the books I dreamed—my child shall write." Eternal deception of Nature! From this attitude come the trammeling affection of parents, the insufferable tutelage, the attempts to solve in terms of their maturity and disillusion the problems of youth and illusion. And once again begins the revolt, the breaking away of youth, the dismay of the parents who find they have a swan not a duckling and vice versa. If you have a child, beware! I say unto you beware. You will try to make your child a poet and he will be a designer of coke-ovens; you will try to make him a lover of natural things and he will desire money. Children—haven't we said it?—are reactions from their parents. But you might try the experiment—a reaction from you would certainly be something interesting. (perhaps the worst might happen—& the child would be a weak echo of you.)

Is this folly or wisdom? After all life and more life—that is the thing. One should refuse no experience which offers itself.

Yes, it is odd how we think simultaneously, but perhaps not so odd as you think. With minds somewhat similarly framed & equipped we are meditating the same problems; not extraordinary then if we sometimes arrive at similar conclusions or, rather, similar moods. All our thought is mood; we think we are dealing with the world with our minds when we are really dealing only with our emotions. So that when we reach one of those arid spots of life devoid of emotion, we have no ideas. That is why we are poets, not philosophers. The ιδεα [semblance] comes to us on Psyche wings, irridescent, an image, things being thoughts for us & thoughts things. But for the philosopher it is not so. He deals with thought as a mathematician with numbers. That is why those who are in love with life are seldom mathematicians. Thought has no meaning for them till it is clad in mortal shape. Poets do not sing the eternal, as bad critics pretend, but the glory of the perishable—beauty, love, intoxication, flowers, moods, the sea, all things that are transcient and lovely. But for the philosopher ideas exist. Even Socrates, who was what we should call a Nihilist, believed in his ideas.

One has so carefully to distinguish between what is primary & what is only secondary, between the essential & the non-essential of life. Harund-al-Raschid,[2] it is said, earned every day his food by making shoes. He kept in touch with reality. But the essential point to him (if I am not mistaken) was not the money he earned but the sense of—how shall I put it?—humanity gained. (Moreover, the wise Caliph, who had listened to poets' tales, knew that monarchs are sometimes dethroned.) The essential thing, after all, was the fun of shoe making when he was fed up with ambassadors, state affairs, harems and palaces & musicians and wars. After all, if you examine life, you will see that in its collective as well as in its individual activity, ennuie is the enemy. Even the war is simply the expression of a continent weary of fifty years of peace—an absurd remedy for vacuity of mind, but one which satisfies the Mrs. Shakespeares[3] and the Huttons[4] & the Rupert Brookes[5] of the world. Nearly every man in this camp now frankly admits that he was wrong in his estimation of the amusement to be got from war. It is my misfortune to have foreseen its ennuie & yet to have allowed myself to be forced into it.

You speak of my desire not to come back from the war.[6] It is perhaps there all the time—a sense of a destiny to be fulfilled. Quem dei amant,[7] you know. But I have rid myself of morbidity and await what often seems the inevitable, tranquilly, almost with indifference. I do not despise my life, but I do not overvalue it. Perhaps something will set me free; perhaps not. In any case, I do not complain.

Will you send the enclosed to Bubb?[8] I forgot for so long to write him.
With all affectionate & tender thoughts,

Richard.

1. Aldington was unsympathetic to his mother throughout his life; see Introduction.

2. Harun-ar-Rashid (766–809), fifth Abbasid caliph, was the lavish patron of the arts who wandered around Baghdad in disguise. His court is the setting for the tales in *The Thousand and One Nights*.

3. People like Olivia Shakespear; see letter 21, note 4.

4. People like Edward Hutton; see Biographical Appendix.

5. People like Rupert Brooke (1887–1915), the English poet best known for *War Sonnets in New Numbers* (1914) and *1914* (1915) which contained a patriotic, sentimental view of war and lost youth.

6. Aldington is obviously responding here to a letter from H.D. in which she has raised the issue of his psychology. While Aldington was not suicidal, his fatalism here has a great deal to do with his efforts to make the war mean something; see Introduction.

7. Whom the gods love.

8. Aldington enclosed a letter dated July 12, 1918 (UCLA), to the Reverend Charles Clinch Bubb, who at the Clerk's Press in Cleveland, Ohio, printed elegant editions of several works by H.D. and Aldington.

29

July 15, 1918

This photograph was sent in an envelope by itself; Aldington is in the front row, far right.

July 16, 1918

Dearest Astraea/

To-morrow I set off on my travels again;[1] the army has at least that advantage—one never stays long in the same place, though frequently the moves are so short that one merely has the trouble of shifting while remaining in approximately the same place. But to-morrow will be a real move. It is sad to leave this lovely village where, though I've had some boredom & depression, I have had also hours of quiet reverie and have had some time for thought & self-collection. As I wrote you[2] I have found a little of my soul that was lost. Very likely I shall lose it again up in that damnable landscape of war, that wrecked earth which is a blasphemy, an insult to the gods. But in any case I have found something here, if it be only a specious wisdom. Dooley dear, j'ai la tristesse des départs[3]—and this is my third trip up the line.[4] I hope it may be my last.

But let us talk of pleasant things. Your correspondence has been a great help and a great pleasure. Through your letters I got into touch once again with that world of ideas which is my world just as much as the world of "stupid poor men"[5] is my world. You have been an immense succour to me and I shall carry back with me a charming image of you in my heart. I hope you will sometimes write me when I am in the line even if I can't write to you anything of interest.

By the time this letter reaches you the papers—if you see them—will have informed you of events whose _noise_ is only too plain here. My luck, so far, has been good. This is the fifth great battle I have just missed.[6] I mustn't boast, though, lest I find myself in it this time tomorrow!

Will you take charge of the enclosed letter[7] which is all I have by way of an agreement with Beaumont. I have written him that in the event of my becoming a casualty, the proceeds of the book & the copyright belong to you. But if you have the letter it will be rather more secure. Don't lose it, will you? I have told Beaumont to send you a copy of the book. Well, I must get to bed now.

Au revoir and my love

Richard.

1. After six weeks of training, Aldington left the base camp for the front line on July 17, 1918.
2. See letter 22, for example, but Aldington is probably referring to the letters of the past few weeks generally.
3. I feel the sadness of departures.
4. Aldington served a period in the trenches during the first half of 1917 and again from the end of April through early June 1918.
5. I have been unable to identify the source of this quotation.
6. Aldington was extraordinarily lucky in missing major battles of the war. The Battle of the Somme began a week after he entered basic training in Dorset on July 1, 1916, and concluded on November 18, 1916, a month before he was first sent abroad. While in France, he served just north of the most intense battle activity, and he left for officers'

training in England just after a major offensive in Flanders began on June 7, 1917. He was in London on leave or in Lichfield during the Third Battle of Ypres, which started on July 31 and continued until mid-November of 1917. He left the trenches for base camp on June 2, 1918, two days before an important Allied counterattack at Château Thierry. The current "great battle" is likely the beginning of the Allied advance which on August 8, 1918, culminated in the Battle of Amiens.

7. Aldington enclosed a letter from Cyril W. Beaumont (see letter 24, note 3) dated June 26, 1918, in which Beaumont offered Aldington a royalty of 10 percent on his *Images of War* (BL).

31

July 18, 1918

This photograph was sent in an envelope by itself; Aldington is in the front row on the far right.

32

July 20, 1918

Dear Astraea/

Just to say that I am back in the line & quite all right. It is very quiet here, quite supernaturally so! There is no news. I had a book from Alec Randall which will be amusing to read.

Somehow I have no thought up here, being immensely lonely without flowers & trees & little creatures or else people I care for. If I could be completely alone in some quiet lovely place, or with "my own kind" again! But that is too much to ask, isn't it? Everything seems too much to ask. It makes me angry sometimes to think of the many people we know who are important enough to be found interesting jobs, while I. But that's rather weak, isn't it? Yet am I an utter fool? I am useless at this soldiering game. I wonder if I'd be useless at everything?

How is Cornwall? I do hope you're happy & well.

Your

Richard

We are those for whom the world has no use,
Guiltless but unneeded.

Was it our fault? All our fault?
Our voice was clear when we spoke,
Fresh and vivid our lives,
Ourselves not unlovely, our thought
Not without kindness for men,
Not without strength.
Was it our fault they did not care,
Our fault they could not hear?

Cast out and forgotten, contemned,
Without root, without purpose, we drift,
Without country—beauty has none—
Without place; we were proud.

O my beautiful,
Your silver is scorned,
Your ivory grace held nothing
By those who root in the mud,
The under-filth of the world.

Come then, be silent,
Glide guilty away,
Either to silence and the dream
We hold more precious than life,
Or to silence & a great light
That will not perish.[1]

1. Aldington never published this poem, which I discuss in my article "Two Poems for H.D.," in *Journal of Modern Literature*, Vol. 15, No. 1, Summer 1989, 174–77.

July 23, 1918

Well, miss, I dunno what things be a-coming to, but us have got ourselves into a regular mess-up. Sicut erat in principio et nunc et semper.[1]

There is a regular sou-wester blowing across France & I can imagine what Cornwall is like to-day—heavy cold seas breaking against the rocks with a flurry of white spray, great gusts of wind roaring over the hills and clouds of rain sweeping over everything, breaking the poor Dryad's[2] flowers and spoiling her quiet sea-pools. Am I right? But perhaps after all the heat & windless days you will not mind the big winds blowing "that the small rain down can rain."[3]

I have heard at last from Gilbert, he was near the line but not actually in it. No doubt he has had his first dose by now—hope he likes it. Lieut. of Engineers isn't a bad job—they do very little fighting. The posts between the British & American E.F.s[4] seem singularly bad—perhaps they are afraid we shall tell the Americans the truth. Heaven forbid.

He says something about hoping to see you soon. If he gets a blighty leave[5] & threatens a descent on Cornwall, you must either turn his flank by wiring for Brigit as chaperone or else attack his center by going straight up to London & keeping him there till his leave is o'er. Have pity on him also—et ille in Averno![6] He will probably be in love with his wife again by now.

I had intended to write more in addition to the letter I wrote you 2 days ago,[7] but once again a kind of mental apathy has seized me & my brain refuses to work. Not from unwillingness to face the problem but because my mind is tired with all this turmoil—& nothing much seems worth while. You spoke, I remember, of my losing all sense of responsibility with Arabella. Of course you are right, but then at least I can urge as an excuse that the times are out of joint, and if I am mad in my way other people are no less mad in theirs. Besides the very madness & extravagance of that passion is the one thing that redeems it from vulgarity. One must have the courage of one's illusions or else life is willed [?] a fit of "shame & loathing."[8]

Another thing—I didn't make A. "promise to be chaste & faithful to me for 2 years." I said if she stayed in love with me for 2 years it would get her round a danger-point when she might do something desperate. God knows I [am] not Sir. Parsifal.[9] I desired the woman (best be frank even if brutal, eh?) but I was not entirely selfish. Perhaps if you knew a little more of life, a little more of the brutality of men, you would not feel so contemptuous. Brigit has assumed that my motives are similar to those of Deighton's friends.[10] So be it, but I protest energetically against that view and maintain that there was idealism & poetry even in the absurdities & cruelties of this affair. I am not an insurance broker, nor am I a soldier—mais assez, on peut bien se faire un idiot ainsi![11]

Anyway here we are—you in Cornwall, A. in London,[12] I in France. I don't know who's having the worst time.

You speak of poverty—dear girl, try living in a hole 30 feet underground with a pint of water per diem for drinking & washing & bully[13] & biscuit for food; do you think poverty really matters? And in any case if I survive the war the government will be bound to look after me to some extent.

What really troubles me nowadays is the semi-drying-up of my impulses to work, though I think I would get them again with idleness & tranquility. But I am very tedious & as bored as a child sometimes.

Richard.

P.S. The faun sends kisses to his dear Astraea, and never, never, NEVER forgets her, nor her girl laughter, nor all the sweet parts of her. When the faun is free again she will love him as she used to.

1. Thus it was the beginning and now is and always will be.
2. One of Aldington's pet names for H.D.
3. The second line of an anonymous medieval poem:

> O western wind, when wilt thou blow,
> That the small rain down can rain?
> Christ, that my love were in my arms,
> And I in my bed again!

4. Expeditionary Forces.
5. A lucky leave which will allow him to go to England.
6. And he in hell!
7. That is, on July 20.
8. I have been unable to identify the source of this quotation.
9. The pure knight in Arthurian legend who finally attains the holy grail. Aldington may also have in mind Richard Wagner's treatment of Parsifal's sexual temptations and purity in his opera *Parsifal* (1882).
10. Deighton Patmore, Brigit Patmore's husband, was a flagrant womanizer and had friends who shared his disdain for fidelity.
11. But enough, one can well become an idiot this way!
12. Arabella Yorke was still living at 44 Mecklenburgh Square in July of 1918 (D.H. Lawrence to Cecil Gray, July 3, 1918, in *The Letters of D.H. Lawrence*, Vol. 3, 261), although she spent two weeks in June with D.H. Lawrence at Mountain Cottage in Middleton (D.H. Lawrence to S. Koteliansky, June 20, 1918, in *The Letters of D.H. Lawrence*, Vol. 3, 256).
13. Bully beef, canned meat which was the daily fare for soldiers in the trenches.

34

July 24, 1918

Dearest Astraea/

You must never feel discouraged because the social order of to-day has apparently no niche to offer you, because you appear to be a sort of outcast, "déracinée"[1] as you like to call it. Only in a very few short épochs has there been a place for the "dreamer of dreams"[2] & even then he has been counted for other things than his dreams—in Athens for his criticism of gods & men, in Florence for his learning, in the Paris of Louis XIV for his support of the monarchy—Euripides, Poliziano[3] & Racine were not loved merely for their poetry but for something extraneous. You, who are purely a poet, would have felt the hostility of any age.

You lay too much stress on nationality—a thing invented by politicians. True the traditions of one's race & people are immeasureably important, but less important than the tradition of one's soil which in turn is far less important than the "tradition of free minds."[4] That universal "Kultur"[5] which belongs to any spirit wide enough to invent it is far beyond any limited "Kultur" or a race. There is more sympathy between a mad Chinese poet & ourselves than between us & a living Australian politician. We must, it is true, go into the lives of the "common people," who are humanity, because they never change; but we must not fall into the error of confusing this love & this understanding with nationality. The people never changes—it applauds Barrabas & crucifies Christ & it is right to do so— and that humanity which Aristophanes[6] laughed at & Petronius[7] sneers at in his patrician way & Rabelais[8] knew and even Browning has glimpses of, remains eternally, or at least as eternally as human life. People who do natural things are less numerous in proportion than in times past, yet they are obviously our companions. And just as Christ loved fishermen & a money-changer and peasants & women of strange temperament, because he was a poet; so do we. Authority and the man of solid virtue, the woman who never errs are nothing to us. We came into the world to interpret sinners (i.e. people who have vivid lives and temperaments) not the righteous, who are so because they are too unimaginative to do anything else.

Life is an adventure & death is an adventure. When Nietzsche told his disciples to "live dangerously," he did not mean among bombs & projectiles & physical dangers but among spiritual adventures. To live according to one's character, to live against the world's way—isn't that to save one's soul?

Someday you are coming back to be my dear Astraea again[9] and all these mad adventures we have been on will make us the richer for each other, make our love the sweeter & keener. You speak of not having a body—you are wrong; you have a beautiful and passionate body. I knew that the last times we were together. And someday you will come back to me with a passionate abandonment and we will live a most poignant adventure together.

You are more wise than nearly all women. Don't be too bitter against me. Someday we will walk along & talk of the clouds & the fields as we did.[10] And the beauty of these things will enter us & feed our love. Ah, my Dooley, did you want me to be like "Caesar's wife"?[11] To shut out the world of experience? Because I do not hate Gray perhaps you think I do not love you? Should I fear the ice who am fire? No, no; I love you & you love me & I know well that the time will come—& soon—when we will be lovers together again, & you will come to me naked & passionate, with a richer abandonment. My dear, dear beautiful child-wife, you don't think that our love could end? One epoch in it has been broken off; we have both suffered, you especially, but there will be new epochs. I don't mind what you say now—I know you must love me as inevitably as I must love you. Other people are nothing to us—just toys on the way. You have never looked into anyone else's eyes as you have looked into mine & I have never looked into anyone's eyes as I have looked into yours.

Yes, have faith and—"escape me? Never!"[12]

Richard

1. Uprooted.

2. Aldington is quoting from William Morris's *The Earthly Paradise* (1868–70), whose classical tales in narrative verse are preceded by a six-stanza apology in which Morris defines his limitations (he cannot console or distract the reader from life's brute realities):

> Dreamer of Dreams, born out of my due time,
> Why should I strive to set the crooked straight?
> Let it suffice me that my murmuring rhyme
> Beats with light wing against the ivory gate,
> Telling a tale not too importunate
> To those who in the sleepy region stay,
> Lulled by the singer of an empty day.
>
> (stanza 4)

3. Angelo Poliziano (1454–90) was an Italian poet known for his Latin odes, Greek and Latin epigrams, and Italian lyrics.

4. Unidentified, probably proverbial.

5. Germany proclaimed that it was fighting the Great War in order to spread its "Kultur"; at this time, the term was frequently used satirically by the British press.

6. The Greek comic playwright (c. 446–386 B.C.E.)

7. First-century C.E. Roman author of the *Satyricon*.

8. François Rabelais (1494?–c.1553), French physician and humanist writer who often drew on classical sources. He portrayed in his work the range of French society during his time.

9. Aldington makes clear here, I think, that it is H.D. who has initiated and defined the current terms of their relationship. Although in many ways Aldington's actions have caused her decisions, she is nevertheless the partner who is insisting on a distance between them. She has evidently in recent letters not only been angry because of his affair but has felt sexually inadequate and insufficiently compelling to her husband. Aldington's response here, which is both apology and reassurance, seems his attempt to insist on a future for their marriage.

10. Aldington enjoyed long walks in the English countryside, and when outside of London, he and H.D. regularly hiked long distances together. He discusses at some length his fondness for walking in *Life for Life's Sake*, 53–58. H.D., too, reveals her enjoyment of this activity in the long walk she details in chapter 9 of *Bid Me to Live*, in which Julia passes most of a day wandering in the rural hills of southern Cornwall.

11. Proverbially to be all things to all people.

12. Aldington is not threatening H.D. here; rather, he is quoting aptly from Robert Browning's "Life in a Love" (first published in *Men and Women*, Vol. 1 [1855]):

> Escape me?
> Never—
> Beloved!
> While I am I, and you are you,
>   So long as the world contains us both,
>   Me the loving and you the loth,
> While the one eludes, must the other pursue.
> My life is a fault at last, I fear:
>   It seems too much like a fate indeed!
>   Though I do my best I shall scarce succeed.
> But what if I fail of my purpose here?
> It is but to keep the nerves at strain,
>   To dry one's eyes and laugh at a fall,
> And, baffled, get up and begin again,—
>   So the chase takes up one's life, that's all.
> While, look but once from your farthest bound
>   At me so deep in dusk and dark,
> No sooner the old hope goes to ground
>   Than a new one, straight to the self-same mark,
> I shall shape me—
> Ever
> Removed!

35

July 28, 1918

Dear wild Dryad/

I'm so glad to know that you're going to "the isles,"[1] though I'm afraid this rain and rough wind will have spoiled a little the lilies of all kinds you were to live with. Two days ago I had a very sad little note from you but instead of answering it I just sent you a faun poem.[2] I'm so glad I did because I know now that the Faun & Dryad[3] will always live & always love each other. You see sometimes the Faun kids himself he's dead & sometimes the Dryad kids herself *she's* dead—& then, like Toddy, they wake up from the "burn-down-dead"[4] and find themselves good & alive again. I hope you'll like the Faun song anyhow.

I wish I'd known you were going earlier—it would have cheered me up lots. Are you staying with the little girl who knows H.D. by heart?[5] Or have you just got rooms? As you speak of Alec & Amy[6] coming down that way I suppose you are not staying with yr: amie.[7] I wish you were in some pleasant house. (Apropos, will you remember I always keep a small balance for you at Cox's? You have only to mention that you need it & I'll send a cheque by return. Don't be proud about this, for I get more pay than I need & I can't use it more pleasantly than for you.)

Amy Lowell's letter[8] strikes me as about the most offensive thing that was ever penned—she is in her fat Boston drawing-room having the impertinence to lecture me in the front line! It takes my breath away. She is absolutely past all decency—and that talking that rot about wishing she were in the trenches. She'd get so stuck in the mud she'd never shift. Amen!

Ah, my dear, how sweet and beautiful you are. Of course I will come to you after the war and we will be "wild & free," and happy "in the unploughed lands no foot oppresses, The lands that are free being free of man."[9] I love you, best-beloved and dearest among all the daughters of the half-gods;[10] you knew that though you forgot than Fauns[11] are queer & wild, with "maggots in their brains"[12] sometimes! Dooley birds[13] get maggots sometimes, only they just trail their wings & look kind of doleful—but it's the same thing in the end!

You must tell me more about this new admirer of H.D. She must be very wise since she can love your poems so much. Has she a name or is she just some belle anonyme? Is she truely of the sacred race[14] or merely one to whom it is given to recognise the gods yet not be of them?

I would like so very hard to kiss you again—that dear small mouth that was made to speak exquisite things just as your curved ears were made to hear "the music of the spheres."[15] But perhaps I should not say this, for silence is most noble to the end. And yet I tremble with pleasure when I think that on the very day of my leaving this prison[16] I shall kiss again the cool fragrant petals of your pale hands and hold against me the tiny points of your sterile[17] breasts.

Over me have swept great waves, yet the great ninth wave[18] has so far missed me; perhaps in the end I shall win through. But, like you, I have been a wanderer upon foreign seas and yearn only to return to "the isles" that are mine by right.

R.

9th R. Sx. B.E.F. is correct address.[19]

1. The Scillies, where Bryher (Winifred Ellerman; see Biographical Appendix) has suggested that she and H.D. go together. Bryher's affection for the Scillies went back to childhood visits; the name "Bryher" is derived from one of the islands.

2. That is, a love poem; unidentified.

3. With these pet names Aldington recalls the early years of their courtship and marriage.

4. Unidentified, but clearly a character in a children's story or folk song.

5. Bryher, who in her memoir *The Heart to Artemis* recalls that she learned H.D.'s *Sea Garden* "by heart from cover to cover" (*The Heart to Artemis,* London: Collins, 1963, 187).

6. Alec Randall and his wife, Amy; see Biographical Appendix.

7. Female friend; this term seems particularly intimate here. Aldington probably sensed the special attraction between H.D. and Bryher from H.D.'s recent letters, and the playful and erotic tone of letter 35 suggests that he is relieved by her beginning a new relationship.

8. Exactly which letter Aldington is referring to here is unclear. Amy Lowell wrote the Aldingtons regularly, sometimes insisting on a sympathy which they found presumptuous given her position of social and financial privilege and her physical distance from their experience.

9. Aldington is quoting from his own poem "The Faun Captive," a draft of which he sent to H.D. on July 8, 1918; see letter 25.

10. Dryads here, who are not quite immortal, but have a special semi-immortal stature.

11. That is, creatures like himself.

12. Proverbially, whimsical or crotchety people had maggots in their brains.

13. That is, creatures like H.D.

14. One of us, a colleague worthy of being considered a particularly close friend.

15. Proverbial, meaning harmony in all things.

16. The army.

17. Aldington is using this word idiosyncratically here to mean "pure." He uses this word similarly, for example, when writing to the publisher Charles C. Bubb about the lesbian verses in *The Love Poems of Myrrhine and Konallis* on July 29, 1917: "I wanted to express the intensity of passion . . . ; I wanted something sterile and passionate and lovely and melancholy. . . . Myrrhine & Konallis are simply the love of beauty, too sensual to be abstract, too remote from biological affection to be anything but sterile" (quoted by Norman Gates in "Richard Aldington and The Clerk's Press," *Ohio Review*, Vol. 8, No. 1, Fall 1971, 23).

18. Proverbially the largest or most destructive in a series.

19. Ninth Royal Sussex Regiment, British Expeditionary Forces. Aldington routinely reminds H.D. of his address, for apparently she repeatedly forgets and asks in her letters to him.

36

August 3, 1918

My dear girl/

Mail, which had been delayed several days, has just reached me. You seem to be in rather a devilish mess,[1] and in a way I am responsible. Distinctly unfortunate that this should happen now as I have been nearly four months in France[2] & haven't much hope of getting back before November! There is the faintest possible chance of my getting back on duty before then and if so I could of course see you & possibly establish your "alibi."

However, the chief point is yourself, your own health and well-being.

Do this:

1. Stay in Cornwall until you know whether Gray is going to be enlisted. (I think he will—most Grade III[3] men are now.)

2. When you are sure of your condition—which, by the way, you should establish at once by consulting a doctor—you must tell Brigit[4] and get her advice & assistance.

3. You must then leave Cornwall. If you stay where you are there may be all sorts of unpleasantness.

4. I don't quite know where to suggest your going—Brigit can help here.

5. You must not worry about the situation—I will accept the child as mine, if you wish, or follow any other course which seems desireable to you.

6. I enclose £5. I will send you as much of my pay as I can. Try & keep it by you for doctors &c. You will need it.

Of course I won't tell Arabella. I can see you must be feeling pretty rotten about things, but you must just feel that this is one more strange experience and not feel badly about it. Cheer up and eat lots—I expect you are frightfully hungry?

Can you give a guess at the date of conception?[5] You see, the devil is that I've been corresponding with Gilbert & he knows I haven't been out of France! I wrote grousing about it only a few days ago. That's rather a blow isn't it? But perhaps that can be arranged—I can tell him I managed to wrangle a couple of days from the Corps School[6] & that I didn't write it to him because of the censor, as I'd been asked to keep it quiet. Let me have as soon as possible the date on which you want me to have been in England.

I really don't know what else to suggest. I am pretty powerless here, as you know. But I will do anything I can.

Brigit is the only trustworthy woman friend you have.

The money question is the most difficult. You can have any cheques[7] that come for me. And perhaps I can borrow some. If necessary I can refuse leave & send you the money I would have spent on that.

Anyway, you must keep on keeping on and not get hysterical or anything. These little matters are not really as grevious as they seem.

With love

Richard.

Address: 9th Royal Sussex. B.E.F.

1. H.D. has written Aldington that she thinks she is pregnant.

2. Aldington left for France in mid-April; he wrote Amy Lowell on April 14, 1918, that he was "off to France once more."

3. Cecil Gray's draft classification. Men were periodically reexamined and reclassified throughout the war, and the British government regularly revised its draft standards as the demand for new troops at the front increased. Gray is about to be called up despite a grade which previously exempted him.

4. Brigit Patmore; see Biographical Appendix. Because of her early marriage and her experience as the mother of two sons to whom she was very close, Patmore was regarded by the Aldingtons and their friends as a woman particularly competent to give advice on such matters.

5. From later letters the date would seem to be July 5, 1918.

6. Aldington was receiving additional training at a base camp in France during the first two weeks of July. It was sometimes possible to arrange leave during or at the end of such training sessions before returning to the trenches.

7. That is, royalty checks.

37

Sunday, August 4, 1918

Dearest Dooley/

I've been getting down to this proposition, and, though I'm anxious not to worry you about it, there are certain points in it which I must put before you since they profoundly modify our various relationships and since upon our present and immediate action depends the tranquility (I won't say happiness) of several lives.

I divide these points into two main headings: Natural and Social.

Let's take the natural first. We assume, do we not, that each man & woman is free to live his own life, to ignore any ordinary rules of conduct when he so chooses. We assume also that men & woman are at liberty to use this freedom in matters of sex. That is merely common-sense & the practice of most civilized communities. But in sexual relationships a woman's part is curious and difficult (so is a man's). That is to say a man has one "mate" & many mistresses; a woman one "mate" & many lovers. But there is a difference here somehow, for a man only loves eternally his spiritual mate, whereas a woman's "mate" is the man to whom she bears children. Am I wrong? Formerly I stood first with you & remained first however many lovers you might have had. But doesn't this event cause a sort of volte-face? Gray becomes your husband & I merely your lover; because the emotions that bind lovers together are exquisite & sterile,[1] like poetry, but a child is a more ponderous link than any beauty. It is there, it cannot be ignored or explained away; it is made out of two people's bodies, is they, cannot be distinguished from them. Therefore I feel most deeply that it is no solution of the difficulties involved for me to pretend that this child is mine. Certainly it solves some immediate social difficulties but it does not solve the natural one, which to us should be the more important. For if I take that step, not only are we all three committed to a lie for the rest of our lives, not only is your child deprived of a real father, but there is immeasurable humiliation for you, humiliation for Gray & even for me. (My dear, my dear, don't let this cold language repel you; I am agonising for you; I will do anything, everything for you, but we must see this thing straight.) Every moment that child is growing within you makes you go further from me & nearer to Gray. Inevitably, you must come to love him more—is he not the father of your child? Inevitably, he must come to love you more—are you not the mother of his child? Inevitably I must drift further from you both—what part have I now that you have come together?

Oh, it is sad, bitter, biting sad, when our love was so deep, so untroubled really by our other love-affairs. But a child! It came to me last night as I lay awake and thought out the situation. The thing I proposed in my first letter[2] is wrong, impossible, cruel—cruel to you, to Gray, to me, cruellest of all to the dear baby-thing you will bear. You have become Gray's; you have ceased to be mine.

You will think: "This is selfishness, this is unkindness, this is cowardliness, this is mere ordinary jealousy." No, dear, it is just truth. You must stay with Gray if he wants it. I think he will. If he behaves meanly then come to me. But now I have no "right" to ask you, no natural or divine right. It's sad, it's bitter sad, but it's true.

Now let us look a minute at the social side. Two lovers meet, kiss, love & part; there is no contract socially, no bond is formed. They are free. But two lovers meet & there is a child—then there *is* a bond, the first social unit is formed, it is ruthless and iron. You & Gray & your child are a social unit, harmonious; any attempt to monkey with that unit only produces chaos. You may have as many more lovers as you choose, he as many mistresses; but you cannot escape that obligation; you ought not to have other children. I may be wrong in this—some people, like Isadora Duncan or Craig,[3] were clearly fitted to disregard that social unit. But aren't we all too poor for that?

I won't go into the disgusting & laborious laws[4] of our country relating to marriage and illegitimacy. You may know that they are a disgrace. The only point is that your child will be given my name unless I repudiate it; that, if I do, it cannot afterwards be made legal. You see the difficulty? It's going to be rotten for Gray to have his child bearing my name; it's going to be rotten for the child also. On the other hand, if you were to divorce me for adultery (with A.) & desertion (!) the child would remain yours & still keep my name! If I divorced you the child would be handed to me & you wouldn't be supposed to have it!!! What a darned farce! I get quite silly when I think of it. The best thing we can do is to avoid the law altogether. You & Gray must live together at least for a time and, if afterwards, things alter you & the little one must come & live with me. It's damned hard luck on Gray, I admit, but then he must consider you & the child first, & it's really better for the child in the long run.

You see I've argued myself round in a circle. It's going to be damnable for us all, because no one will believe that yarn[5] about my going to Newhaven on leave. Who the devil would go to Newhaven on leave? And heaps of people— A.[,] Mr. Whitall, Gilbert, Beaumont, Alec, Amy, Frank, Ezra, May Sinclair[6] know perfectly well I've not been out of France since I landed. Best be honest and say what's happened and say that I'm eccentric enough not to commiserate but to applaud you, that even this makes no real difference to us. Damn it, Dooley, I am fed up to have lost you. I was an idiot to let you go away with Gray, but the omens were unfriendly. I never really thought you would have a child with him. And, Dooley, I can't ever really love this little one—there's our own sweet dead baby[7] I'll never forget. I should always hate this one for being alive. No, no; we *can't* act this lie. I won't. You are a free woman; act as such; be brave and tell the truth; you loved Gray because I had a mistress & you two have had a child. You have a right to have a child with anyone you want; but don't let's act this lie. Always, always I will be devoted to you; I will do all I can with my money &c. But this other life-long lie I will not act. I will not. Your people in America must be considered, of course, but the Atlantic is wide, the war lasts—you need say nothing to them, but must we sacrifice our lives for them? Even if you had to tell them the truth they will blame me (& rightly) not you.

In any case we can't get around Gilbert; he knows enough of the army to know that such a leave as you speak of is impossible. The right thing to do is to have the child, not to pretend it's mine but of course not to flaunt the fact that it's Gray's. If Gray is exempted[8] go away somewhere quietly with him & have the child—I will try to see you both before this happens (sometime in November or December) & we can talk things over quietly. If Gray is enlisted you must try to get Brigit to be with you. Someone you must have; perhaps America will be inevitable. If I am asked I shall say quite simply that the child is not mine, but that you & I are just the same to each other. [(]Which is true, as least as far as I am concerned.) We will get as comfortable a time for you as possible. You must just become a primitive creature and for God's sake have a *healthy* child! Don't go & compromise its life by worry, intrigue or bother. I will send you £5 a month as long as I am in the army, more if I can; Gray must try to do the same. That will help you to live cheerily, and if possible I will give you £20 extra towards nursing expenses.[9] Later on, if you and Gray wish to marry, we will discuss it. But the main thing at present is your own health, well-being & peace of mind. There will not be so much to trouble about if we face things squarely. *You are to tell Gray at once;* you understand? It is most unfair not to tell him. He can write to me if he wishes—you know I will be courteous and understanding. It's really more his pigeon[10] than mine, for, as I have explained above, I'm now secondary in your life. I only step in if he fails. But as an old friend I claim to do everything I can to help you through this rather rocky period of your life.

Write me freely, & never doubt my love.

God bless you, dear.

Richard.

1. That is, pure; see letter 35, note 17.
2. Letter 36.
3. Duncan (1878–1927) had a tempestuous affair with Gordon Craig (1872–1966), English scene designer and theorist, who was the illegitimate son of Ellen Terry and Edward Godwin.
4. Aldington's discussion of English laws relating to marriage, divorce and illegitimacy in this and subsequent letters is sound. There were no strict rules for divorce in 1918; a husband could divorce a wife on the basis of her adultery (establishing the affection of both parties and the opportunity), but a wife could divorce on the basis of adultery only when it was coupled with cruelty or desertion. "Non-access" of the husband was sufficient proof of a child's illegitimacy.
5. H.D. has apparently suggested in a recent letter that Aldington and she pretend to have met during a short leave in Newhaven, a small, unattractive town whose only real function is as a port for ferries between England and France, primarily Dieppe.
6. Arabella (Dorothy Yorke); James Whitall; Cyril Beaumont (see letter 24, note 3); Alec Randall; Amy Lowell; Frank Stewart Flint; Ezra Pound; and May Sinclair (1863–1946), a literary friend of the Aldingtons. See Biographical Appendix.
7. The Aldingtons' child died at birth on May 21, 1915.
8. Cecil Gray's military status is still unclear.

9. The costs of delivery and postpartum care.
10. Business.

38

August 5, 1918

My dear/
Your letter postmarked Aug 1st has just come. I don't understand at all.[1] Please see a doctor at once. I've been living hell these last 48 hours, thinking of your anguish & distress, thinking that this strange event had separated us perhaps for years. Please, please, *please* find out & let me know. I can stand the truth—I've faced the whole problem for us both. But I'm just grasping at the hope you may be mistaken.

You will wonder why I seem to lay so great a stress on your having a child with G, when I approve of your being his mistress. My dear, no man can take you from me by being your lover & I'm only too happy for you to have a pleasant companion, a lover, to keep you gay & well and interested while I'm here. But I do lose you if you become a mother, naturally & inevitably. It was for precisely that reason I stifled my desire to have a child with A. That desire was very great but it was madness—it meant binding A. very closely to me or else behaving very cruelly. Am I right? You must really get this affair put straight. One way or the other. I'll face *everything* with you & stick by you, dear. Don't have any doubt of that. I spent terrible hours thinking how confused you must be feeling. Have this child if you are pregnant—we will arrange things somehow. Do get my attitude correctly—I'm not angry or jealous or "honorable" or any such bilge, but only profoundly grieved because I suddenly realised that your maternity would naturally & inevitably cut you away from me & join you closer to G. And I don't want to lose my Astraea—queer wonderful creature that she is! You've just got to understand me properly here or you will be making a bad blunder in psychology. I love you & I want you to be happy & have lovers & girl lovers[2] if you want, but I don't want to lose you as I should if this happened. Gray would be a worm if he let you go when you had his child in your womb. Now wouldn't he? You know he wouldn't do such a thing; he wants to have you with him.[3] And you & I would just be friends or lovers, not imperishable sweet comrades as we have been.

O my dear, I pray I don't hurt you by what I say. I want to be so tender, so all-embracingly compassionate—but while this thing is in doubt I haven't the right.

Your
Richard

P.S. Shorter's article[4] need not worry you. Why change H.D.? You are bound to get this sort of thing. Let them print your photograph—you don't care. What the devil do these people matter?

1. Evidently H.D. has written that she may not be pregnant, that she is not certain.

2. Aldington knew about H.D.'s erotic relationship with Frances Gregg before their marriage (see Introduction) and is evidently aware of H.D.'s now potentially erotic relationship with Bryher.

3. There is no evidence to suggest that Gray ever wanted to marry H.D., to live with her for an extended time, or to participate actively in the role of father or provider for their child. It would seem that Aldington is projecting himself into Gray's situation here.

4. Clement K. Shorter (1857–1926) was editor of the illustrated weekly *The Sphere* and a friend of the Ellerman family (see Biographical and Periodical Appendix). H.D.'s photograph was never printed in *The Sphere,* and while Bryher may have proposed something to H.D., Shorter never wrote an article about her in his column. He did mention Amy Lowell and discussed Carl Sandburg as an imagist in "A Literary Letter" on August 3, 1918 (90), and on October 5, 1918, he included a photograph of the Aldingtons' fellow imagist John Gould Fletcher in a brief profile of his work.

39

August 8, 1918

Have a bad cold—will write to-morrow.

Love—R.

Be gay & cheerful—all will come right.

This postcard was enclosed in an envelope; Aldington is standing in the second row, second from the right.

40

Dearest Astraea/

I have been hoping so much to have a letter from you but none has come. I suppose you have not understood my letters—it was only to be expected. Never mind. We will go on loving each other, won't we?

You'll write me soon I hope & tell me truthfully how you are. Remember, I still don't know.[1]

Dear girl, I do pray that you are happy *whatever* has happened; & be sure I want to do all for your happiness, not for myself.

I kiss you—and I want you so hard sometimes, often, always!

Richard.

1. Aldington is still unsure whether or not H.D. is pregnant.

41

August 12, 1918
(First of 2)

Dearest Astraea/

Your two letters of the 7th & 8th have just come. I feel very confused and a little mad, yes, quite a little mad. Things seem so inextricably confused, so tragically in conflict that I cannot think except "what does it matter? what does anything matter?"

I don't understand yet whether you are ill or just enceinte[1]—either is sad. But the saddest thing of all is—us. Where are we? What are we doing? What do we want? I really don't know what I want, except perhaps to creep away by myself & try to construct the illusion of peace. The war is driving us all mad. But you, how is it with you? I feel in your letter pain & scorn. Yesterday I had one very similar from A. She "will not write again until I answer."

Put it I'm a pathological case—to be in love with two people is, I suppose, a disease—still, I must try to carry on. If I don't, there's nothing for me but a revolver bullet.

I love you so much that it is an agony. I love Arabella. This is really madness. You see it would be all right if I didn't care, now wouldn't it?

I am so sorry you are ill. You must see the doctor & get to know what is wrong & then we will do all we can to get you well & to look after you. I am glad Gray will look after you, but I don't like him going to his mother.[2] These mothers![3] They are only less imperative than their daughters!

Dear Dooley, you are a jolly good sport and I admire you immensely. You have a hell of a long furrow to plough if what you fear is true. But I will do anything I can. What can I do?

You speak bitterly of "one afternoon"[4] in my November leave. One afternoon! O my dear, my dear. What is there to say? "Ah me, pain, pain. Pain ever, forever."[5]

The news from the line[6] is very good, don't you think? It ought to prolong the war quite a lot.

I have two or three French scientific books to read; it helps to keep one sane. I have a work of materialistic philosophy "Intelligence & the Brain,"[7] which is somewhat alarming. It appears that our aptitudes & characters are determined by "lobes" & "lesions"! Tiens![8]

Let me know how you are getting on. Is it very hot in Cornwall? It's positively scorching here, but I have a pretty "cushy" sort of job.[9]

Au revoir. I wish I didn't feel so damned discouraged about everything.

Richard.

P.S. If you see John[10] please be very reticent about me—I don't care to have my affairs discussed with him.

I suggest it would be better not to see Arabella.

R.

1. Pregnant.
2. Gray apparently left Cornwall in early August for his mother's flat in London in part to escape local conscription. Reflecting on Gray's death in 1951 from complications as a result of heavy drinking, Aldington commented in a letter to H.D. on February 23, 1952, on Gray's desire to avoid military service: "Gray's heart was so bad in the war—perhaps for war purposes?—that I was much surprised he lived so long."
3. Aldington's distrust of mothers certainly has its roots in his unpleasant relationship with his own mother, although his relationship with H.D.'s mother seems to have been positive and warm (see Introduction). He is perhaps particularly skeptical here because of his experience of Dorothy Yorke's mother, who was manipulative and imperious.
4. H.D. has evidently suggested in her most recent letter that they meet only "one afternoon" during Aldington's anticipated leave in November 1918.
5. Unidentified.
6. The successful Allied effort at the Battle of Amiens began on August 8 and concluded on August 11, 1918.
7. Unidentified.
8. Goodness!
9. "Cushy," meaning easy, safe, was military slang which became common during World War I.
10. John Cournos; see Biographical Appendix.

42

August 12, 1918

Dearest Astraea/

My long letter,[1] written a few days ago, has very likely hurt you. I realized that at the time but it seemed so essential to "clear up the situation." I gather from your last letter that Gray is still away, & that you haven't told him. Really, Dooley, it's damned unfair not to tell him. He's got to readjust himself to this state of affairs and I consider that he now has a sort of "right" over you. If he fails you, o my dear, my dear, I am there "semper eadem."[2] I wish I could comfort you, my pretty one, and have you sleep gently in my arms. Of course, dear, you will always be my lover, won't you? And we will have each other in spite of all your husbands & children & so on. That I never for a moment doubt, but somehow this other thing has to be settled somehow. I fear that your having gone 3 weeks over your time is a pretty sure indication. What do you think? Have you tried giving yourself several orgasms in one night? As you know, that helps a delayed period very much. I wish I were with you for I understand that delicate little part of yours so well—I could make you glad & perhaps start you going again. I wish you weren't pregnant, Dooley; & I'm still hoping you aren't; but I'm facing the whole thing as if you were. The American idea[3] would perhaps be good, though it seems hard to have you go. I don't know that the Scillies[4] would be the best place for you—the doctor there is probably incompetent. But you must find out soon whether you are enceinte or no, & you must tell Gray. I feel rather annoyed with him—dash it, he might have been more careful. Though perhaps he didn't know *how* careful one must be.

You must write and tell me all that happens. I wish I could be more use to you, but chained here and depressed myself I feel very useless, as if I'd failed you. You must "stick it,"[5] Dooley; you are a dear wonderful creature & are made for great exquisite experiences. This is a hard time for you, but with courage you will come through[6] & life will be good again.

Tell me if you want more money. Anything I can do, count as done. Keep cheerful, exercise, eat, don't read too much, bathe, & don't forget to have a tremendous affair with yourself *at once*—the excitement of the spasms may start you. Have as many orgasms as you can, even if you don't want them—go to bed after lunch, say, and do it then. If that doesn't do any good, you can pretty certainly decide that you are enciente. Don't talk to your flower too often—it is a strain on the nerves. What I mean you to have is a sort of orgy straight off to stimulate you. Otherwise, only do it once or twice a week—& don't forget to think of me! I think of you when I have mine.

Your
Richard.

1. That is, letter 37.
2. As always.
3. H.D.'s plan, in reserve since 1914, to go home to Pennsylvania for the duration of the war.
4. Her plan to visit the Scilly Islands with Bryher.
5. Keep on with it, hold out.
6. Aldington echoes here the title of D.H. Lawrence's first volume of poetry, *Look! We Have Come Through* (1915), whose erotic verse explores both the tensions and the affirmations of marriage.

43

August 14, 1918

Dearest Astraea/

After I got your letter of the 8th I went & played a most strenuous game of "table tennis," got very hot, had a bath, changed, meditated, and am now in as sane a mood as a sheep in wolve's [sic] clothing can be.

I like your letter. It is clear & firm and puts things well. But at once on reading it there came into my mind the chief cause of our unrest, the "unknown" quantity. It is not these extraneous love affairs which separate us but the uncertainty of my tenure, the fact that for more than two years[1] we have known each other only in snatches. Dear one, above all things I want to be your lover, to help you if I can, not to hurt you. (There are nights when I simply writhe with shame & anguish thinking of the poignancy of those moments last December when you sat alone by the fire singing softly to yourself. That was terrible, terrible, Dooley; it was like some Greek tale—Oenoene.[2] It was the bitterness of all life. And that night my spirit was yours though my body was another's. I never deserved such love; but I pay a little for it every day with tears I shed inwardly, with pangs I do not speak of. My Dooley—"and I am no more worthy to be called"[3] your love.)

You say I am a child of Zeus,[4] and about me indeed there is a sense of Fate; what of life I deny the gods force upon me. But we have spoken of that.

My dear, you, like me, like all artists, have a diverse nature, have not one personality but several. Therefore I am inadequate to you & Gray is inadequate to you. I believe you & I complete each other more closely than most people— at least, we did; the last 2 or 3 years may have changed us. But there is a side of me which, as you know, goes hankering after unredeemed sensualism; & there is a part of you which is always seeking something purer & more spiritual than me. You may reproach me with carnal tastes as I reproach you for "living a world ahead"[5] (which simply means ahead of me), but these tendencies in us remain, cannot be hidden. We must look upon each other with the tenderness, the understanding, the tolerance of Rénan.[6]

You speak of forming some new attachment.[7] There, you are presuming upon Fate. Love is a chance and one does not create it by imagining one is in love with a person. On the other hand, should you find someone with whom you were in love, it would be inevitable. I never worrried about G.—I knew he wasn't human enough for you. But someday I may anguish over you as you over me. But your woman's instinct here deceived you; you didn't see that I *loved* you & *desired* the other. You would not take your mythology far enough; and you saw a "rival" (horrid word!) in the nymph surprised in the brake. Yesterday I read this: Ἐγὼ γὰρ αμπελίδος ὄρχον ἐλάβας. εἶτα μοδχίδια δυκίδων παραφυτείδαδ ἀπαλά, κ.τ.λ.[8] and I knew, in a way, that it was your voice speaking. And then: τί δοι καλὸν εἴργαδται;[9] It was a reproach, infinitely sweet, from the lost lips of Euridike,[10] a reproach for my yielding to the powers of brute force, an exhortation to

· 127 ·

remember that clear light we used to speak of. And do not think that this love of mine for you is just abstract, just "literature." You are young and beautiful and attractive and charming; and I love you also in the rich earth way, the desire of the flesh for the flesh, the look in your eyes when you love me, the touch of your chaste mouth upon my over-heavy, over-eager lips.

There is no doubt that I love you; there is no doubt that _were I free_ [11] I would be with you, look after you, love you. But, alas, I am not free. There are still two more years [12] at least for you to face without me, or with me at long irregular intervals. I shall be 28 then, a little bitter, disappointed, my work perhaps ruined, my mind infinitely agitated, myself useless for making money. Dooley, Dooley, I'm not worth the waiting for.

And then as to Arabella. [13] She is passionate & thinks, acts & lives by instinct. Perhaps she will be persuaded, but I fear that in the end there must be a break. I dread that, Dooley, partly from constitutional cowardice but partly also because she will feel so badly & perhaps act rashly. God forbid that I should exaggerate myself, but permit me the vanity of stating that this is the first time she has known a European who was both an artist and one who has that sense of "decency" towards women which some Englishmen strive for but which is not common in the regions of the Boulevard du Montparnasse. [14] Forgive this self-gratulation. But if she comes to think I've behaved meanly she loses what little moral sense she has left. And, damn it, Dooley, I believe in women having all the lovers they want if they're in love with them—but I don't like to be responsible for the making of a halt. Your wisdom & your woman's instinct can help me here enormously. Don't think me a "prig"—I don't deny that I am to blame in this matter. But—you understand?

Well, I must break this letter off abruptly—it is very late and I've been so interrupted that I fear I have been very incoherent.

Keep wise and cheerful. And get well, dear.

Love from
Richard.

1. The time since Aldington entered the army in June of 1916.
2. A nymph of Mount Ida whom Paris loved before he met Helen.
3. Luke 15:19, 21; on his return home, the prodigal son declares to his father, " 'I have sinned against heaven and before you; I am no more worthy to be called you son.' "
4. That is, essentially a Greek.
5. Unidentified.
6. See letter 13, note 4.
7. H.D. may have written Aldington about her possible erotic response to Bryher, but it is more likely here that she has suggested that he may fall in love with someone else if he hasn't already fallen in love with Dorothy Yorke.
8. "For I cut down the row of grapevines, next I planted the tender stalks of figs, etc." Aldington is quoting from Aristophanes' _The Acharnians_, line 995.
9. "What fair thing have you done?" Cf. Plato's _Gorgias_, 521e.
10. When Eurydice, the beloved wife of Orpheus, dies, he lamented her with songs

on his lyre, seeking her in the underworld. On the condition that he not look back, he was permitted to lead her out, but looking back to see if she were following, he lost her irrevocably.

11. Aldington underlines this clause four times.

12. Aldington felt that the war would last at least until 1920, a common feeling among soldiers at the front until November 1918.

13. Aldington feels a particular responsibility toward Dorothy Yorke, in part because of her having been deserted by a former lover in Paris before coming to London in the summer of 1917.

14. A central street in a district of Paris on the south (left) bank of the Seine, which was a center for artists and bohemian life.

44

August 18, 1918[1]

Dearest Astraea/

Having descended in the enclosed poem[2] to a more than Rummelesque sentimentality I see nothing for it but to dump the result upon Walter.[3] Perhaps sometime when you have nothing better to do you would type the enclosed & send it [to] Rummel, saying that if it inspires him to melody he is welcome to make any use of the work (free of all charge!) & if not, he has waste-paper baskets and razors. Apropos, I suppose they (W. & T.)[4] are still at the Rue Rayuouard? Quelle vie! Thank God we never sank into such iniquitous domesticity.

Four months ago to-day[5] I was on a charmed steamer midway between the two countries. Time does pass somehow, you see. I hope that before another 4 months have passed I shall see you again. Will you still love the fat and faithless faun?[6] But one cannot arrange life or it becomes merely a system. We retain enough spontaneity not to know how we shall behave— yet I hope you will say again: "Is this Richard?"

Let me know how your health is and please allow me to pay *all* doctor's fees for you. See a specialist if necessary and tell him or her to send the bill to me. Please tell me about yourself. Write and let me see what you write—or have I lost that privilege?

I kiss your Dryad flowers,

Your
Faun.

1. Aldington addressed this letter to Cornwall, but it was forwarded from Pendeen on August 22 to London, where H.D. had gone to stay with Amy Randall, Alec Randall's wife, at 3 Christchurch Place, Hampstead, four houses down from where the Aldingtons had lived from the fall of 1914 through the summer of 1915.

2. Unidentified.

3. Walter Morse Rummel was a pianist friend of Ezra Pound's; H.D. had heard Rum-

mel play in Philadelphia. His performance and behavior generally appeared elegant and accomplished. H.D. and Aldington came to know him in Paris in the summer of 1912; see Biographical Appendix.

4. Walter Rummel and his wife Thérèse Chaigneau, who married in 1912.

5. On April 18, 1918, Aldington left for France after nine months of intensive training and leave in England.

6. Throughout his adult life Aldington had a tendency to gain weight; H.D. was always slender and tended to remark on Aldington's shape.

45

August 19, 1918[1]

I love you, I think of you, I want you—wait for me.

Richard.

1. Like letter 44, this note was also addressed to Cornwall and forwarded to London.

46

August 21, 1918[1]

Dearest girl/

I understand so well how unhappy you must feel while there is this uncertainty.[2] Once you know one way or the other things will be clearer and the courses of action more defined. Somehow I still think you are perhaps not enciente. If you were you would surely feel very well and contented; but if you are in pain it must mean that there's something more wrong than just pregnancy. You must go see a specialist in town—at my expense, please, dear. Have the bill sent to me. If you don't do this I shall feel you are "cutting" me.

I think these interminable days are among the most abominable of my life. If only it did the slightest little good.

When you see Brigit you must be careful to let her know all about everything so that she can give you advice after proper thought. I don't know that it's necessary to tell Arabella—unless you particularly want to. The fewer people who know at present the better. Perhaps, if you find you are enceinte, it would be wise to speak to her. But it's entirely up to you—I have said nothing, have hinted nothing.

You must not be too generous in your desire to let everyone be "free"; after all, "freedom" does imply a voluntary admission of responsibility. G. cannot possibly evade the fact that he is the father of your child. Army or no army[3] that fact remains. You know, Dooley dear, I do want to do anything and everything for you, but it doesn't seem as if [I] have the "right" to do much. This makes life seem very queer. O my dear, I do so want to do the right, the tender, the gracious thing—you know?—my heart is good enough. But I cannot quite see how. I wrote Brigit a curt little note—as we are not on particularly good terms—begging her to be very careful as to what advice she gave you, because I feel all your life's happiness depends on what happens now. I seem to bring unhappiness to everyone I care for—it drives me mad to think of such unhappiness falling on the little girl I saw in Brigit's room six years ago.[4] I feel very angry with Gray sometimes—because it's just like a sloppy musician not to be precise and careful. God, I feel deadly sick to think what you are going through—poor dear, my dear little girl child Astraea. You have suffered too much already that this should come on you.

Keep a good heart, my dear; nature, in her infinite kindliness, is perhaps preparing for you some exquisite recompense for these bitter years. It is perhaps weak selfishness for me to regret that your child is not ours. But "no man escapeth his fate by lamentation,"[5] and I must accept this, the bitterest thing that has ever happened to me. Between you & me as always there is great love, a perfect love. I do not see the future clearly, yet I do know I shall never love anyone but you inevitably. Though we be oceans apart I never forget you. Be brave, be strong, have your child and I will try to care for it for your sake—if you want.

Sleep, dear; don't think; just be a happy mother.

Your

Faun.

1. Like the previous two letters, this letter was also addressed to Cornwall and forwarded to London.
2. About whether or not H.D. is pregnant.
3. That is, whether Cecil Gray is conscripted or not.
4. Aldington recalls here having met H.D. at a party at Brigit Patmore's in early 1912.
5. Unidentified.

47

August 25, 1918

Dearest Astraea/

You are very wise to be going to town[1]—I insist on your going to a good doctor at once. There may be something seriously wrong with you and you must have it seen to at once. Do you understand? Give my name and address (B.E.F.)[2] to the doctor & I'll pay his bill by return.

Now for God's sake *don't* go live in some dull little room[3] in town. Stay somewhere cheerful and let me make up any deficiencies in your accounts. Miss Weaver[4] owes me a few pounds over the P.T.S.[5] & I should be getting some money from the U.S.A. soon.[6] Please do not go to any rotten little place.

I see from your last letter that you are not at all happy and I am quite grieved at this. Moreover I am frightfully disappointed that your trip in Cornwall has not built up your health. I was hoping you'd get quite well again.[7] You must forgive me if I am often forgetful of your physical fragility, but you know people of "rude health" are very selfish in that way. And with the improvement in food & conditions one gets as an officer I have now become "very fit"—very sunburned, not quite so fat, fresh and very "male"! The last two months have been the most agreeable I've had for over two years. I've been very worried about you and about things generally—but what I mean is that life has been pretty cushy here[8] and yet strenuous enough to be healthy.

I don't see why you should run away from London because there's a chance of my getting leave.[9] You needn't really worry—there's not much chance of my coming this year. And Arabella though jealous has amazing patches of sanity for a woman—and in any case why the devil shouldn't I do as I like? Are you going to make me waste 2 days leave travelling up & down from London to the Scillies?[10]

My dear, I get fed up with G. & van Dieren.[11] It makes me think of what we used to call "holy Ezra."[12] (Apropos, poor old Franky[13] is a "Tommy" in the Rifle Brigade at Falmouth! He's in a B1. battalion,[14] so I guess mending roads & frightening Boche prisoners will be about the extent of his military excesses.) Of course it's damned rotten for a man of Gray's sensitiveness & talent to be shoved into the A.P.C.[15] But he won't have more than two years of it and must look on it as imprisonment for art's sake!

I know I am glad to be out here now—there is an immense stimulation in these victories,[16] especially when you are not fighting them! My present situation is ideal—I get all the excitement with a minimum of danger. I never thought the Allies had the brains or the guts to do what they've done. The Boche is really rattled—he's getting pushed all ways; there are rumours that he is retreating, retreating, retreating everywhere.[17] I know it's all rot and so on, but it's like a bull fight or a fierce football match; and after one side has been conspicuously beaten & stuck it there is something pleasing in seeing them turn round & give the other man hell. They have a simple amplitude about things nowadays; if the Boche sends a shell over they send back 5, does he drop a bomb, a telephone message gets 10 dropped on him; does he raid with a company, we attack with a brigade. And so on. I feel pretty sure we shall drive him back to the Meuse[18] next year, be in Germany in 1920 & have peace by the end of that year—i.e. in just over two years.[19] I don't know if you read the papers, but perhaps you know the armies have taken 100,000 prisoners & more than 1000 guns in about six weeks? Stuff to give the troops, who by the way have the same cynical boredom in victory as they have in defeat. Of course most of us will get killed, but it will be an amusing experience. So you must cheer up and get through the next two years somehow and then we'll be happy ever after. Do you ever write anything nowadays? You are such a shy bird, one never hears anything of you.

Au revoir, dear girl. I love you very, very much and I want you to love me—and I'll do *anything* to make you happy. Don't feel too sad; one does I know, and hates people who say "be cheerful," but it's worth being cheerful on one's own. Anyway, we're not immortal, old thing; we're "on leave" from eternity, so may as well have a good time.

Get well—take yourself in hand; you must. Hang it, you're young & sweet & fresh—"I say unto you mourn not for the kingdom of heaven is at hand."[20]

Richard

1. On the basis of postmarks on forwarded letters it would seem that H.D. left Bosigran in Cornwall for London before August 22, 1918. She evidently left somewhat precipitously, for she did not inform Aldington of her new address in time to avoid the forwarding of letters 44, 45, and 46. Letter 47 is correctly addressed, so Aldington has heard from H.D. that she is staying with Amy Randall at 3 Christchurch Place, Hampstead.

2. British Expeditionary Forces.

3. The housing shortage in London in 1918 was serious, and since giving up her flat at 44 Mecklenburgh Square in early August (H.D. wrote John Cournos on August 7, 1918, that she had given up her room there), H.D. is in a somewhat awkward situation and realizes that she cannot continue to stay with a friend.

4. Harriet Shaw Weaver, editor of *The Egoist*; see Biographical Appendix.

5. The Poets' Translation Series, which included six translations that appeared initially in part or in their entirety in *The Egoist*. The Egoist Press published the pamphlets in 1915 and 1916; Aldington was general editor as well as translator of the first (*Anyte of Tegea*), fourth (*Latin Poetry of the Italian Renaissance*), and fifth (*The Garland of Months by Folgore Da San Gemignano*) volumes in the series.

6. Probably money from *The Dial*, in which installments of Aldington's "Letters to Unknown Women" had appeared in March, May, and June.

7. H.D. was periodically ill, and her physical health was often related to her emotional state. She had not been well since returning to London from Lichfield in late November 1917.

8. Aldington's boast here of good health and physical comfort cannot be taken very seriously. He is obviously trying to reassure his wife and to relieve her of having to worry about him. Officer or no, Aldington's experience at the front was far from pleasant.

9. While the Aldingtons are comfortable writing to each other, H.D. has evidently decided that she would prefer not to see Aldington in London and/or that she would prefer not taking the chance of seeing him and Arabella together—a possibility if the three of them were in London at the same time.

10. H.D. is still considering spending some time in the fall visiting the Scilly Islands with Bryher (see letter 34). Such a plan, however, does not preclude a visit from Aldington, whom she obviously here still wants to see on his next leave.

11. Bernard van Dieren (1887–1936), a composer unceasingly championed by Cecil Gray, who was also a personal friend.

12. Ezra Pound at his most pontifical, informing others categorically of what art was and who was artistically worthy.

13. Frank Stewart Flint; see Biographical Appendix.

14. A battalion of men fit for service abroad in garrison or provisional units, but not for front line service.

15. The Army Pay Corps, which employed men trained in accounting or unfit for any sort of physical service. There were several central offices in the United Kingdom where pay records were kept and from which paychecks were issued.

16. The Allies were victorious at the Battle of Amiens (August 8–11), and on August 21, the Allies initiated the Second Battle of the Somme and the Second Battle of Arras, both of which were going favorably.

17. During the summer of 1918 the war, which had become static and entrenched all along the western front by 1918, finally began to move forward in a series of Allied successes that would enable British forces to reach the Hindenberg Line by mid-September 1918.

18. A river located in the Ardennes region of France, northwest of Verdun and southeast of Cambrai.

19. The many months of stasis at the front had not prepared the soldiers for the rapidity of the war's conclusion, and Aldington's estimate here was a typical response.

20. John the Baptist says, "Repent, for the kingdom of heaven is at hand" (Matthew 3:2) and Jesus says the same words later (Matthew 4:17); it is probably these words that Aldington is recalling, despite his misquotation.

48

August 31, 1918

Dearest Astraea/

I feel kind of baffled I admit. Wish I'd get brain fever or something and not have to think.

The only thing I am sure about is that I don't want you to have an operation.[1] I beg and implore and beseech you not to. You are not strong enough; it is most fearfully expensive & difficult; it would harm you very much physically and do your mind irreparable harm. Please believe I am absolutely sincere in this; look at B.;[2] she is not the gay sweet creature she used to be. But not you—no, no, no; I can't bear the idea and your being cut. Promise me you won't?

I don't know why A. wants to be married to me.[3] Except that sense of possession. Psychologically she is right—I am not a lover but a husband.[4] Too many scruples.

This is absurd. What complications.

You felt she was hostile to you? I gathered that from an over-tone emanating from your last letter. A pity. Still it is only natural.

Yesterday, before I had your letter I wrote her saying that I intended to accept paternity of the child[5] if you wished and that I would always want to see you because you are very dear to me. I tried to explain and more how it was that you will always mean a great deal to me and how she has given me so much. I admit ruefully that the present position is untenable; both flanks are gone & the center is wavering. Quey?[6] Which is the best position to retreat to? (I'm afraid you were damned unlucky in marrying me, Dooley.)

Now, look here, dear one; no, hang it, I can't suggest that.

A. writes rather fiercely that she won't let me accept the child as mine! (Gesture of tigress preserving her young.) Good girl. But suppose I insist? It is rather charming of her, though, don't you think?

I don't know that I like the farm idea.[7] A mother ought to suckle her child if she can and have it live near her. You would have fits all the time thinking it would get hurt if it was away from you. I know what mothers are. And your child *must* be brought up among gentlefolk.

As a matter of fact, dear, the whole problem is insoluble. I think the only possible solution is the one you suggest—to break with both of you and go live by myself. I shall be miserable, but I can get a post-office job after the war and that will keep me from thought & ambition.[8] I care too much for both of you to take either without the other. Best quit. You will have your child; Arabella will marry someone; I will learn German and devote myself to philanthropy.

You can tell Arabella that it is not possible for us to marry since you are not able to divorce me (adultery alone is insufficient in England) and I refuse to divorce you. I will write her the same if she asks me, but she doesn't. I am rather surprised that you say she still persists in the "all or nothing" attitude. Perhaps it is only logical and normal; yet granted the somewhat peculiar circumstances perhaps some concession might have been possible. Curious.

I have been very much at fault, weak and over-anxious not to wound. To you I have under-estimated my passion for A., to A. I have under-estimated my tenacious devotion to you. You might, if you choose, call me a liar & a blackguard; I should not feel it truthful to dispute it. I have said passionate and intense, no doubt foolish things to A., and have led her to expect more than it is in my power to give. To *want* to give everything is not the same as having the power; my nuances were not precise. I have made a mess of things. You, poor darling, are up against it; A. will be very angry with me (which I shall dislike) and will say bitter things (which will hurt me very much) and I shall feel very lonely & lost. But the only straight thing is to quit and see neither of you.

Cheerio,
Richard.

Later.

Have written A. the substance of this: ie. that I intend to accept the child as mine, but that I will not see either of you two again. It is the only possible solution.

I will send you the money I mentioned.[9] Please accept the Dial cheque[10] which I returned endorsed to A. yesterday.

R.

1. That is, an abortion.
2. Brigit Patmore.
3. Aldington is apparently commenting on H.D.'s concerns in a recent letter. It would appear that H.D. and Dorothy Yorke have met in London and discussed Aldington.
4. Aldington was always essentially monogamous and had a strong tendency to bond with a partner against all others. His self-evaluation here is very perceptive and anticipates his erotic relationships with women for the rest of his life.
5. While Aldington initially reassured H.D. that he would not tell Yorke about the pregnancy (see letter 36), it is clear here that he has told her, as he inevitably had to at some point.

6. Aldington is likely thinking of the Spanish "Que?" meaning "What?"

7. H.D. is considering putting the child in a nursery soon after birth.

8. Aldington is thinking of Frank Flint's situation: his civil service job with the post office worked against his creative thinking and writing of poetry; see Biographical Appendix.

9. See letter 47.

10. See letter 47.

49

September 1, 1918

My dear Astraea/

I am sitting out of doors to write this in a deep lane with banks covered with sunny flowers. The wind and the clear sky give me sanity and calm. And I am more than ever convinced that what I wrote you yesterday is the only possible course for us to follow. It is true, as I wrote Arabella, that all the colour goes out of life, all the interest. But I gain calm and a certain liberty of the spirit and a sense of justice. I have still some evil hours to go through, to struggle with my loneliness, my affections, my sensuality. Yet I believe I can do this. The B.E.F.[1] gives me at least a temporary protection under which I can "grow a shell" to use your phrase. It is better for us all to live apart, and not to see each other. I don't think there is any necessity for me to see either of you in November.[2] I can go to Paris or not go anywhere, and by the time the war is over we shall all be pretty used to the state of affairs. You see there was a time when I cared so much, so very much. But now I don't care; I should not be strong enough, I know, to resist if I saw either of you, but from here, my "Hindenberg Line,"[3] I can laugh at you—you can't come to me & I need not come to you unless I want. I think I am master of the situation? After the war, if there is an afterwards, it will be easy for me to evade you both.

I maintain what I said before: I will accept your child as mine and give it my name. It is too great a burden for a sensitive child to brand it with bastardy. And I won't have it. The little creature has done no harm and that at least we can do for it.

I will send you one third of my income whatever it happens to be.

I will not see Arabella any more than I will see you. It is all over, napoo,[4] fini—understand? Neither of you. I can do without you, and I must do so and you will both have to do without me—which I guess you can do.

My present job is to get on with the war, which I shall do to the best of my ability. Afterwards I shall do what I think best—almost certainly it will not be literature, nor women. There will be plenty of jobs for discharged officers. So I have no particular worries about my future. I hope you will be happy and I hope Arabella will, and I hope you will both forgive me for having loved too much and now not at all.

Richard.

P.S. I endorse September cheque.[5]

Later.

Your letter of 26.8.18 has just come. I am sorry about the Lawrence business[6] for your sake; but people are like that. I suspected the Gray business too.[7] Artists! My God, quel canaille.[8]

But I see no reason to alter what I have written above. Look on me as a sort of eternally absent friend; you can rely on my discretion and help at any juncture and in any circumstances.

I am deeply sorry for you, but I can do no more.

R.

1. British Expeditionary Forces.
2. Aldington anticipates a three-week leave in mid-November.
3. Aldington's strategic and entrenched position of safety.
4. An English corruption of "il n'y en a plus," meaning finished, dead, gone.
5. Aldington regularly sent his army paycheck to H.D., who periodically sent him funds from her bank account.
6. After the Aldingtons' return to Mecklenburgh Square from Lichfield in late November 1917, D.H. Lawrence's relationship with H.D. became very intense (see Introduction). If we can trust *Bid Me to Live*, she and Lawrence maintained an intimate correspondence (their letters have apparently not survived) that continued throughout her time in Cornwall. Lawrence's failure to respond with equal passion to H.D.'s overtures effectively precluded this aspect of their relationship. In addition, Lawrence's affection for Dorothy Yorke, of whom he was consistently fond, probably led him finally to distance himself from H.D. Yorke visited the Lawrences for two weeks at their cottage in Derbyshire in June (D.H. Lawrence to S.S. Koteliansky, 20 June 1918, in *The Letters of D.H. Lawrence*, Vol. 3, 256). It was through Yorke, for example, rather than through H.D., that Lawrence probably knew, as did very few others, that H.D.'s child was Gray's and not Aldington's (D. H. Lawrence to S.S. Koteliansky, 7 April 1919, in *The Letters of D.H. Lawrence*, Vol. 3, 349).
7. Aldington finds Gray no more faithful to H.D. than Lawrence.
8. What riff-raff.

50

September 2, 1918

Dearest Dooley/

I hope you are feeling better all round and that Brigit has been a comfort to you.

You must forgive me if I write only a little letter or none at all; I am rather unhappy and exhausted with a great struggle.

Let me know how you are, if you want anything &c.

Don't trouble about L. and G.[1] If I can I will provide for the child—I would rather, if it can be done, that you didn't take G.'s money.[2]

Richard

1. D. H. Lawrence and Cecil Gray.

2. H.D. is apparently considering asking Gray for money to pay for childbirth expenses and later maintenance, but despite pressure put upon him, primarily by Brigit Patmore and Bryher, Gray could never be coerced into giving H.D. any funds toward child support. Patmore's letters to H.D. and Bryher during the 1920s (BL) chronicle the women's unsuccessful efforts to persuade Gray of his financial responsibility.

51

September 8, 1918

Just to say that I have not forgotten your birthday.[1] Perhaps it would be too cynical to offer you congratulations, yet at least I can salute you with a gesture.

Life is very strange and pitiful. These bitter days we are all three suffering, this pain and discontent, seem very useless; one can only keep in mind the immense background of human misery and reflect that we are now in harmony with it instead of in contrast.

Of course one must not take things too tragically; there is something attractive in Anglo-Saxon imperturbability. Yet I have a precise sensation that what Browning would call "the poetry of life" is over. No doubt I shall continue to live and act and perform all the little fruitless gesticulations of existence, but the flash has gone from the gun, the perfume from the flower, the ecstacy from music. I shall never again live in the old intense way, never be thrilled by beauty as before, never wait for a woman with a beating heart and dry lips, never *live* again.

O my dear, this is a sad bitter little birthday note, but you must accept it. We have become middle-aged before our time, and it is more gracious to leave the stage at once than to importune spectators with a diminishing charm. This moment comes into all lives. I did not think it would come so soon to me; I hope that it has not come to you. But directly we cease to live in ecstacy, youth has gone. I have had nearly ten years; and of many beautiful things given me by the Fates the most beautiful has been to love & to have been loved.

I am firm in my resolution and I have this one hope in life—that it will make things easier and more tranquil for you. I shall not see Arabella again, as I promised you; nor will I ever have another mistress. I will do all I can for you and your dear child—dear to me, because it is part of you—but you must not expect to see me again; the middle-aged like to avoid pain!

Richard

1. September 10. H.D. celebrated her thirty-second birthday in London at dinner with her old friend May Sinclair and a new friend, Clement Shorter, editor of *The Sphere,* with whom she had begun to correspond in July 1918, and whom she had recently met after her arrival in the city (see Biographical Appendix).

52

September 20, 1918

Dearest Astraea/

Thank you for your letter and for sending Amy's.[1] She makes one impatient and I intend not to write her again. The woman's a fool. Harmless, but a fool.

I haven't heard what address you are going to, so am writing via 3 C.C. Place.[2]

As you may remember I am here until October 8th,[3] so naturally there is no news to give. I am dull but comfortable. May have more to report this time next month.

I hope you are well and that everything is progressing well. Look after yourself and keep fit.

What are you doing about coal[4] for the winter? I suppose you know it is strictly rationed? Don't forget to look after this.

Love from
Richard.

1. H.D. regularly forwarded letters from Amy Lowell, who often wrote letters to both the Aldingtons jointly.

2. 3 Christchurch Place, where H.D. has been living for almost a month, although she is now planning on moving to a place of her own. In an undated letter to Amy Lowell sent from this address in September 1918, H.D. conveys her current situation and intentions. Although the letter is guarded and omits mention of much that is emotionally central to H.D. at this point, it deserves quotation in full:

c/o Mrs. Randall
3 Christchurch Place N.W.
Hampstead

Dear Amy,

I was sure I wrote you and I had an idea R. too wrote, as he said your article was far, far too kind and he was awfully touched by your generosity. But word keeps coming from time to time of things not received, so I imagine you never knew how really touched we both were. How could you doubt that?—Now I hope this reaches you, as I appreciate your writing me, after my apparent neglect—also I want to thank you + for R., for the check. I will write again. This is just a scrap to catch the next post out.

I have just got back from Cornwall + am hoping to go away again somewhere nearer London. Above address always will reach me—also 44; though I have given up my room there, books etc. still stay + post is forwarded. But I shall send you my country address as well.

I am writing Fletcher—have not seen him yet. Will give you news of him. I dined with Clement Shorter last night. He is a fine old man—very generous + open-minded, though, of course, a bit conservative + old-fashioned. I think your book gave him his first impulse toward modernity. He thinks a lot of you, as you already know. I met the Bryher girl in Cornwall. She is about 24. I think, too, shows great promise. She simply worships you + your work. I go to see her this afternoon + will write you further of her. She comes from wealthy people. Do not tell her I told you as she is very queer about it. But her wealth could make no difference to *you,* nor to any real friend. She imagines any kindness + interest come *only* because her father is reputed "the richest man in England." Of course, one can understand, but if she is any good at all, her father's position won't hurt her. (Her name is not Bryher.) Of course, I did not know this when I met her, and my interest was genuine. Yours, too, I am sure is.—She was worried: Did I think Miss Lowell was offended etc. I assured her you would be pleased by her appreciation + now I will tell her I have heard direct from you. She wants to meet people who write. Clement Shorter + H.D. is the extent at present of her literary acquaintances. I will try to find people but you know how disappointing most "writers" are—and everyone is in the war almost. I told her if she went to America, I was sure Miss Lowell would be very kind to her. She is wild to go away. But it seems impossible now—and her people are dead against it.

The Lawrences are in the country. You probably hear from Lawrence. Flint is in the army—I don't know anything about him. I am forwarding the letter. R. has a jolly job now, back of the lines in signal work. No doubt you will hear from him. I have not seen the Pounds. London is rather more lively than when I left—more hope in the air, and food problems not so serious.

Well, good luck. I will write again.

Love to Mrs. Russell + to you.
from
Hilda.

3. Aldington is still at base camp receiving special training in Signal School 8th Corps.

4. The British government introduced wide-scale rationing in 1918: sugar was rationed in January; in April ration cards were issued for meat, butter, cheese, and margarine; in July ration cards were replaced by coupon books and only tea, cheese, and bread were unrestricted. Coal was also rationed in 1918 and electricity and gas supplies reduced.

53

September 22, 1918

Dear Astraea/

Have had a letter from your little friend Winifred Ellerman.[1] She seems to have the right spirit, and I've encouraged her to work at Greek with the idea of her doing something for the P.T.S.[2] if we can get it going again. Has she showed you any writing? It seems most enthusing to find someone who understands things; she realized what "Captive"[3] means, "Syracuse, the quarries &c."[4] Has anyone else, I wonder? Anyway, thank you for getting her to write—it was "like your gracious way"[5] once more. Perhaps you will bestow upon her with my blessing all the Bubb booklets[6] if you care, if you haven't given them already.

I have had some money[7] from Miss Weaver for the P.T.S., some I will send Franky[8] & your cheque[9] I enclose herewith.

Hope you are getting on well, & that you are happy.

Love from

Richard.

1. Bryher; the letter has apparently not survived.

2. The Poets' Translation Series; see letter 47, note 5.

3. Aldington's poem "The Faun Captive," a draft of which he sent to H.D. in July; see letter 25.

4. Aldington also wrote to Bryher on September 22, 1918, thanking her for her initial letter and elaborating on her understanding of "The Faun Captive":

> You are the first person I know of who has understood that indeed it does mean "Syracuse, the whole expedition, the fight in the harbor, the quarries." It is the bitterness of that abominable captivity felt again, resentment against the invasion of one's spiritual life. For we, who care for beautiful things . . . , are in perpetual conflict, in which too often we are worsted. (BL)

In quoting Bryher's letter back to her, Aldington confirms her gloss on the poem, which recalls the destruction in 413 B.C.E. of the Athenian fleet in the harbor of Syracuse during the Peloponnesian War (Thucydides, *History of the Peloponnesian War*, Book 7, chapters 69–71).

5. See letter 26, note 5.

6. Booklets of work by H.D., Aldington, and others, published by Charles C. Bubb at the Clerk's Press in Cleveland, Ohio. These included reprints from the first Poets' Translation Series as well as H.D.'s *The Tribute and Circe* (1917) and Aldington's *The Love Poems of Myrrhine & Konallis* (1917) and *Reverie: A Little Book of Poems for H.D.* (1917).

7. Probably royalties from the first Poets' Translation Series.

8. Frank Stewart Flint; see Biographical Appendix.

9. H.D.'s portion of the royalties sent him by Harriet Shaw Weaver.

54

September 27, 1918

My dear Astraea/

Your plans[1] seem to me excellent and sensible, and you should pass a fairly comfortable winter I think. Take exercise & keep normal. The arrangements for food and warmth seem O.K. It is not precisely the ideal existence one formulates but it is the best you can do under the circumstances.

Will you note that after Oct. 4, letters should be addressed 9th Royal Sussex, & the "Signal School 8th Corps" discontinued. I go up the line on the 8th.

I am very glad to find that you are cheerful and, as you say, "without resentment." Yet, when you say that, I wonder if you have completely "got" my attitude. God forbid that I should re-touch new wounds, but as I was catagorically definite with Arabella, so must I be with you. I want you to understand that in the actions & determinations I have taken I have been moved by affection for you rather than any bourgeois sense of duty. That is clear, isn't it? But I want you to understand also that this affection is purely that of friendship. Your friend- ship seems very valuable to me & I am anxious to retain it, but on no misappre- hension. So far as you & I ever being lovers again or living together as husband & wife, you must understand that it is fini, fini, fini. Now I am not trying to force you into anything. I am proud that you should bear my name; glad if you correspond with me on matters of art & literature & life; happy to meet you as one meets an old friend. You are quite free to make any kind of "liaison" you choose, providing some sort of elementary social camouflage is used; I don't wish to interfere with you in any way. Be as "free" as you can in a world of slaves. If you care to give & accept friendship upon these terms, I am only too happy. It is purely up to you. But I cannot have you being pleasant to me if I feel there is any idea in your mind of the old relationship being renewed. Because that is now impossible. You may think me idiotic and affirming more than I can carry out. But women are not so essential to life as they imagine; and in any case—well, there's no need to be offensive, is there?

I think I've made my point clear, and made it so with as much consideration as is consistent with precision.

It is no use our being humbugs, my dear. Things can't ever be the same again, so why carry on with something patched-up, a makeshift? I have at last "sorti mon beau tranchant,"[2] as you see & cut the Gordian knot of this affair. Arabella knows precisely how I stand & we have now ceased to correspond except at rare intervals. But there is no necessity for you & I to adopt this severity, unless you are anxious to eliminate so eccentric a person from your circle. We have many points of common interest not at all affected by the state of our hearts. You don't need any reiteration of my admiration for your work (though, since we are being so devilish frank, it wouldn't hurt for you to improve your spelling & punctua- tion!)[3] or for your personality and fine mind. So, as I have said, if you care to carry on, on this purely friendly basis, I am delighted. If not, it is up to you.[4]

Now then; I believe this is really the last postcript to this almost year-old affair. I am conscious of being less pleased with myself than I could wish, yet on the whole I have been fairly frank & not altogether inconsistent. Your going-off with Gray was of course a mistake—never, in future, have an affair with a man if you are not both in love with each other. If you had been in love passionately with G., all right; but just slipping off like that—wrong, dead wrong. Probably you will now write & say that you *were* passionately in love with G. In which case I shall just note down that all men are liars, especially women.

For myself, as I wrote you, there seems to be no particularly brilliant future. There is nothing I particularly want, and that is very dull. Yet I have gained a certain balance, a certain possession of myself, and a measure of certainty that no person in the world is essential to me. That is a great gain, for to put one's happiness into the hands of another is indeed a handing of hostages to the future.

You will, I hope, pardon the frankness and perhaps offensiveness of this letter—it is for the truth's sake. I hope to hear from you.

Ever yours
Richard.

1. Aldington directs this letter to H.D.'s new address, about which she has written him so that no letters are misdirected or forwarded. She has also evidently shared with him her plans for the next few months: she has rented Peace Cottage at Speen, near Princes Risborough in Buckinghamshire, and has asked her American girlhood friend Margaret Snively Pratt with her baby to join her for the fall and winter. Pratt had been living in London with her year-old daughter while her English husband, Bernard Pratt, was fighting at the front. Years later Pratt wrote to Bryher about H.D.'s arrangement: "I think the reason she had me stay with her in Speen before Perdita arrived was because I was so normal, not poetic" (Margaret Snively Pratt to Bryher, 3 February 1975, BL).

In leaving London for the country, H.D. was acting less impulsively than in her somewhat precipitous departure from Cornwall: she had an attractive cottage in a village that offered her the relative peace of rural England within a short distance of London. Her new friend Clement Shorter had a large country house nearby at Great Missenden. The situation seemed to both Aldingtons sensible and stable.

2. Gotten out my good cutting edge.

3. H.D.'s spelling and punctuation were extraordinarily bad.

4. Aldington was more decisive in general than H.D., and more able to stick with a course of action once decided upon. H.D.'s palimpsestic method in her writing was also characteristic of her life: she was less able than Aldington to let go of friendships and experiences in fact and memory. Thus while she initiated the separation Aldington is defining here (see letter 48), the decision and responsibility he indicates are hers will be difficult for her to manage clearly and consistently.

55

September 30, 1918

Dear Astraea/

Enclosed Oct. cheque.[1]

I have Miss What's-her-name's poems;[2] I don't know quite what to say about them. They leave me quite unmoved. I expect I have lost my flair for these things.

No further news. I go up the line on the 8th. Address to battalion after 4th.

Ever yours
Richard.

1. Aldington routinely sent H.D. his army pay, which is the excuse for this letter. This and many of the letters which follow are often occasioned by Aldington's excuses for the continued correspondence.

2. Bryher's poems, perhaps those which later appeared in *Poetry* in October 1920 (Vol. 17, No. 1, 136–137), under the group title "Hellenics": "Blue Sleep," "Eos," and "Wild Rose," or similar poems inspired by Bryher's relationship with H.D. and imitative of the latter's style and subjects. These poems were signed "W. Bryher," and Aldington is obviously exasperated here about whether to call Bryher "Miss Ellerman," "Miss Bryher," or "W.B.," as she sometimes signed herself during this time in initials that echoed H.D.'s. In an undated letter to Bryher (probably written in mid-September 1918), H.D. indicates that Aldington is interested in seeing some of Bryher's work and writes: "I am sending him the three poems you sent me. He will understand and appreciate them." In the same letter H.D. urged Bryher to send Aldington the manuscript of her novel; see letter 56. She continued: "He would be so pleased to see the MS. and is, I assure you, an impersonal + just (even if beautifully generous) critic" (BL).

56

October 6, 1918

Dear Astraea/

I like your little friend's book.[1] She is immature, but in some ways startlingly like you. I hope you will see her sometimes & lead her in the right paths. Her liking Amy[2] so much is a weakness—let's hope she'll grow out of it. I've dropped notes to May & Brigit[3] to ask her [to] tea—she may need to know pleasant women. Really, I have enjoyed her enthusiasms & I thank you for getting her to send me the m.s.

I have not heard from you in answer to my long letter.[4] But I feel sure you will see the wisdom of my plan. Don't think, because I wrote bitterly, that I will ever be anything but tender & affectionate to you. But can we do anything but be friends, dear friends? There must be no more humiliation for either of us.

I heard from Arabella yesterday; she is "touchante,"[5] but I can see she still dreams of "possession." And that will not be. I will not sell my tatters of freedom, my mind, my love of beauty, for any other passion. No doubt she would be an excellent wife; but that is precisely what I don't want. You are not a wife; you are a dryad. And I am ever so safe by being married to you. None of these human women can then steal the faun from himself, because he is a wanton.

Don't think I am resentful. I have told you frankly that I wish things were different, but I accept fate—and you are, & always have been, free to do what you choose. You must not mind if, in the future, I see you without the child; I would not have asked you to look at Arabella's.

I am glad that you'll be comfortable at Speen.[6] And I hope Margaret[7] won't get on your nerves. Still she can give you many hints.

My dear child, you must save more than £10—at least £50. I should be getting some money from my book[8]—you must have that and the money from Poetry,[9] if it comes.

Flint says he may get me some stuff into a new Anglo-French review,[10] so if he asks for any stuff of mine send him the "Faun Captive" & the "Fantasy in Three Movements."

Don't forget to write to 9th Royal Sussex again now. Leave out "Signal School."

Affectionately

Richard.

1. Bryher sent Aldington a draft of her autobiographical novel *Development*, published by Constable in 1920. Aldington was genuinely pleased with Bryher's prose and wrote more expansively to Flint on the same day as this letter to H.D.: "Hilda has found a new Imagist, a girl in London who is mad about our work, and has a most wonderful mind. I have seen a m.s. of her prose. It is young (and foolish) in parts, but she has a superb gift of realisation of beauty & a clear imagist method of writing." Aldington then quoted from *Development* at some length and concluded: "A prose H.D. She has pages of quite magnificent stuff. Of course, the book is far too much concerned with literature; but she is now quite crazy about life & if she avoids certain obvious perils will do good work" (HRC).

2. Amy Lowell. Bryher's affection for Lowell's work was untempered. Aldington wrote Bryher on October 5, 1918:

> You love an ideal Amy. I know her well, know how good she is; but she won't last you. . . . You like her love of life more than her art. You are quite right; but someday you will strike the essential falseness there. Amy has not known great love or great grief. She is vivid and delightful, altogether miles above that deadly Georgian crowd; but she is not of the immortals. You can say I hate her because she has too many dollars & a motor car & a suite at The Berkeley. Not a bit; these things are extrinsic. She is just too comfortable. (BL)

3. May Sinclair and Brigit Patmore.

4. Letter 54.

5. Touchy.

6. Where H.D. is now settled.

7. Margaret Snively Pratt; see Biographical Appendix.

8. Aldington's *Images of War: A Book of Poems* was published by Cyril W. Beaumont in early 1919.

9. *Poetry* owed Aldington for poems it had accepted and would publish in November 1918 (Vol. 13, No. 2, 67–71), under the title "Prayers and Fantasies I–VIII."

10. Aldington was able to place several poems in *The Anglo-French Review*, which began publication in February 1919.

57

October 13, 1918

Dear girl/

I am back[1] at the Div: Rest Camp in another part of the line, but still many miles from the fighting. Still as this is unconquered land it is interesting to take trips to places now "famous in story." Strangely enough the country is not nearly so destroyed as the kind I have known before. The villages are wrecked, it is true; no life, except soldier's, exists over vast tracts, dotted with shell holes & crosses, pitted with the holes of myriads of field mines, where only the whirr of partridges & the noise of starlings break the silence. Desolation, yet not unpleasant. It fits my mood of tranquility and self-possession—a land that has lost much, yet is free. For as Landor says: "If the souls of the citizens are debased, who cares whether its walls & houses be still upright or thrown down?"[2] The converse also is true.

I send you with this a book of songs I picked up on a battlefield, dropped by some poor lad who lost his life in this struggle. How bitter it is to reflect that the fight is for wealth & power & greed only, not for freedom, not for love, not for the future, not for anything true or great or noble. Yet somehow I grow to a mood of acceptation; not just timidity or resignation, but a knowledge that fools are many times too strong for the wise, & that we must use what little wisdom we can gather from the parsimonious gods to endure the pains unnecessarily inflicted on us by the carelessness of others. I feel ready for anything.

You must read the little book I send you. Some of it seems to me very beautiful, though I can only guess the meaning. This (p. 16) I like:

> Der tag ist nun vergangen
> Die güldnen Sternlein frangen
> Am blauen Himmelsfaal.[3]

which makes one think of the old Germany of romance & tenderness, apple-cheeked girls & young men called Johann Wolfgang or Ludwig von Beethoven— Ludwig who would not lift his hat to an emperor! This also I think very sweet and beautiful:

> Unsern Ausgang segne Gott,
> Unsern Eingang gleichermasson,
> Segne unser täglich Brod,
> Segne unser Thun und Lassen,
> Segne uns nut selgem Sterben,
> Und mach uns zu Himmelserben![4]

And there are quite a lot of other things worth reading, especially the Volksleider[5] at the end.

I hope you are going on well. It is some days since I heard from you, but communication here[6] is rather more complex than at the Signal School.

Affectionately
Richard.

1. Aldington recalled this experience of returning to the front years later in a brief essay which he sent to his friend, Eric Warman, probably enclosed in a letter to him dated November 19, 1958:

In the autumn of 1918 I was sent down the line to go through a course which was supposed to qualify me to be a Company Commander. The course was hurried at the end, and we were told we had to rejoin our units at once, there had "been another battle." We knew what that meant. Although all officers, we had to march on foot the last part of our journey—all transport needed for the advance, that advance of which we had heard so often for so long that we no longer believed in it. We bivouacked the first night on the old Somme battlefield, between Bapaume and Cambrai, just where our old front line had been at the time of the March, '18, attack. I persuaded two or three of my brother officers to take a walk in the dim autumnal afternoon, with the flames of burning Cambrai and other towns or villages bearing witness that at last "the advance" was a reality and not paper propaganda.

Forty years later I cannot forget what we saw. As far as we could see, just over against what had been our positions in March were battalion graves—every two or three hundred yards, the grave of a battalion. They were not ours, they were Germans. Over each was a huge cross bearing the date 21/3/18. Then in front was the grave of the Colonel or Major; behind him the regimental officers; then the N.C.O.s and men—fifty, sixty, a hundred, sometimes more. And looking over that ghastly dreariness of the Somme, we could see that these cemeteries, these battle burial fields, went on as far as the eye could reach. And Cambrai, burning, lighted our way back to camp, as we stumbled over the debris of the German army.

. . . Having seen that, I know what Death is. In that desolation nothing lived. Even the rats had been killed by the gas, and if birds drank the water of the shell-holes, poisoned with mustard gas, they died. There stood smashed guns and broken tanks like wrecks in that ocean of shell-holes. As had been the case a month or more before, on the old battle-line, the ground was covered with a bewildering chaos of abandoned German equipment—camouflaged German helmets, rifles, entrenching tools, bombs, gas masks, water-bottles, overcoats, hairy packs, cartridges. Here and there, occasionally, the equipment of one of ours, dumped by the stretcher-bearers or the burying parties. The utter silence, save for the faint hissing of the engine, the utter desolation, the ugliness, the sense of misery, the regret of all our lost comrades. (SIU)

2. I have been unable to trace this quotation.

3. The day has now passed / The little golden stars break / Upon the blue heavens.

4. May God bless our going out / And likewise our coming in, / Bless our daily bread, / Bless what we do and do not, / Bless us with blissful dying, / And make us Heaven's heirs!

5. Folk songs.

6. Aldington left Signal School on October 8, 1918, and is now moving eastward toward the front line. The Allies were advancing rapidly in October of 1918 and Aldington is travelling through territory which was recently "no man's land" between Allied and enemy trenches and territory recently occupied by the Germans.

58

My dear/

A paper came, the first in four days. What does it mean?[1] Can it be? Dare we hope? Is this torture, this age-long nightmare ending? I dare not hope it, dare not or I should give way utterly. When I heard that there was even a chance of peace—"terms accepted"—I was dumbfounded. We had heard nothing. No newspapers, you see. This is a great desert. Miles & miles. No news. But that one newspaper—terms accepted. It can't be; I can't believe it. The hope, the chance overwhelms me. Some of them are talking of "good times." O, it is mad. We must pray to be sane. I went out & stood leaning my head on the cross over a dead German's grave and cried, yes cried like a weakling. It is too much. O my God, if only it is true.

They speak of what they have lost. A brother, money, a mistress. I say nothing—I have lost my dreams, only my dreams. Yet I am thankful. Oscar Wilde came out of prison broken, penniless, almost friendless. I shall leave (if this peace comes) this harsher prison, no less broken than he, but with a good heart, a great heart. It does not matter if I must hold out my hand for bread to my inferiors, if I must be a beggar.[2] At least I shall be free & perhaps my lost dreams will come home to me. O to see with clear unafraid eyes once more the calm light upon calm waters, sun, wind & trees and the ecstacy of beauty, the presence of the gods. It will not matter if I be lonely & friendless & poor, shamed some ways & desolate, if only once more we have peace, if only once more we can feel the gods near, and the divine dreams return.

There will be people about you speaking foolishly & haughtily of "victory." Turn from them—remember, as I do, the myriad dead and give them, if you can, your tears, as I do. Perhaps yet the nations will be saved from utter destruction; perhaps greed will triumph & distrust & malice & ambition separate men. But at least we can hope and at least, thank all the gods, no man has died at my hands.

Affectionately,
Richard.

P.S. Tell me it is not all a lie. There is hope of peace?

1. Germany formally requested an armistice on October 4, 1918.
2. Aldington is acutely aware that he has no job, no means of support, waiting for him once he leaves the army.

59

Dear Astraea/

We are out of the line for a few days rest, yet are in a village which has not seen Allied troops since August 1914. To-day we took down a board which said "Sachen Strasse" & put up one which said "Sussex Street."

There seems to be no other news except that I have been made signal officer[1] for the time being, the other signal officer having been wounded in the last "show." It is much pleasanter than being with a company.

Have you seen Bennett at all? He is an officer in our brigade whom I asked to write to you when in town. You should have heard from him by now.

May Sinclair writes very pleasantly. She is of course full of "victory." I am sending her (ironically) a German helmet.

I have a little German testament for you, picked up at "XYZ"—.[2]

I hope you are well. Will send you November check (post-dated) before we go in the line again.

Affectionately
Richard.

1. Aldington was made an acting captain.
2. Because of military security, Aldington cannot reveal his precise whereabouts to H.D.

60

October 23, 1918

Dear girl/

I haven't written for a day or so, chiefly because I haven't had any paper. The advance is so rapid, that even here (10 miles behind line) we have been without everything except bare rations. Things are slowly improving, though, now.

I am glad you are happy in your new place.[1] I trust you will keep well and strong and learn how to look after your child. Margaret[2] can tell you many things of course.

It is unfortunate that Gray is in his present position.[3] Of course, one respects his resolution, but I doubt its utility. He will probably be in "durance vile"[4] after we have got free again. And there always remains the plain fact that once war starts one should help to keep its horrors from the people one cares for. Whether he serves safely in prison as a deserter or dangerously in France as a soldier, he will be equally cut off from his music; in the first case he is useless, in the second at least he is preventing his wife & child[5] suffering the horrors that one sees here. But I do not condemn him; I regret the circumstances & hope he will emerge untouched from his ordeal, whatever it may be.

Well, I have had a very long spell out of the line & don't so very much dislike going back to it again. At least there seems now some chance of a solution, though not that ideal solution one hopes for. I scarcely think it will last more than another year.[6]

In addressing letters please omit "D Coy"[7]—I am now on B.H.Q.[8] as signal officer.

Affectionately
Richard.

1. H.D. has now settled in at Peace Cottage near Speen, where she has been living for almost a month.

2. Margaret Snively Pratt.

3. Although Cecil Gray's military status (IIIB) protected him through July 1918, he became increasingly fearful about being forced into military service and evaded local conscription by leaving Cornwall before August 1918 for his mother's home at 13B Earl's Court Square, London. He must have been in hiding at this time.

4. With this familiar phrase Aldington suggests that even after the war's end, Gray may find himself in prison as a conscientious objector or merely as a draft evader, a deserter.

5. That is, H.D. and her unborn child, both of whom Aldington considers bonded to Gray in some spiritual way.

6. Like many soldiers Aldington was convinced, despite recent Allied victories, that the war would continue for a long time.

7. D Company.

8. Battalion Headquarters, to which Aldington, as acting captain and highest ranking signal officer, was now assigned.

61

October 26, 1918

Dear Astraea/

As I promised[1] I am sending the November cheque. You must stick another penny stamp on it, or it will not be paid. Sorry I haven't one to put on.

It is quite interesting up here and I am hoping to see more interesting things soon.

There is no particular news to write. I had a very friendly note from Paul Nash,[2] excusing himself for the delay in providing drawings for my book. Humbug, no doubt, but expressed with a "sheen" of sincerity.

Au revoir,
Richard

1. See letter 59.
2. The artist working on illustrations for Aldington's *Images of War*; see letter 24, note 4.

62

October 27, 1918

Dear Astraea/

Thank you for your letter of the 22nd. I am glad you are well, though, no doubt, you have bad moments sometimes.

I don't think you should take Amy Lowell too seriously. Whatever she may or may not have done to cheapen your work & reputation you are still too un-known for it to make the slightest difference to you. If you want to write, write;[1] if you don't want to write, don't. But what Amy Lowell does, says or thinks is really of no particular importance to you.

As to leave; it will probably be some weeks before I get it, but, if I do, it will be better in many respects for us to meet somewhere in town.[2] I shall probably stay with my father & Molly[3] & go down to Rye[4] for a week-end's shooting & riding. It will not be wise for me to come to Speen for just one day; it would make Margaret very suspicious and would also arouse the curiosity of the villagers.

I have rather lost count of time, so I don't quite know how long you have been enceinte—if it will embarrass you to come to town, we might meet on neutral territory, Brigit's[5] perhaps. But I will write you from town *when* I get there.

Of course, I shall not stay with Arabella; though I may meet her on terms of decorous & amiable frigidity.

Any news of Gray? He is a fool to resist. The war won't last more than a year & he'll never get to France. Why not put up with it? Still, he's free to do as he pleases.

Things are very interesting here as I wrote you, though sometimes too tragic. I saw a French child to-day—but, never mind, we won't speak of these things. Keep well & strong & happy.

A very pleasant compliment was paid your country to-day. The whole of our Brigade marched into a village with the bugles playing "Over There," the Amer-ican war song. Quite graceful don't you think?

I sent you the little cheque[6] yesterday. I'm sorry it's so small.

Herewith letter from Nash explaining delay in publishing my book.[7]

Affectionately
Richard.

1. That is, to write poetry; the issue is not whether H.D. will correspond with Amy Lowell. The Aldingtons maintained a regular exchange of letters with Lowell, although by 1918 their letters had become less frequent than when the three were working closely together on the imagist anthologies. H.D. had been experiencing a difficult time with her work since early 1918, confronting now apparently for the first time the writer's block which she would periodically encounter later in her life. She had also resolved not to publish for a while, in part questioning the quality of what work she felt able to produce, in part as an act of protective retreat from the personal intensity of her life, which was at this time—and would continue to be—the emotional center of her art. On the same day (October 22, 1918) that she wrote Aldington about Lowell, she also wrote Lowell a letter which deserves quotation in full:

> Dear Amy:
> I am sorry my note seemed mysterious and queer. I believe Winifred Eller-man has written you. She had a romantic idea that she wanted to be on her own + I understood that—feel the same myself. I believe she is of German jew (as you suggest) extract. I have seen her only about three times.

Its very sweet of you to suggest my publishing—but I hope not to do that again—for a long time, if ever. I want to keep in touch with literary people for R.'s sake until he is free of the army—and I hope to continue to be in touch with you always in a friendly way—But I suppose like Fletcher I am a pathological case + I may as well accept the fact. I am very, very anxious for R. to have his chance of a "career" once the war is over—and I shall do everything to help but I have been putting off publishing poems—I don't really over-criticize my work—but what is good will be good in ten years. I am only writing you an ordinary little note.

Miss Ellerman is very, very simple—an undeveloped, lonely child.

I hope Mrs. Russell is well—R. is up the line again but the news is awfully good.

In great haste
with love
always
Hilda.

I have not seen Fletcher for six months—nor do I hear from him. I am very happy in the country here—beautiful beech forests—you really must visit me here one good day.

2. In London.
3. Aldington's father and sister Margery had a flat in London during the war.
4. Aldington's mother maintained the family's home at Rye in Sussex.
5. Brigit Patmore was living temporarily in Brighton at this time.
6. Aldington's army paycheck.
7. *Images of War.*

63

November 1, 1918

Dear Astraea/

Herewith blank cheque—only to be used if I am killed. It will save any trouble about duties &c. Just go to Cox's & find my balance & make out cheque accordingly. Don't forget to put another penny stamp on it.

You are entitled to a pension in the event I mention—see you get it.

We go over the top[1] in a couple of days. Hence these gloomy words!

Cheerio! The war's nearly over, I think. So you'll be all right.

Richard.

1. From the front line of trenches into no-man's-land. Aldington was part of a successful British advance that began on November 4, 1918.

64

Dear Astraea/

I am very sorry you feel that way about things,[1] but there are many reasons for it. I scarcely know what to say about it. We are fighting & advancing all the time—no rest, but we don't mind if only it's ending the bally[2] business. So you see I'm not very clear as to the best thing to say.

No doubt I have changed. It is not my fault, but a misfortune over wh: I've no control.

As to G.[3]—I don't blame him. Influenza is rotten—had it myself in July.[4]

I shan't be back until the end of the month, & don't want to come specially. This is very interesting & exciting—new towns & villages every day, enthusiastic welcomes by French people, &c &c. And then what have I to come home to? I arrive at Victoria[5]—where am I to go? What am I to do? Arabella puts one part of London "out of bounds" to me—old sentiment puts another. You are hurt and unfortunate, I know; I sympathise deeply & do all I can. But my life also is ruined. I am the only man in this battalion who is not anxious about leave!

I will like to see you & talk quietly. I will try not to hurt you, but you must remember it is seven months now since I touched civilisation.

Don't let me hurt you. Keep proud. As to money it is not worth being proud about.

In great haste
Richard

1. Evidently H.D. has written Aldington that she feels he has changed and that he is to a degree responsible for the problems they are now struggling with in their marriage.
2. A euphemism for "bloody."
3. Cecil Gray is apparently avoiding a confrontation with H.D., evidently refusing at this point to see her because he is ill with the influenza that soon became epidemic in postwar London.
4. See letters 18 and 24.
5. Victoria Station, in central London.

65

Dear Astraea/

I go on leave tomorrow & hope to reach London about the 16th or 17th. If you will write me and fix a date, place & time for meeting, I will be there. Only address[1] will be 68 Queensborough Terrace, London, W2.

Affectionately
Richard.

1. The address Aldington gives is of a private hotel in Paddington.

66

Sunday

   I am not seeing *anyone* to-day. Excuse my breaking appointment.
                           Richard

*T*he relatively perfunctory nature of Aldington's letters in early November suggests the new plane he thought he had established in his relationship with H.D. The process which initiated this somewhat detached and practical but finally unstable territory began as early as September 8 (letter 51), exactly one month before Aldington was due to leave signal school and to begin his return to the trenches. With H.D. then in London and her plans to retire to Speen crystallizing, Aldington evidently felt that her situation had achieved a stability that did not depend strictly on him. Anticipating his return to the line, Aldington began the difficult task of once again getting his affairs in order to face the real possibility of imminent death: "Dearest Dooley" (letter 50) and "Dearest Astraea" (letter 60) of September 2 and 20 give way to "Dear Astraea" and the somewhat jaunty "Dear girl" or to no greeting at all. Aldington could not, however, have anticipated the armistice on November 11, and was unprepared for the overwhelming emotional tension of his long awaited leave, which followed soon after. Just when he thought he had perhaps negotiated the terms of a peace, a workable, controllable stance from which he could deal with the problems of his marriage, he discovered, as letter 66 suggests, that he was by no means so much in command of his own responses as he had earlier supposed and had insisted to H.D. The three difficult weeks of Aldington's leave deserve detailed attention particularly because of the gap in the Aldingtons' correspondence caused by their proximity.

In *Life for Life's Sake* Aldington recalls his specific experiences during the last days of battle and the events that quickly followed the armistice. On November 4, 1918, he remembers, "I was looking at the luminous dial of my watch in the gray dawn and giving my headquarter signallers the order to advance. As far as the eye could see to north or south a huge curve of flashing gunfire lit up the sky, and the old familiar roar and crash of drumfire beat on the ears" (191). He continues:

> My job that morning of the 4th was not to kill Germans, but to see that as my battalion advanced I kept my battalion headquarters in touch with brigade and both flanking battalions with a minimum of break and delay. For this purpose my field service message book and those of the other relevant officers contained two pages

of mysterious letters and numbers, showing my different positions and those of the other stations at quarter-hour intervals, until the final objective was reached.

I hadn't to worry about what was going on. What I had to do was to lead my little group of men forward for about five hundred yards, cross a road which my map assured me was there (it was), set up a lamp signal station at once, establish contact in three directions, send and receive any messages; and at 6:15 a.m. precisely move on to another point. These manoeuvres were carried out with such clockwork precision that, except when moving, we were never out of touch with the other stations for more than two minutes. I got through the German barrage with the loss of my corporal and one man, passed dead and wounded and surrendering Germans, and lost my knapsack. Our trench mortar bloke covered himself with glory. Somewhere, somehow he had pinched an old horse, and brought his clumsy mortar walloping into action at just the right moment to knock out two machine-gun nests which were punishing one of our companies. By 7:30 a.m., we had advanced two miles, captured six guns and two hundred prisoners, and could see the enemy retreating with undignified haste in the distance. Field guns galloped up, and went into action.

We had another weary week of marching and actions with rear-guards before our armistice, and when it came it was undramatic and undemonstrative. Yet it was not without deep feelings. There was an uprush of confused, poignant emotions—relief, gratitude, a stir of hope, a belief that this was the end of the war, an overtone of profound sadness as one thought of the silent ruined battlefields and the millions who never saw the day for which they had fought. And one's own insignificant little life, saved, but in ruins. (191–192)

The "ruins" of his own life were, of course, deeper and more personal than this memoir reveals, and the arduous days of travel to England on his first leave in many months did not calm his nerves. Aldington recalled the details of his trip to London with vivid specificity:

There had been no leave for several months, and my name was at the head of the roster. On the morning of the 12th I was handed a leave warrant in the orderly room, with the laconic and somewhat cynical advice to get to rail head as best I could. During the long period of trench warfare, rail head had been only a few miles behind the line, but now it was at least sixty and nobody in front knew exactly where it was. The best bet seemed to hitch-hike to Cambrai by jumping an army truck, but unluckily I couldn't find one going that way. Heaven knows how many trucks I rode on that day or where we went, but for hours and hours I was driven over an interminable landscape of ruined villages, battered trenches, wrecked guns and tanks, and a huge amount of scattered equipment of all sorts abandoned by the fleeing Germans.

Somewhere in the early afternoon I passed through Quesnoy, which was full of Australian soldiers cleaning up the debris of war and some of the filth characteristic of places which had been German rest billets; and at dusk reached the headquarters of another Corps somewhere in the advanced Somme area. That night I slept, along with other officers returning on leave, in a large and rather chilly marquee tent; and some time on the next day got to Cambrai, only to find that the leave train had left and I should have to wait overnight.

Not long before, I had been among the first troops to enter Cambrai, while it was still being shelled and was on fire. The streets then were littered with dead men and horses, fallen telegraph wires and the debris of ruined houses. Even in that confusion I noticed two things: the Germans had invariably fired the beautiful old Flemish houses, and the glowing woodwork still showed the beautiful Renaissance designs of the carving; and as we went along the streets of unshelled houses, we could see that they had been looted and that in the centre of each room was a pile of clothing, books, pictures, broken furniture, torn cushions, and similar objects on which the Germans had urinated and defecated. I am quite sure of these facts, because I saw them myself. In 1917 on the outskirts of Lens we discovered the same peculiar form of German insult in trenches and dugouts they had been forced to abandon by the Canadian advance at Vimy. On that afternoon of the 13th of November I went round the town and verified what I had seen. I could not go into any house—that was forbidden—but I could see easily through the smashed ground-floor windows. Moreover, I could not find a single one of the old Flemish houses unburned.

That night Cambrai was full of officers returning on leave, and we were billeted in a large hospital which was not required for the wounded. It was still a strange and delicious experience to sleep in a real bed again, but about 5 a.m. we were roughly awakened by orderlies, who rushed in and shouted the sensational news that the German armistice commission had revealed the existence of a time bomb in the building due to explode in an hour. There was no need to urge us to dress rapidly. After a very quick breakfast we entrained in a hurry; the train moved out a couple of miles from town and waited. And waited several hours. I then had ample time to reflect that Cambrai had been in our hands for at least three weeks and that no time bomb could be devised to last for such a period; so evidently that was a little joke of the authorities to make sure we didn't oversleep and miss the train.

How slowly the train moved! At sunset we had only got as far as Pérone, whose ruins looked gaunt and tragical against a gray sky cut with a blood-red rift of light from the setting sun. We did not reach Boulogne until dawn of the 15th, and there I saw a curious and moving sight—French soldiers who had been prisoners of war since 1914. They still wore tattered uniforms of red and blue, which looked positively historic, they were so different from those of the later armies. The faces of these men were pinched and yellow with privation, and there was an eerie, slightly insane expression on them.

In all it took me about eighty hours to go from the Franco-Belgian border to London. (192–194)

It is apparently from Cambrai that Aldington writes H.D. on November 13 (letter 65), asking her to determine a time and place for them to meet, but when he finally arrived in London late on November 15, he was physically and psychically exhausted and unprepared to see her for several days.

H.D. heard of the armistice on November 11 at Speen, where she and Margaret Snively Pratt and her one-year-old daughter had spent a relatively calm and insulated autumn. Although she had celebrated her birthday in London at a small party with her old friend May Sinclair and her new friend Clement Shorter, the older, rather staid editor of the illustrated weekly *The Sphere*, by the end of September she was settled in the tiny cottage in the country. She took walks in the neighborhood and received presents of roses, nuts, and jam from the old-fashioned and gentlemanly Shorter, who often shared tea with her when spending weekends at his country house less than four miles from Peace Cottage. Bryher also came to tea perhaps once or twice, but H.D. did not have many visitors and tended to organize her days with Margaret Pratt according to her baby's schedule.

H.D.'s letters to others during this period reveal the tenor of her life during the fall of 1918. On October 11, she wrote to Shorter that she and Mrs. Pratt "are walking over to see your garden as soon as we get a good day. . . . It rains + rains, but I love this country and the air is miraculously fine + bracing" (UR). On the same day she wrote to Bryher, encouraging her epistolary relationship with Aldington: "Do send him a line about books etc. He must not lose hold on his literary life + he gets so discouraged. . . . We must all make an effort, once the war is over, to renew some interest in the real living beauty of the so-called classics." H.D. was enthusiastic, it would seem, about her husband's plan for the second Poets' Translation Series, and looked forward to the communal effort. By mid-October H.D. was also past the first trimester of her pregnancy and evidently felt physically better than she had for some months.

The period was, of course, not without emotional strain for her. While it seems likely that she had told Margaret Pratt about her pregnancy, her tall, slender frame would allow her to conceal her condition from others until at least the middle of December, and she never told Pratt that the child was not Aldington's. Amazingly Pratt writes to Bryher on August 8, 1962: "I read of the death of Richard Aldington. I didn't know that he had another daughter. . . . Did Perdita keep in touch with her father when they were both living in New York?" (BL). The painful problems and shifting nature of the Aldingtons' relationship were intensely private matters for H.D. and she dealt with them alone and in personal letters to her husband; later, she would deal with them in her art. She must have anticipated his approaching leave in November of 1918 not only as a confrontation but as an opportunity for expression, a time both for a formal reworking of the grounds of their relationship and for an intimate sharing at this point impossible for her with anyone else.

The violence of world events had continued to impinge on H.D.'s private life as well. On September 25, 1918, her older brother Gilbert was killed in France in the Battle of St. Mihiel. She did not hear of his death until her mother wrote her, and she responded with deep sadness on November 4, 1918. H.D. felt real affection for her brother, but she was also distant from him and had not seen him since she left the United States in 1911.

H.D.'s relationship with Bryher was only beginning and its nature and boundaries were still unclear to them both. They were not often in the same place at the same time. They had been near each other in Cornwall in July, but Bryher was evidently at her parents' country house at Eastbourne in Sussex when H.D. moved into town in late August. Bryher remained in Sussex when H.D. moved to Speen at the end of September, then moved into London in October while H.D. remained in the country. Their friendship was thus primarily epistolary throughout 1918 and apparently focused on Bryher's literary work and travel plans: she was eager to visit America and wanted H.D. to come with her to the Scilly Islands, which she had enjoyed since childhood; it was not until December of 1918 that the two women would imagine traveling together to Greece or that Bryher's planned American itinerary would include H.D. The friendship was between, on the one hand, an ingenue, a developing child still living with her parents, a pupil eager to learn about literature and to meet the people who created it and wrote about it and, on the other, an experienced older woman (Bryher was twenty-four, H.D. thirty-two) living on her own, who was a poet, had published and been a part of a significant literary movement (imagism), who knew other writers and could tell her what to read and discuss writing with her.

H.D. found Bryher stimulating in her youth and novelty, but throughout 1918 she shared Bryher with Aldington: she sent him the younger woman's work at a time when she was not sending him anything of her own; she encouraged Bryher to participate in Aldington's plan for translations on which she was also working; she paralleled Bryher's writing with Aldington's, pointing out to her their shared subjects and sensitivities. H.D. apparently initially understood Bryher as a part of her marriage. She welcomed her as a person who did not exist as an intimate so much on her own terms as an alter ego: Bryher was H.D. unfettered with her pregnancy and husband; Bryher was a daughter, the unborn child whose birth H.D. anticipated with confused feelings; Bryher was Aldington, another literary mind inspired by her and writing out of the context of their friendship. But for all the psychological complexity of this relationship for H.D., Bryher was by no means H.D.'s confidante in 1918, and H.D. kept her at a distance. At the time of Aldington's leave in November, Bryher did not know her friend was pregnant, and H.D. did not tell her that the child was not Aldington's until after her birth.

On November 11, 1918, H.D. wrote Bryher that she was coming to London on Friday, November 15, and suggested meeting her at her parents' home for lunch on the following day: "Your enthusiasm has helped me—and once I hear from R., I will know definitely about my future work and life" (BL). The letter is chatty and indicates little of the apprehension H.D. must have felt. While implying to Bryher that Aldington will somehow define "her future work and life," she also implies that it is merely details (logistics perhaps of his demobilization or their living arrangements) that need to be settled. The letter is replete with indecision but gives the impression of haste and good spirits rather than psychological equivocation: "I shall probably come up this weekend or early next. I shall write you in a day or so when I decide. . . . I find I am coming Friday."

H.D. probably did have lunch with Bryher on Saturday, November 16, and she had planned to see Aldington the following day when she received his note at the Lancaster Hotel, 66 Upper Bedford Place, where she apparently remained during the two weeks she spent in London before returning to Speen at the end of the month. Exactly what occurred when they did meet and how often they saw each other are not clear. Certainly they met privately, probably more than once, and Aldington saw H.D. at least once at the Ellermans', where he also met Bryher and Sir John Ellerman, her father. He wrote Amy Lowell on December 8, 1918, that Bryher was "very enthusiastic about you & about us all & seems a person of decidedly fine temperament." On Sunday, probably the 24 of November, H.D. wrote to Clement Shorter:

> I feel so very sorry but Richard was suddenly called away. He had hoped for another week, and we had made all our plans accordingly. I am feeling so tired with the continual rushing about we had last week that I will return at once to Speen. I wonder if you understand how really disappointed I am? And when I come to London again in a month's time,—will you let me have a little talk with you about work?
>
> With best wishes and sincere regrets on the part of Richard
> and
> Hilda Aldington
>
> (UR)

While Aldington's leave was due to end on December 1, he managed to arrange an extra week, and H.D. is clearly making excuses for them both in her letter to Shorter. As is clear from Aldington's letter to her on December 6 (letter 68), she also hoped to see and probably did meet with Gray in London. Aldington could not now give her what she wanted and needed in terms of emotional support; he was required to return to the front and had no money beyond his army pay, which he was already sending her. Nor could he make decisions for her—which may in fact have been what she was asking of him. He had with deep reluctance but finally with committed acceptance agreed to define the relationship on her terms (see letter 48), and he felt he could not now renegotiate. H.D. left abruptly for Speen and did not see Aldington again before his return to France.

67

December 1, 1918

Dear Astraea,

I haven't forgotten you, you see. I was sorry you left town[1] so suddenly, but I have no wish to interfere with your movements. Nor am I going to remonstrate any further on the subject of provision for your future; it is really up to you. No more than Cain am I my brother's keeper. Get from Gray what you want or what you can; and call on me in any emergency. I shall not fail you.

I am planning to restore the P.T.S.[2] Are you willing to collaborate? The whole thing would be on a larger scale than before & I would pay a royalty on all successful translations. Let me know if this agrees with you & what choruses[3] you would care to do.

Affectionately
Richard

P.S. I have extension of leave[4] until the 5th, but have not written "W. Bryher."[5]

1. H.D. left London precipitously in the last week in November and is now again at Speen in Buckinghamshire.
2. The Poets' Translation Series. Aldington intends to edit a new series of translations like the earlier series published by the Egoist Press in 1915–16.
3. As the third pamphlet in the first Poets' Translation Series in 1916, H.D. had translated selected choruses from Euripides' *Iphigeneia in Aulis*. For the second pamphlet of the second series she translated choruses from Euripides' *Hippolytus*, which appeared with her earlier work in 1919 as *Choruses from Iphigeneia in Aulis and the Hippolytus of Euripides*. H.D. wrote Bryher on November 11, 1918, "I have an idea for some new Greek work"; this work was likely the translation of choruses from *Hippolytus*.
4. Aldington was probably hoping to remain in England so as to be demobilized quickly. Unluckily, two days after he finally returned to France, the War Office issued an order permitting all officers on leave to remain indefinitely in England and to be demobilized from there.
5. Winifred Ellerman.

68

December 6, 1918
E.F.C.[1] Officers Rest House and Mess

Dear Astraea/

I'm staying here[2] on the way back to the division. Train is delayed 6 hours. Cheerful prospect.

Look here. I hate to bother you but I want my books away from Miss James.[3] Will you have them at Speen or shall I store them somewhere? I want now a Greek dictionary,[4] the epistolae of Alciphron[5] sent out to me. If you will not be in town yourself could you drop Miss James a note and let Arabella get them? You see I am very much handicapped by not being able to get at my books, but I thought it better not to go to 44. There would have been too many explanations.

As to yourself. I hope your interview with Gray[6] was satisfactory and that you feel more tranquil about things. We will leave all discussion[7] until you are well again. It is not kind to worry you about things when you are enciente. It was wrong of me to allow you to talk. Just try to think of nothing but getting through with this. Has Brigit fixed up that place for you?[8]

When you do start work again I should think that the choruses,[9] or an entire play, would be your forte. We ought to get some big publisher to take up the whole series.[10]

Will you let me know about those books? Perhaps for the time being you could let me have your small Greek dictionary[11] & keep my large one, as transport is not so difficult for you.

Later I may ask for other books.

Affectionately
Richard.

1. Expeditionary Force Canteen.

2. Aldington was at a base camp in France on the way back to the Ninth Royal Sussex Regiment, now at Monchin in Belgium.

3. The Aldingtons' landlady at 44 Mecklenburgh Square. Although H.D. gave up her London flat in early August 1918, Miss Elinor James agreed to store the Aldingtons' books, papers, furniture, and linen.

4. Earlier, Aldington had been working without reference books from his own library, often without any books at hand at all or only with whatever odd volumes he was able to purchase in French towns or to borrow from fellow soldiers. Any books he had at the front before this time were expendable and were frequently left behind or lost during battle or while advancing. He now realizes that he will have both some time to work and some order in his life so that books and papers will not be routinely lost. He is also aware of the necessity for literary work, as he must begin to find a position to support himself as soon as he is demobilized.

5. The letters of Alciphron, a sophist of the second or third century c.e., were supposedly written by ordinary Athenians during the fourth century b.c.e. and reveal Alciphron's wide reading of classical literature. Aldington intended to translate Alciphron's "love letters," probably those written in the voices of courtesans, for the second Poets' Translation Series, although such a translation was never published; see letter 70.

6. H.D. apparently saw Cecil Gray in London in late November.

7. That is, of the future of their marriage.

8. H.D. intended to move from Speen to a nursing home (a maternity hospital) in London before the baby's birth (due in mid-March). Brigit Patmore was making arrangements for H.D. to enter St. Faith's Nursing Home at the appropriate time.

9. See Letter 67, note 3.

10. The second Poets' Translation Series; see letter 70.

11. H.D. owned a copy of the abridged edition of Liddell and Scott's *Greek-English Lexicon* (Oxford: Clarendon Press, 1916); it is now in the Bryher Library in East Hampton, New York.

69

December 12, 1918[1]

Dear Astraea/

I heard from Miss Ellerman[2] & am writing to her. Did you tell her to like the line "Sleep that is whiter than beautiful morning"[3] or did she find it herself? She says she likes "Red & Black";[4] I hope she realizes what it means!

As to P.T.S.[5] I would like to see Hutton[6] & talk it over with him. I would like to bring translations out in a uniform cover at 6d & 1/–. I want Latin, Greek, French, Italian, Russian, Spanish & perhaps modern Hebrew things. I want to be general editor, to make you Greek editor, Frank[7] French, Storer[8] Latin, myself Italian, John[9] Russian, and Ezra Spanish. I will undertake to "manage"[10] all these dissonant elements. I want to pay authors or other translators 10% on what they do, & I propose that you & I do at least ⅛ of the translations. They will be published three at a time or perhaps six, to attract notice. Moreover, in most cases they will be accompanied by the text.[11]

Now don't give this scheme away, as if it is known, it will be cribbed. I think Hutton could be trusted, but not Dent[12] or any other publisher; I think Constable[13] ought to do it as it will be the choicest piece of scholarship of modern times, if properly done.[14]

I will like to have the poems you speak of.[15] I'm sorry I can't get you the German book[16] as I am at a place called Monchin[17] between Lille & Valenciennes. But if you write to Nutt,[18] Shaftesbury Avenue, he will get it for you through Holland. It will cost more than published price but that is inevitable.

It is not so bad here,[19] but I'm trying to get away;[20] have written some letters with that intention.

I hope you have come to a satisfactory arrangement with Gray;[21] your letter is a little vague on that point.

Affectionately,

Richard.

1. After his return to the front, Aldington's letters took longer than previously to reach H.D. British troops were moving eastward rapidly and his letters are seldom stamped at the field post office on the same day on which he dated them. Additionally, H.D. was now spending a good deal of her time in town without having told her husband of her address, so his letters are forwarded to her from Speen. This letter was dated by Aldington December 12, 1918, postmarked at the field post office on December 16, 1918, stamped for forwarding at Speen on December 19, and redirected to the Lancaster Hotel, 66 Upper Bedford Place, London WC2.

2. Bryher.

3. I have not been able to identify this quotation. It may be a line from Stendhal's work or a line from a draft of Bryher's own *Development*, which she had earlier shared with Aldington; I have not, however, been able to find this line in the published version of her novel.

4. Stendhal's famous novel, *Le Rouge et le Noir* (1830), depicts the French social order under the *Restauration* (1814–30). The central character, Julien Sorel, is a carpenter's son who combines an admirable sensibility with cold ambition. He eventually is condemned to death as a result of his passion for two women.

5. The second Poets' Translation Series; see letter 70.

6. Edward Hutton.

7. Frank Stewart Flint.

8. Edward Storer; see Biographical Appendix.

9. John Cournos; see Biographical Appendix. Despite the difficulties in their personal friendship (see Introduction), Aldington assumed that he and Cournos could still work together professionally. Similarly, he assumed that despite the problems in his marriage, he and H.D. could continue to be helpful to each other artistically as critics and fellow poets.

10. Aldington was experienced in such management of personalities; his work on *The Egoist* (1913–17) and with first Ezra Pound and later Amy Lowell on the imagist antholo-

gies (1914–17) had taught him a great deal about "dissonant elements" and how to manage them. His later work on a final imagist anthology, which appeared in 1930, as well as his edition of *The Viking Book of Poetry of the English-Speaking World* (1941), attest to his competence as managing editor of the series he proposes here.

11. The six translations eventually published included Aldington's *Greek Songs in the Manner of Anacreon* (No. 1) and H.D.'s *Choruses from the Iphigeneia in Aulis and the Hippolytus of Euripides* (No. 2) in 1919 and Aldington's *The Poems of Meleager of Gadara* (No. 6) in 1920. None of the translations included the original text.

12. The publishing company of J.M. Dent.

13. Constable and Company published H.D.'s *Sea Garden* in 1916 and the British editions of the three anthologies *Some Imagist Poets* in 1915, 1916, and 1917.

14. Aldington is probably thinking of other contemporary efforts to define the canon by publishing a series of "classics" for a wide audience. The democratic impulse to freeze and to interpret such works inspired *The World's Classics* series published by Oxford University Press, for example, as well as the Everyman series in the United States.

15. Aldington is probably referring to the choruses from Euripides' *Hippolytus* on which H.D. is now working.

16. Likely a translation of Euripides' *Hippolytus* or a commentary on the text.

17. In *Life for Life's Sake* Aldington calls Monchin "a straggling Belgian village" (195); it was five miles from Tournai.

18. David Nutt, the London bookseller with whom Aldington had an account.

19. Actually Aldington was quite frustrated by his life in the army after the armistice. He wrote Ezra Pound on December 8, 1918: "I am teaching Tommies to read the newspapers & do multiplication sums. . . . This education scheme is bullshit at its purest" (BL).

20. That is, to get demobilized.

21. H.D. apparently met with Gray in London in late November, but no financial settlement or other formal arrangement was ever made.

70

December 13, 1918

Dear Astraea/

Re P.T.S.[1] I enclose a rough draft of my proposal.[2] Will you and Winifred Ellerman take it to Shorter[3] and get him to lay the proposal before Constable & Co.? Don't let this Scheme out of your hands except to Shorter & make him promise not to give it away. If you will get him to take it to Hutton[4] they should be able to wrangle it for us. Remember we sold 3000 of the others[5] with no advertisement & without any machinery of distribution.

I will deal with Miss Weaver & keep all these translators at work. I should use people like Whitall[6] for dull things that have to be included, Amy[7] for modern French &c. I want Greek & Latin work only from you; Greek & French from W. Bryher; French from Amy (she translates French well.) French & Italian from J.G.F.;[8] French, Italian & Latin from Flint; Latin & Italian from Alec;[9] Greek

& Latin & [sic] Storer; Greek, Latin, French & Italian from myself. If we do Russian & German, Alec & John will have to find translators.

Can you do this at once? Get Miss Ellerman down, tell her I have got this plan out, with work for her to do; & together sit on Shorter's neck. Get him to persuade Hutton, & there should be no further difficulty. Lay stress 1. On unique plan. 2. Former success. 3. That this is work of permanent value. 4. Will bring kudos to a publisher. 5. Will not be a financial loss. 6. It is cheaper to get out 10 of these little books, which will always go on selling, than to publish one bad novel.

I need scarcely add that it will give us all something to work for.

Your translations are here.[10] Will write you more later.

Ever Yours
Richard.

P.S. We must have a pukka[11] contract with Constable.

enclosed with letter 70:

Scheme for Poets' Translation Series

Object: To give the public at small cost versions of choice, though often little known, poetry & prose.

Translations will be made by people who have produced work of some interest & distinction; their endeavour will be to rescue this literature from the philologists, to present it purely as a work of art, to "give the words of the original as simply & clearly as possible."[12]

Series will include not only authors who wrote in Greek & Latin but those who used the languages of modern Europe; new foreign authors as well as those of older times will be included. When complete the Poets' Translation Series will form a choice collection of Belles Lettres.

General Editor: Richard Aldington

Greek editor: H.D.

Latin   ”   :   R. Aldington

Italian   ”   :   R. Aldington

French   ”   :   F.S. Flint

(if desired)

Russian ”   :   J. Cournos

German ”   :   A.W.G. Randall[13]

List of Translators:

R. Aldington, H.D., F.S. Flint, Amy Lowell,[14] W. Bryher, E. Storer, A.W.G. Randall, J.G. Fletcher and others.

Following are proposed for publication in the series; others will be added:

Greek. Choruses from Ion,[15] Hippolytus and Iphigeneia in Aulis of Euripides,[16]

Meleager,[17] Anyte,[18] Sappho,[19] Asclepiades,[20] Anacreon,[21] Leonidas,[22] Aelianus,[23] Alciphron (Love-Letters).[24] (Nearly all complete.)

Latin. Renaissance Latins (2 vols),[25] Mosella,[26] Columella on Gardens,[27] Gotteschalcus,[28] Tibullus,[29] Gallus,[30] some of Ovidius,[31] Commodian of Gaza,[32] & other classic, silver & church Latinists.

French. Villon,[33] du Bellay,[34] d'Orléans,[35] Remy de Gourmont,[36] Mallarmé (prose poems),[37] Rimbaud,[38] Laforgue,[39] Samain,[40] de Règnier,[41] Ronsard (?),[42] Marot,[43] pre-Villon lyrists, Symbolistes[44] & Parnassiens,[45] living people, Spire,[46] Vildrac,[47] &c. (Flint will add to these.)

Italian. Lorenzo di Medici (part of),[48] Folgore da San Gemignano,[49] Poliziano (songs),[50] Cecco (sonnets),[51] Cavalcanti (?),[52] new versions of Trecento poets,[53] Carducci (some),[54] Leopardi (some),[55] Molza[56] & Bembo[57] & the other "pastorals" including Tuscan work of Navagero[58] &c., the poetry from Il Decamerone,[59] Boiardo[60] (perhaps) and others.

Terms. Books should be published at 6d. & 1/- in neat coloured stiff paper covers; should be known as Poets' Translation Series; should be published at least 3 at a time; should eventually include not less than 50 vols & not more than 100. Series to be advertised as a contribution to modern taste, not as a stunt or any darned Amy Lowell business[61]—no vulgarity.

I pick my own books & my own translators; if the publisher knows better, let him find them. I accept suggestions from anyone if I think them good.

Granted all this I consider I can make a good show of this,[62] bring kudos unto any firm & not lose their money but even make some, in view of the fact that these things will sell permanently.

N.B. The Egoist[63] will do the above, but not on a big enough scale for me to give my time to it.

R.A.

[The following is crossed out:]

Notes

1. With regard to Russian & German I need to consult Randall & Cournos to get out list.
2. With regard to prose, I can get out a list later when I have time to think.
3. Present lists are incomplete—I have no books here.
4. Within a month I can hand over enough work to make at least 6 vols;[64] thereafter can guarantee 5 per month at least.
5. I should be general editor & all work would pass through my revision; I guarantee nothing obscene, Cubist[65] &c. I would get a certain sum for my work as editor to cover expenses of correspondence, buying books &c, 10% per copy to all translators, including myself.

[The following note was written on a torn slip of paper and enclosed in letter 70.]

Any foreign books you may need, whether Greek or French—any of Renée Vivien[66] for example—you may need; order from David Nutt, Shaftsbury Avenue, W.C.1. & tell him to charge them to me. He will send you any catalogue you may want.

1. The second Poets' Translation Series.
2. See below.
3. Clement Shorter; see Biographical Appendix.
4. Edward Hutton, editor at Constable and Company.
5. The set of six pamphlets in the first Poets' Translation Series, published by the Egoist Press in 1915 and 1916.
6. James Whitall.
7. Amy Lowell.
8. John Gould Fletcher; see Biographical Appendix.
9. Alec Randall; see Biographical Appendix.
10. H.D. has sent Aldington her translations of selected choruses of Euripides' *Hippolytus*.
11. Real, genuine.
12. In the first number of the first Poets' Translation Series, Aldington described the purposes of the project: the translators "will endeavour to give the words of these Greek and Latin authors as simply and clearly as may be" (Richard Aldington, *Poems of Anyte*, London: the Egoist Press, 1915, 7).
13. Alec Randall.
14. While Aldington felt that Lowell's verse was often weak, he was always impressed by her command of French and familiarity with French literature.
15. *The Ion* (c. 412 B.C.E.), a play by Euripides (c. 485–c. 406 B.C.E.), has a complex plot concerning the discovery of the parentage of Ion, son of Apollo and Creusa. The drama is considered one of the most beautifully written of Euripides' plays. H.D. eventually published her translation as *Euripides' Ion* in 1937, but as Aldington suggests here, work on this project began before the end of 1918.
16. In Euripides' *Hippolytus* (c. 428 B.C.E.) Theseus's second wife Phaedra's unrequited passion for her stepson Hippolytus is expressed in particularly powerful language; in his *Iphigeneia in Aulis* (c. 405 B.C.E.) Agamemnon's sacrifice of his daughter is a plot on which the sometimes static choruses have little bearing. H.D. translated *Choruses from Iphigeneia in Aulis* in 1915 and it appeared as the third pamphlet in the first Poets' Translation Series in 1916. It was subsequently included in a slim volume entitled *Choruses from Iphigeneia in Aulis and the Hippolytus of Euripides*, which appeared in 1919 and is one of the six books in this scheme that was actually completed.
17. Born in Gadara, Meleager (fl. 100 B.C.E.), the Syrian poet and philosopher, wrote epigrams and other poems, many of them erotic, over a hundred of which appear in the Greek Anthology, the greatest surviving collection of classical literature and a work both Aldington and H.D. knew well. Aldington published his translation, *The Poems of Meleager of Gadara*, in 1920 as number 6 in the second Poets' Translation Series. In 1930 he included this translation in his collection of translations *Medallions* (London: Chatto and Windus) and commented on Meleager's "exceedingly rich, voluptuous poems," noting that he omitted only those which were revisions or which were so erotic that they "could only be printed in an enlightened country" (13, 14).

18. Born in Tegea, Anyte (fl. early third century B.C.E.) was a well-regarded lyric and epigrammatic poet. Eighteen of her Doric epigrams, many of them in the spirit of Sappho, appear in the Greek Anthology. Aldington's translations of her work appeared as *The Poems of Anyte of Tegea* in 1915 as number 1 of the first Poets' Translation Series. It was reprinted as part of the second series, and Aldington included it in his collection *Medallions,* calling her "one of the great woman-poets of Greece" (3).

19. Born in Lesbos, the Greek poet Sappho (born 612 B.C.E.) lived in Mytilene with a group of female companions whose lives and marriages she celebrated in her verse. She was sensitive to nature and her subjects are usually personal, while her treatment is lyric, direct, melodious, and powerful. Edward Storer translated some fragments of Sappho for number 2 of the first Poets' Translation Series.

20. Asclepiades of Samos (fl. 290 B.C.E.) was one of the greatest epigrammatic poets of the Alexandrine period.

21. Anacreon (born c. 570 B.C.E.), the Thracian poet, wrote witty and fanciful verse concerned mostly with pleasure. Aldington's translation, *Greek Songs in the Manner of Anacreon,* appeared in 1919 as number 1 in the second Poets' Translation Series. When he reprinted this translation in *Medallions* (1930), he commented:

> This translation was entirely a "war work," as it was started in a camp and finished, after a long interval, in the village of Taintignies near Tournai. A small and imperfect dictionary was the only one light enough to carry on active service; the translator is aware that this fact, added to lack of practice in Greek during those years and the general effect of unpleasant surroundings, rendered the translation less accurate and spirited than is desirable. (57)

22. Leonidas of Tarentum was one of the greatest Greek epigrammatists of the Alexandrine era. He wrote sad poems about the life of the poor, with whom he identified. Nearly a hundred of his epigrams appear in the Greek Anthology.

23. Claudius Aelianus (c. 170–235) taught rhetoric in Rome and wrote in Greek, publishing collections of excerpts and anecdotes of a paradoxical or moralizing character. His works were popular among his contemporaries and are known for their Attic purity of diction.

24. Second- or third-century C.E. sophist whose letters are essentially dramatic monologues in the voices of ordinary Athenians of the fourth century B.C.E. and recall fourth-century B.C.E. comedy, especially Menander. Aldington was interested in translating the love letters himself; see letter 68, note 5.

25. Aldington published his translation *Latin Poems of the Renaissance* (1915) as number 4 in the first Poets' Translation Series. He did not complete a second volume, but included a much expanded collection of translations in *Medallions* (1930).

26. Already translated by F.S. Flint as number 6 in the first Poets' Translation Series.

27. Lucius Junius Moderatus Columella was a first-century C.E. Latin writer on agricultural subjects. Book 10, dealing with gardening, of his *De Re Rustica* (60 C.E.) is written in verse as a tribute to Virgil.

28. Gottschalk (810–869) was a medieval monk who wanted to leave monastic life but was repeatedly prevented by the authorities until he became an itinerant preacher. What little verse of his survives apparently grew out of his enforced suffering and his sense that people are predestined to evil as well as to good, a heretical doctrine which finally led to his imprisonment.

29. Albius Tibbulus (48?–19 B.C.E.), Roman elegist.

30. Gaius Cornelius Gallus (c. 69–26 B.C.E.) was a friend of both Augustus and Virgil. Although once well-known for his love elegies, only one pentameter of his verse survives.

31. Publius Ovidius Naso (43 B.C.E.–17 C.E.) was during his life the leading poet in Rome. In the early twentieth century his *Art of Love* and *Metamorphoses* were well-known in many English translations; Aldington is probably proposing to translate Ovid's less popular works, such as the love poems in *Amores* or the epistolary verse in *Heroides,* which contains poems in the voices of legendary women writing to absent husbands or lovers.

32. Commodianus, a Christian Latin poet of the third, fourth, or fifth century C.E., known for his rough metrics in which quantity played little part.

33. François Villon (1431–?), French poet; see letter 22, note 3.

34. Joachim du Bellay (1522–60), French poet, a Latinist rather than a Hellenist. Many of his poems had earlier been translated into English by Edmund Spenser.

35. Duchess d'Orléans, Princess Charlotte-Élisabeth de Bavière (1652–1722). Her letters, written for the most part in German, provide political and social commentary on court life.

36. See Biographical Appendix.

37. See letter 23, note 2.

38. Arthur Rimbaud (1854–91), a violent and unstable poet of genius. He was a strong influence on the symbolists and on modernism generally, both in England and on the continent. Championed by the French poet Paul Verlaine (1844–96), Rimbaud is known for his exploration of the unconscious and for his experiments with rhythm and syntax.

39. French symbolist poet Jules Laforgue (1860–87) advocated vers libre and was an important early influence on T.S. Eliot.

40. See letter 14, note 13.

41. Henri de Régnier (1864–1936), French symbolist poet and novelist who advocated vers libre and drew on classical forms and themes.

42. Pierre de Ronsard (1524–85), French renaissance poet and humanist who drew on classical authors as models.

43. Clément Marot (1496–1544), French poet of the early Renaissance.

44. These French poets rejected traditional conventions of theme and technique in their verse, advocating vers libre and emphasizing sensory impressions and the role of images in poetry. The movement began about 1880 and reached its height ten years later. Aldington was particularly interested in the symbolists Mallarmé, Verlaine, Rimbaud, LaForgue, Régnier, and de Gourmont, all of whom he wants to translate here.

45. A group of poets active between about 1860 and 1880 who admired the scientific positivism of the period, rejecting romanticism for restrained, objective, and impersonal poetry in rigid rhythms. Later symbolists rejected this movement, although several, notably Mallarmé and Verlaine, initially identified themselves as Parnassiens.

46. André Spire (1868–1966), French poet, editor, biographer, and bibliographer, whose poems Aldington published in *The Egoist* and through the Egoist Press and with whom he corresponded between 1915 and 1955. The surviving letters are at SIU.

47. Charles Messager Vildrac (1882–1971), individualist French poet and dramatist associated with the Abbaye commune and press.

48. Lorenzo de Medici (1449–92) was a Florentine poet-prince whose Petrarchan sonnets and other verse reveal a wide range of subjects and literary experiments with meter and form.

49. A contemporary of Dante, Folgore da San Gemignano (fl. 1305–16) wrote a series of sonnets for the months of the year and another for the days of the week. Aldington translated *A Garland of Months by Folgore da San Gemignano* as number 5 in the first Poets' Translation Series in 1916.

50. Angelo Poliziano (1454–94) was among the poets whose work Aldington translated in *Latin Poems of the Renaissance,* in which two of Poliziano's poems, "Simonetta" and "Epitaph for Giotto, the Painter," appear.

51. Cecco Angiolieri (c. 1260–c. 1313), the first master of Italian humorous and realistic verse.

52. Guido Cavalcanti (c. 1250–1300), a close friend of Dante, wrote about fifty poems and is particularly known for his difficult canzone on the nature of love.

53. Lyric thirteenth-century poets who wrote primarily in the Tuscan dialect, among them Cavalcante and Dante, although Aldington is probably thinking of many less stellar writers, such as Brunetto Latini (c. 1220–c. 1296) and Cino da Pistoia (c. 1265–c. 1337).

54. Giosue Carducci (1835–1907), primarily a classicist, wrote ten volumes of poetry and essays on literary criticism and history.

55. Giacomo Leopardi (1798–1837) was well-grounded in Greek and Latin literature; his lyric poetry and moral dialogues in verse reveal a somber, even distraught personality.

56. The minor poet Francesco Maria Molza (1485–1544).

57. Pietro Bembo (1470–1547) had great influence upon his contemporaries, although his own poetry and prose, primarily in the form of dialogues, was essentially minor, imitative, and classical in impulse.

58. Andrea Navagero (1483–1529) wrote highly regarded Latin verse often translated into English, while his few Italian poems are less well-known and Petrarchistic. Aldington translated several of his Latin poems in *Latin Poems of the Renaissance* and expanded his selection of Navagero's work in *Medallions.*

59. Giovanni Boccaccio (c. 1313–75) wrote his great *Decamerone* in the early 1350s, a collection of a hundred various, primarily humorous tales. Aldington published his translation, *The Decamerone of Giovanni Boccaccio,* in 1930.

60. Matteo Maria Boiardo (1441–94); his unfinished epic of Arthurian love, *Orlando innamorto,* was completed by Ariosto in his *Orlando furioso.* Aldington may be considering translating Boiardo's highly regarded Petrarchan lyrics.

61. While Aldington, H.D., and Pound initially welcomed Lowell's publicizing of imagism and praise for its principles and poets, they were embarrassed by her pushiness and tendency to appropriate control of the movement while not always embodying its tenets in her own work.

62. Aldington's experience in coordinating the English contributions to the imagist anthologies of 1915, 1916, and 1917 had given him experience in the business of editing, as had his work for *The New Freewoman* and *The Egoist* and his initiation of the first Poets' Translation Series of six titles. His practical mind and disposition to detail made the task he proposes here a logical direction for him to pursue.

63. Because of failure to secure other funding, the six translations which did appear as part of the second Poets' Translation Series were published by the Egoist Press.

64. Aldington intended to reissue several translations already published on a smaller scale by the Egoist Press as part of the first Poets' Translation Series. Among the works he mentions here, H.D.'s *Choruses from Iphigeneia in Aulis* was in fact reissued in an expanded volume with the choruses she was currently translating from Euripides' *Hippolytus* as Number 3 in the second series. Aldington's *The Poems of Anyte of Tegea* (Number 1 in the first

series) was reissued with Edward Storer's *Poems and Fragments of Sappho* (Number 2 in the first series) as Number 2 in the second series. Aldington's *Latin Poems of the Renaissance* (Number 4 in the first series) was expanded and became Number 4 in the second series. Flint's *The Mosella of Decimus Magnus Ausonius* (Number 6 in the first series) was with his translation of *Columella on Gardens* formally advertised in *The Egoist* as Number 6 in the second series, but did not materialize. Four other volumes, among them translations by Storer and Randall, were also advertised but never completed.

65. Aldington disliked Cubism's emphasis on form; see letter 22, note 7.

66. Pseudonym of the poet Pauline Tarn (1877–1909), companion of Natalie Barney. Her French verse in very pure forms was influenced by Baudelaire, and she shared Barney's interest in Sappho.

71

December 15, 1918[1]

Dear Astraea/

Thank you for your promptitude in sending the dictionary;[2] I am afraid that, in this mess of Christmas, it will be some days before it arrives. I am handicapped here in all manner of petty ways—lack of ink & paper, no fuel[3] to warm the room I work in, irritating little military jobs unsuspectedly thrust upon one. I have but one prayer: to get away from this hated uniform & this hateful race.[4] I don't think I can live in London; even Paris seems too near England!

As regards my books[5] I think they had better stay in London. You see if they are there I can go over them & pick out those I want to keep. Perhaps Alec[6] could take charge of them; of course you are welcome to all you want for your own use, but I prefer that the majority should stay in London. Probably I shall not require many of them in which case I can distribute them.

Alciphron[7] is in the Teubner edition.[8] Alec could find it in five minutes if he had the books.

Glad you are working. I like the new translations[9] very much—am making careful notes to send you. Let me know if anything happens in re the proposal for the new P.T.S.[10]

May write to Fred.[11]

Ever yours
Richard.

1. This letter was addressed to Speen, postmarked December 17 at the field post office, and forwarded to the Lancaster Hotel in London.

2. H.D. had evidently written Aldington that she has sent the dictionary he requested (letter 68), but the package will arrive separately later.

3. In *Life for Life's Sake*, Aldington recalls that after his return to the front in early December of 1918,

> I spent twelve endless and miserable weeks, in bitterly cold weather, with a foot or more of snow, and no fuel except a bit of coal dust and an occasional

tree which I bought from the estate of the local count . . . [who] charged about three times as much as his wretched trees were worth. However, we were glad to have them at any price, for without the wood we couldn't even have had our food cooked. (195)

4. The British. Aldington blamed the British for the war's physical, emotional, and spiritual effect on him. His anger with England never diminished and can be seen as the impulse behind most of his novels (notably *Death of a Hero* in 1929, *The Colonel's Daughter* in 1931, *All Men Are Enemies* in 1933, *Women Must Work* in 1934, and *Rejected Guest* in 1939). His eventual rejection of England for homes in the United States and France has its roots in this wartime anger and blame.

5. The books stored at 44 Mecklenburgh Square which Aldington suggested H.D. might move to Peace Cottage in letter 68. H.D. went through them carefully, writing Bryher on December 17 that she had "spent a rather discouraging morning over the books" (BL).

6. Alec Randall. Aldington periodically acquired an enormous number of books and because of his many changes of residence (he never owned a house and travelled frequently throughout his life), was periodically forced to dispose of portions of his library by selling volumes or giving them to friends. Aldington's decision to make a selection from his current library and to store the majority of his books in London does not necessarily indicate that he intends to separate from H.D. after his demobilization.

7. See letter 70, note 24. Aldington indicated that he wanted to translate Alciphron himself in letter 68.

8. Teubner published critical editions of Greek and Latin authors in Leipzig beginning in the late nineteenth century.

9. H.D.'s work on selected choruses from Euripides' *Hippolytus*.

10. The new Poets' Translation Series; see letter 70.

11. The Australian writer Frederic Manning (1882–1935) was both a poet and a classical scholar.

72

[December 17, 1918][1]

Dear Astraea/

This is a very lovely translation,[2] unique, personal, vivid. No one but you could have done it. I have marked a few minor corrections of punctuation, spelling & grammar, chiefly to preserve you from the fools who will see that & nothing else. Work of your sort must be utterly impeccable. Certain lines from their concision are ambiguous—expand them a little & make your meaning plain, unless the original demands ambiguity. Avoid inversion, the stocatto, & repetition "why, why" &c or use them very sparingly. Note that your use of "absolute" is incorrect & makes it a noun.

I need not apologize to you for these remarks.[3] You, as an artist, know how much work on my part they mean! And I would not make them except that I want your work absolutely flawless. I think this translation an improvement on the Iphigeneia.[4]

May I have it for the P.T.S. if we get it going?

Now, _don't_ touch this translation except to make the corrections marked.

Ever yours
Richard.

1. This undated letter was addressed to Speen and forwarded to H.D. at the Lancaster Hotel in London.

2. H.D.'s translation of choruses from Euripides' _Hippolytus_.

3. Aldington's criticism of others' writing was often specific and authoritative. H.D. was used to working closely with her husband and understood both the essential justice and the kind impulse behind Aldington's response to her compositions. In "Heliodora," she gives a vivid account of their mutual effort, his criticism, and her ability both to "take it" and to profit from it. "Heliodora" first appeared in _Heliodora and Other Poems_ in 1924, though it was obviously written several years earlier.

4. H.D.'s 1916 translation of Euripides, _Choruses from Iphigeneia in Aulis_.

73

December 21, 1918

Dear Astraea/

I was very glad to get the Dictionary[1] & Bough.[2] Thank you for sending.

Will write Miss Ellerman in re P.T.S. You will have had my letter by now in connection with it.

You are very good to think so charmingly of my future, but really, dear child, you must think of your own. Keep warm & well fed this bitter weather. I must find out from Brigit if she has got that twilight-sleep place fixed up.[3]

You will forgive my not sending anything for Xmas. I'm sending to no one, as I can't afford it. Cheque[4] of course will go off on Jan 1st.

I do hope that trip to Greece comes off.[5] Some arrangement could be made about the child. Of course it will live & you will love it very much & you will be happy even if it is messy & noisy.[6]

I am sure you will be all right. And I'm glad you want to work again; it is the most satisfactory thing. I hope you will realise that my criticisms on your Hippolytus[7] are meant in the right spirit.

Don't worry about "Double Maitresse."[8] I can't work much here—too cold.

Affectionately
Richard.

P.S. A. wrote she had seen you & you looked better & gayer. I am glad.

It was rather hard coming back here, but I keep as happy as I can.

1. The Greek dictionary Aldington requested in letter 68.

2. Likely one or two volumes of James Frazer's *The Golden Bough*, which appeared in a twelve-volume expanded edition in 1913. Part 4, in two volumes, entitled *Adonis Attis Osiris*, would have been of particular interest to Aldington in 1918.

3. Brigit Patmore was making arrangements for H.D. to enter St. Faith's nursing home to have her baby, due in mid-March. There H.D. could give birth with "twilight sleep," a combination of morphine and scopolamine first introduced in Germany in 1907 as an anesthetic during childbirth. The medication was still considered novel in 1918.

4. Aldington's army pay, which he routinely sent to H.D.

5. H.D. has evidently written Aldington about Bryher's idea of traveling with H.D. to Greece after the baby's birth. On December 17, 1918, she had written Bryher in response to the plan: "I am very, *very* excited about Delphi! But I must have two years preparation." On December 18, 1918, she continued enthusiastically:

> I bought myself one of these modern Greek manuals—and it amused me so much, I thought you must have one. It will save us some time to ask fluently for "candles, matches and hot water," and as there will be none of the above-mentioned in the wilds of Arcadia and the crags of Parnassus, our energy will perhaps be wasted. But I should like to feel, should occasion arise, that I *can* say to my laundress in the vale of Tempe, "You don't put enough starch in my collar!"

The two women did make the trip in February of 1920, not returning to England until the summer.

6. Aldington's reassurance here is apparently in response to a letter from H.D. in which she recalled their own child (see Introduction) and shared her concern that she might not be able to love this baby. H.D., like Aldington, tended to perceive the coming child in the context of the one they had both lost. She wrote to tell Bryher of her pregnancy in these terms on December 18, 1918: "Three years ago, I had a sad illness + lost my little child. I am expecting to have another towards the end of March.—Do not take this too seriously, as you know my views on the average parent, and if arrangements can be made, an old nurse of Mrs. Patmore's children will take, at times, entire charge, so that I may continue my work. . . ." In an undated letter in early January of 1919, H.D. told Clement Shorter of her pregnancy and placed it in the same context:

> I am making arrangements to enter a nursing home in March or early April. I had a very sad confinement about three years ago and lost my child, so I feel it very wicked to worry yet about this one's life and future. . . .
>
> Do not refer to this. I cannot talk about it, as I was so sad and ill the last time.

7. See letter 72.

8. The best known novel by Henri de Régnier, *Double Maîtresse* (1900) is a psychological work set in the late seventeenth and early eighteenth centuries. It is characterized by an elaborate libertinism and written in a highly decorative, precious style.

74

December 24, 1918

Dear Dooley/

I heard from A. that you had lunched together. She seems very "triste," don't you think? I fear she is rather alarmed at the number of articles I send her to type!

Glad you & Shorter had such a good time. Perhaps you can do prose regularly for something after your confinement?

As to articles for Massingham.[1] The "Letters to Unknown Women"[2] May Sinclair has, since she wrote me she would try to place them. I want to write "critical dialogues" about books. I have actually done: 1. The Tenderness of Dante.[3] 2. Les Chevaux de Dioméde.[4] 3. A Soldier's Library.[5] 4. The Scholar's Italian Book.[6] Arabella has the first three & I have the last. I have planned tentatively these: 5. Anacreon.[7] 6. Folgore da San Gemignano.[8] 7. Scenes & Portraits.[9] 8. La Double Maitresse.[10] 9. Rimbaud.[11] 10. Landor's Classical Dialogues.[12] 11. Campion & Quantity in English.[13] 12. Sea Garden.[14] 13. Villon.[15] 14. Alciphron's Love Letters.[16] Of course I might not do all or any of these but I shall do some. An article on The Future of Poetry[17] I am having sent to Harriet.[18] I don't know whether these dialogues would suit Massingham. Perhaps he might have a look at them, though I thought Hutton would perhaps like one or two of the Italian ones for his review.[19] Still there would be no harm in Massingham seeing them. I have done three dialogues & an article[20] since I came back here,[21] as well as several poems & poems in prose.[22] So there is no doubt about *quantity* if the quality is O.K.

I don't know about social or political articles. I did one about the election[23] but lost it somewhere. If I do any now I will send them.

Have you any news of P.T.S.? I am working, rather slowly, on Anacreon[24] & Alciphron.[25] It is good steady plodding. I hope the scheme comes off; it would be great fun. Of course, I want W. Bryher in it, but she must learn Greek & improve on her Lament for Adonis.[26]

I hear we are going to Tournai on the 7th Jan—always a little nearer Germany! I do hope I can get free soon.

Hope you are well and cheerful as your letters sound.

Affectionately
Richard.

1. Henry William Massingham (1860–1924) was a well-travelled journalist who edited *The Nation* from 1907–23.
2. Although Aldington was publishing this series in *The Dial,* he is here, as was his legal right, seeking English publication; see letter 19, note 2.
3. Probably never completed.
4. Probably never completed.

5. This article may well have become "Books in the Line," which appeared in *The Sphere*, April 12, 1919, 26.

6. Probably never completed.

7. Aldington was translating Anacreon at this time.

8. Probably never completed.

9. Probably never completed.

10. Probably never completed.

11. Probably never completed.

12. Probably never completed.

13. This article probably became "Campion's 'Observations,' " which appeared in *Poetry*, Vol. 15, No. 5 (February 1920), 267–271.

14. Probably never completed.

15. Probably never completed.

16. Aldington was translating Alciphron at this time.

17. Aldington's article "The Poetry of the Future" appeared in *Poetry*, Vol. 14, No. 5 (August 1919), 266–269.

18. Harriet Monroe at *Poetry*.

19. Edward Hutton edited *The Anglo-Italian Review* in 1918 and 1919.

20. Not identified.

21. That is, since approximately December 6, when Aldington returned to France after his last leave.

22. Not identified.

23. Polling took place on December 14, 1918; Lloyd George's coalition government obtained a sweeping majority.

24. See letter 70, note 21.

25. See letter 68 and 70, note 24.

26. Bryher's *Lament for Adonis: Bion the Smyrnaean* (London: A. L. Humphreys, 1918). Bryher's translation comprised only five pages of this fifteen-page book; the rest was made up of the Greek text, reproduced with acknowledgement from William Heinemann's Loeb Classical Library edition, and a five-page introduction. Bryher relied heavily on J. M. Edmund's translation in the Loeb edition and voiced as her own Aldington's principles of translation as expounded in the first Poets' Translation Series (see letter 70, note 12). She wrote: "In this translation I have endeavored to recapture the spirit of the poem rather than to render it word for word into English, to use no archaic prose or needless inversion, and to reflect, as closely as may be, the thought of the poet himself" (5). Aldington reviewed Bryher's translation in *The Egoist* (Vol. 6, No. 1, January–February 1919); his approval is restrained:

> It is a pleasure to know that the principles of translating laid down in the prospectus of The Poets' Translation Series are being followed by other translators. That this "literary-literal" method has a distinct advantage over all others is proved by a very sensitive version of Bion's *Lament for Adonis* recently published [in November] by Miss Winifred Bryher. . . . she is on the right track. . . . The translation is not perfect . . . but it contains beautiful phrases. . . . (10)

75

December 28, 1918

Dear Astraea/

Do you mind concentrating your mind for a few minutes on the convolutions of bureaucracy?

Now then.

1. Was Miss Weaver's letter[1] correctly worded. i.e. did it state catagorically that I was in the employment of The Egoist[2] before August 4th 1914 & that she was prepared to re-employ me?

2. Was the letter sent to the correct place, i.e. the Local Advisory Committee[3] of the Department of Appointments (for officers *only*) as laid down in the procedure for Demobilisation of Officers?[4]

If the answer to either of these two questions is in the negative, will you communicate at once with Hutton & request him to inform you:

A. Exactly how the letter should be worded and

B. Exactly where it should be sent.

On receipt of above information will you hand it on to Miss Weaver with the request

A. That she will write a letter in the correct form. And

B. That she will forward it to the correct address.

With reference to application already made—will you tell Hutton how it was worded & where it was sent & ask him if it is valid or if a new application should be sent. I am not sure whether "Ministry of Labour"[5] *is* the Department of Appointments or something different.

All this is tedious & elaborate but unless the procedure is rigidly adhered to I shall not be posted as a "slip man"[6] & shall hang on here until I am as old as Rip van Winkle.

Thanks for card—will write more soon.

Affectionately,
Richard.

1. Aldington has asked Harriet Shaw Weaver to write a letter to the military authorities on the basis of which he might be demobilized.

2. See Periodical Appendix.

3. This department arranged the release of officers who had jobs waiting for them.

4. Demobilization was arranged by selected categories, regardless of rank. Men in occupations considered to be of national importance, such as miners, were the first to be released.

5. This was not the same as the Department of Appointments. The Ministry of Labour concerned itself with the release of soldiers in nationally important occupations.

6. This was a man for whom a productive job was waiting and who could be released,

on the orders of his commanding officer, at the same time as men in "pivotal" occupations. The "slip" refers to an employer's certificate confirming occupation.

76

Dear Astraea/

I am so pleased that you feel more secure about the future. No, I won't take any of little Miss E's gifts,[1] but I shall ask you to let the monthly £5[2] stand over this time. I had so many stupid expenses here this Christmas—all kinds of things, Christmas cards, charities, god knows what—that until I see my pass-book I don't quite know where I stand.

Are you hurt by the alterations I suggested in your Hippolytus?[3] Surely you are beyond, far beyond, that amateur stage!

I have written John[4] about P.T.S. Am working on Alciphron[5] & making lists of poets to be translated. I have also done some dialogues & articles[6] which will do to show as specimens in London. I hope that Hutton's efforts will be of some avail.

The French are only demobilising down to men of 40! So I don't think there is much chance[7] unless some special kind of appeal is made. It is humiliating & maddening to be kept here, but there you are—were I wealthy, like the Sitwells,[8] or merely syphiletic like Lewis,[9] the case would be different!

I am in correspondence with your little Ellerman friend & advise her about books &c. Have set her a P.T.S. job.[10]

Other things are as usual.

Hope you are fairly cheerful.

Affectionately
Richard.

1. Throughout her life Bryher was generous with presents of modest sums of money or luxuries.
2. The portion of his pay that Aldington routinely sent to H.D. rather than keep for his own use.
3. See letter 72.
4. Probably John Cournos.
5. See letter 68, note 5.
6. See letter 74.
7. That is, a chance of a speedy demobilization.
8. Edith (1887–1964), Osbert (1892–1969), and Sacheverell (1897–1980) were known for their extravagant personalities and freedom to experiment in literature because of family wealth.
9. Percy Wyndham Lewis.
10. Aldington advised Bryher about her translation in a letter he wrote her on December 22, 1918:

Hilda writes that you are thinking of doing Theocritus. You have courage! Do you know what I think? That it would be better to leave him until you know more Greek & have read more Greek poets. If you start off with one of the greatest, the lesser poets, beautiful as they are, will not move you. Whereas, if you start by the lesser poets you will be all the more dazzled by the loveliness of Theocritus. I wish you would do an epigrammatist for the Translation Series: Will you? I will give you four to choose from: Plato, Lucian, Callimachus & Antipater of Sidon—just the epigrams in the Anthology. You will need Jacobs' Anthologia; (& for the time being you can have my copy, which Hilda will lend you) and the latest edition of Liddle & Scott's Lexicon (containing all the special anthology words) and a good Greek grammar. The Latin translation in Jacobs' will help you to be sure you have the precise literal sense, & for the rest I am secure in your own taste. You will find it a hard job if you are conscientious. The right word is never in the dictionary, & will elude one's search.

Will you do this? I would so much like to have you in the Series. . . .

On January 1, 1919, Aldington again urged her to translate a minor poet:

I wrote you about the translations, & gave you a choice of four beautiful poets, any of whom would dazzle this century. Lucian, Plato, Callimachus, Antipater of Sidon. Which is it to be? Plato is perhaps the most intense, Callimachus the most polished, Lucian the cleverest, & Antipater the most decorated! Indeed I want you to be a translator in this series, & I know your work will be a great help. . . .

77

January 2, 1919

Dear Astraea/

Thank you so much for sending me "Hymen."[1] It is delicate and fragile, with an air of much less maturity than your earlier work in Sea-Garden.[2] There is a most exquisite child-like quality in the earlier songs, & the more sensual tone of the last three strikes one as a totally different impulse. The introduction of rime is not displeasing, because it is used with skill & tranquility; tho' "sips" & "lips" gives me just a faint displeasure.

The prose descriptions between the songs do not interest me; I should very much like to see the procession as you describe it & to hear the music, but it is a little out of my "galère"[3] to criticise this part of your poem. Yet, as they are part of your idea they should be retained. It seems a pity to waste it on "Poetry and Drama,"[4] yet I cannot think of any other periodical which would take it. Show it to Shorter & ask him. If there is no English periodical, then I should certainly send it to Harriet[5] with the prose part, as she'll then have to pay you more! I think that without saying anything to her you could publish the poems separately in the Sphere[6] under separate titles. Here they are: 1. Song for Hera.

2. Ivy & Crocus. 3. Winter-Rose. 4. Hyacinthes. 5. Bride-Song. 6. Laurel. 7. Bridal Song. 8. Cyclamen. 9. Epilogue. If they would take the lot—as they ought—& print one each week, Harriet wouldn't know & you would get some money. (Excuse this commercialism!) Then I think it should be issued as a little book at 1/−, with a short note by someone or other, perhaps Willy Yeats.[7] He would surely say a word if we asked nicely! That is my advice: Get Harriet to print the <u>whole</u> thing; the Sphere or some other English periodical the <u>Songs</u>; & issue it later in book form. It is worth this publicity, though, as you say, it hasn't the epic intensity of your other stuff. If you can't get an ordinary publisher, I will put up the money for the Egoist[8] to bring out a few hundred copies, & we can probably get someone to do it in the U.S.A.

Will write again soon. Am retaining the ms. for a day or so longer.

Affectionately
Richard.

P.S. Hippolytus[9] I returned some time ago.

1. "Hymen" was first published in *Poetry*, Vol. 15, No. 3 (December 1919), 117–129; it was later collected with other poems in *Hymen* (1921).
2. H.D.'s first volume of poetry, which appeared in the fall of 1916.
3. Literally, a slave ship, penal servitude; metaphorically, hell.
4. Harold Monro edited eight issues of the quarterly *Poetry and Drama* between March 1913 and December 1914, when publication was suspended because of the war. Aldington visited Monro at the Poetry Bookshop during his November leave and evidently discussed with him the periodical's revival. Monro began to publish the journal again under a new title, *The Monthly Chapbook*, in July 1919. In January 1920, the title was changed again, to *The Chapbook*, which continued until 1925. Aldington published here regularly after the war. Monro was committed to new directions in criticism, poetry and poetic drama. He published Edward Storer's verse play "Helen," for example, in the June 1914 issue.
5. Harriet Monroe.
6. See Periodical Appendix; neither the whole of "Hymen" nor individual poems ever appeared here, nor did parts of "Hymen" appear separately in any journal.
7. William Butler Yeats, whose literary stature and interest in both poetry and dramatic forms would have made him a suitable choice. However, no note preceded the poem when it appeared in book form in 1921.
8. Although Aldington did not need to "put up the money," the Egoist Press did publish *Hymen* (which included "Hymen" as well as other poems) in England in 1921; Henry Holt published it in America in the same year.
9. H.D.'s translation from Euripides' *Hippolytus*; see letter 72.

78

January 3, 1919

Dear Astraea/

Herewith your "Hymen."[1] I have been over it several times & have corrected a few spelling errors & made a note or so. Words surrounded by a circle thus:

(maidenhead) are those I think should be either omitted or altered, you will see which in each case. I believe it may be taken as an axiom in poetry that in nine cases out of ten repetition of a word weakens the effect. Apropos the word "maidenhead"[2]—this does *not* mean virginity, "maidenhood" but is an Elizabethan word meaning the sex of a maiden. Is that precisely what you wanted to say at that point? It is a trivial thing but worth considering.

I think I like the thing more now I've got to know it & the prose intervals are more attractive to me. You must have it re-typed by a professional typist—your own copy is full of little blurs & errors which distract the attention & will cause mistakes in setting up the type.[3] Moreover it looks better. Have it done in duplicate. The songs for the Sphere[4] you can do yourself, but do them slowly & correctly, with a two-line space between each line—trivial but again necessary. And, moreover, don't submit your m.s. *ever* until I have been over it; you make little careless errors in spelling & syntax &c which fools pick up as a weapon against an original artist. Remember, H.D. cannot afford to be anything less than perfection.[5]

Richard.

1. Aldington is returning the typescript of H.D.'s "Hymen"; see letter 77.
2. H.D. kept the word "maidenhead" in the stanza in which women sing:

> From citron-bower be her bed
> Cut from branch of tree a-flower
> Fashioned for her maidenhead.

Three stanzas later, H.D. used the word "maidenhood":

> That all the wood in blossoming,
> May calm her heart and cool her blood
> For losing of her maidenhood

(H.D., "Hymen," in *Collected Poems, 1912–1944*, ed. Louis Martz, New York: New Directions, 1983, 108). Since the original typescript of "Hymen" has not survived, we cannot know exactly what revisions Aldington suggested nor what changes H.D. may have made as a result.

3. H.D.'s typing was oddly spaced and irregular; she frequently omitted words or letters, and her spelling was indeed very bad. Aldington's advice seems quite justified.

4. See letter 77.

5. It is important to realize here that Aldington is equating "perfection" with "H.D.," his wife's carefully fashioned literary persona. He is under no illusion that his wife is, can, or should be perfect, nor does he ever measure her as a person against any standards of "perfection." In fact, Aldington criticizes H.D.'s own "ardour for perfection" in letter 13. It is also worth noting, however, that Aldington is here voicing an aesthetic idea shared by his contemporaries. In March 1913, Pound wrote to Harriet Monroe about the lack of artistic standards in America: "Who in America believes in perfection, and that nothing short of it is worth while?" In March 1915, Pound wrote to Monroe again on the same subject, insisting that the artist's "only respectable aim is perfection" (Ezra Pound, *The Letters of Ezra Pound*, ed. D. D. Paige, New York: Harcourt Brace, 1950, 14, 56).

79

See inside also
B.E.F. January 6, 1918[1]

Dear Astraea/

Your choruses[2] must be delayed or lost in the post—I sent them off before Christmas. They probably got submerged in that insipid mass of sentimentality.[3]

Have you another copy? I thought the choruses excellent, & only ventured on a few verbal alterations—mostly spelling & grammar! And inversions, of which you have too many.

I am glad that you feel more courageous. Your prospect is not pleasant & the courage you show is admirable. I cannot believe that so clear & fine a mine [sic] can be wasted, & I expect with confidence great things from you. One gets exceedingly depressed at times. And then exceedingly & unreasonably exalted. It is all very foolish. Of course, I am fretting about being demobilised, but when I am I really don't see how I'm going to make bread let alone butter to put on it. Frankly, we poets are anachronisms; the world has no place for us & the sooner we recognise it the better. Yet it is impossible for us, by reason of our temperaments, to succeed in any other capacity. We are fated to make a mess of our lives. When I see what a mess mine is in, I shudder. I see absolutely no solution anywhere, & very little but hardship, wretchedness & distress for the future.

Wherefore, I return to my writing table & continue my translation of Anacreon,[4] remembering that the Royal Sussex[5] never lost a trench!

Affectionately
Richard.

Later.

Your letter of Jan. 1st arrived. And from Miss Weaver. My God. All I can say is, My God. I am surrounded by fools and super-fools. Does she, do you, does *any* sane person imagine that the Govt. will release an officer to take up an appointment of £36 a year? Are you mad? Couldn't she have the sense to put a reasonable figure? I told her that there was nothing binding in it. Do you know what this means? That the application will certainly be rejected, that no effort on Hutton's part or my part or anyone's can alter it, that I shall be sent to the army of occupation[6] & not be released, perhaps, for years?

Well, I suppose it's not your fault; but it is the last straw. It's no use grousing is it? But my only chance of life is gone, wrecked. What a blasted fool the woman is. Tell her and her bloody paper[7] to go to hell, will you. I have [not] the patience to write to her.

Another two years of this hell!

Cheerio; be good.

R.

1. In fact, January 6, 1919.
2. H.D.'s translation of selected choruses from Euripides' *Hippolytus.*

3. That is, the Christmas mails.

4. See letter 70, note 21.

5. Aldington had served with the Ninth Royal Sussex Regiment since early 1918.

6. Sixteen British divisions formed the Army of Occupation in 1918–19. If a soldier's unit was attached to one of these divisions, and he were not in a high priority demobilization category, he would have been obliged to continue his army service. Reallocation of troops began in early February, 1919.

7. *The Egoist.*

80

January 7, 1919

Dear Astraea/

Excuse me for the hasty way I wrote you yesterday. My excuse is that I am on the verge of a complete mental collapse[1] & the news from Miss Weaver[2] simply stunned me, since I know that my release is now an impossibility. You could not expect the W.O.[3] to release an officer to take up a position at £36 a year. Now could you?

And the worst of it is no other application can now be made.[4]

I have written Hutton & await a reply from him, before taking decisive measures. I will *not* endure another year of this.

Yours
Richard.

1. There is no question that Aldington is here suffering from "shell shock" (what is now called "Post Traumatic Stress Disorder"). Throughout these letters he tries to shelter H.D. from his nervousness, depression, and guilt, but occasionally—as here—he is frank and open, even desperate.

2. See letter 79.

3. The War Office.

4. Late in 1918 the War Office changed the procedure for demobilization to the simple release of soldiers on the basis of length of service: those who had served longest would be released first.

81

January 9, 1918[1]

Dear Astraea/

I have an idea. Do you think that Shorter could get me a hack translation job while I'm here? I mean the translation of some French novel or tedious memoir or something which a publisher is going to do & for which he would pay the ordinary translator rates. And could you find out 1. If Marshall Foch "Principes de Guèrre"[2] has been translated, 2. If not, whether any publisher would give an order for its translation by me. I have the requisite military knowledge as well as the power to put the French into English. If I could get the job it would help to pass time here & also get a little money.

Excuse brief letter—I have such extraordinary head-aches[3] these days that I can scarcely write.[4]

Your
R.

1. In fact, January 9, 1919.

2. Ferdinand Foch (1851–1929), marechal de France, became General-in-Chief of the Allied Armies during the last year of the First World War. His *Des Principes de la Guerre: Conférences Faites en 1900 à L'École Supérieure de Guerre* (1917) was translated by Hilaire Belloc in 1918.

3. Aldington was plagued with intense headaches that began about this time and lasted well into the twenties. They are a characteristic element of the experience of "shell shock." In *Life for Life's Sake,* Aldington recalled that after his return to the continent in December of 1918, "I began to notice some of the after effects of the war. I slept badly, was subject to meaningless but unpleasant moods of depression, and was in a frenzy of impatience to get out of the army. And it seemed to me that my mind had deteriorated, because of the difficulty I found in concentrating on mental work" (195). Years later Aldington recalled his psychological and physical distress when commenting on Henry Slonimsky's difficulties with insomnia in a letter to him on November 8, 1941:

> A physical symptom naturally suggests a physical cause, but from my own experience I do believe that insomnia may have a psychological basis. I suffered rather badly from it February through May of 1919, after I was demobilised. True, my general health was rather poor after the hardships of two campaigns mostly on half or even quarter rations; but I think the real cause was a combination of public and personal disappointments and miseries. (SIU)

4. The word "wright" is crossed out here.

82

January 13, 1919

Dear Astraea/

Sea-Heroes[1] is the best of these pieces;[2] needs a little working over. Be quite sure of the spelling & meaning of these words before sending the poem out.

Who is "she"[3] in the third strophe? Greece, Carthage, England?

I don't think I'd send it to Harriet[4]—try one or two English papers first. Why shouldn't The Nation[5] give you a showing? Don't despise these English weeklies. They are <u>read</u>. If you got your Hymen poems in the Sphere[6] & then three or four others into The Nation, it would help you enormously, I mean in getting known.

Simaetha[7] is quite good & should make a good link in a series. Thetis[8] is a little weak in spots—it doesn't say much & the mood is uncertain. Still it has undoubted beauties. I think it needs more work.

Just received the prospectus of "Art & Letters,"[9] new series. *If* they can make a "do" & get their subscribers it might be worth while going on with them. I gave them a couple of poems. But I doubt very much if they get anywhere. The prospectus is largely my fault. I don't think Read[10] put things as tactfully as he might!

Cheerio,

Richard.

1. H.D.'s poem "Sea Heroes" was first published (as "Sea-Heroes") in *Coterie*, No. 4, 1920, 44–46, and collected in *Hymen* in 1921.

2. "Simaetha" and "Thetis"; see below. After a long period during which H.D. found it difficult or impossible to write, she was now working productively again not only on translation from the Greek but on her poetry. On February 1, 1919, after a hiatus in their correspondence, H.D. wrote Amy Lowell about her difficulty:

> It has been impossible for me to work for some time—but I believe I can now begin again. Richard's position out there was, for so long, so exceptionally dangerous—and my people at home were broken by my brother's death in France—and you can imagine being alone here + not able to get across to them, pretty well wore me to shreds. But the first shock over, my people seem strong again, and R. is safe—and I am seriously getting back to work.

H.D. is not being fully open here about all the pressures which have made writing difficult for her, but she acknowledges the period of unproductive work and suggests the beginning of a new period of creativity.

3. The reference for the pronoun in the third stanza of "Sea Heroes" remains vague.

4. Harriet Monroe at *Poetry*.

5. See Periodical Appendix.

6. See letter 77.

7. "Simaetha" was first published in *Contact*, No. 3, 8, in 1921 and appeared in *Hymen* later the same year.

8. H.D. evidently agreed with Aldington about the weaknesses in this poem: she revised "Thetis" extensively (as evidenced in the typescript, BL), did not publish it serially, and included only part of it in *Hymen*.

9. Edited by Frank Rutter with Charles Ginner and H. Gilman in 1917, this journal of visual and literary art suspended publication in 1918, then recommenced in 1919–20, edited by Rutter and Osbert Sitwell.

10. Herbert Read (1893–1968), poet and literary critic. Aldington may have met Read as early as his November leave in 1918; they became good friends during the years after the war. In 1917, Read's critical and aesthetic theories shaped the character of *Art and Letters*. When the periodical resumed publication in 1919, T.S. Eliot's theories became the dominant feature of the journal.

January 21, 1919

Dear Astraea/

Thank you for your letters & for all you have been doing for me.[1] The news is excellent.

Now, Mrs. Yorke[2] is a good common-sense woman & offered to help, so I've sent her the forms[3] with precise directions. She will take them to Weaver, get them filled in, & get them stamped &c.

You are _not_ to worry any more about this or about me; above everything you are not to stand in queues &c. You know perfectly well you shouldn't.

I'm am [sic] "bucked"[4] with Shorter's letter—I'll love to do some work for him; & I'll write Amy[5] almost at once. I've finished rough draft of Anacreon[6] & am carefully rewriting.

M.S.[7] also has a small temporary job for me, so I'll be all right.

You have fixed up twilight sleep[8] O.K.? Please be tranquil in your mind & let the child be a pleasure to you—I don't mean having it, which is as Euripides says,[9] but afterwards. Don't feel that it is anything but fine to be a mother; because it is fine, and is one of those simple pure things that fools like Lawrence & Pound do not understand.

So glad you have promise of work.[10] It is splendid. You'll be O.K.

Enclosed Feb: cheque.[11] I send it early, as an officer going on leave is taking mail. Excuse, therefore, hurried letter.

Yrs.

1. H.D. had been doing her best to arrange for Aldington's demobilization; she had written to Harriet Shaw Weaver at _The Egoist_ about the possibility of Aldington's getting his old job back; she had spoken with Clement Shorter about Aldington's situation in the hope that he might employ Aldington in some capacity at _The Sphere_ or use his influence to persuade other editors or publishers to give Aldington some formal contract for articles or translations. H.D. had also, evidently, visited the War Office in an attempt to see exactly what needed to be done to secure her husband's release.

2. Dorothy Yorke's mother, Selina Yorke, was a strong, forceful, even domineering woman who was very close to her daughter and anxious to look out for what she saw as Dorothy Yorke's interests.

3. Employment forms required for Aldington's demobilization.

4. Encouraged.

5. Amy Lowell.

6. See letter 70, note 21.

7. May Sinclair.

8. See letter 73, note 3.

9. In _Medea_, Medea tells her children, "I labored, travail worn, bearing sharp anguish in your hour of birth" (1030–1031).

10. That is, that H.D. is beginning to write again.

11. Aldington's paycheck, which he continues routinely to send to H.D.

January 29, 1919

Dear Astraea/

Thank you for sending me Myrrhine.[1] I have written Mrs. Yorke[2] to try to get that "slip"[3] through, but I rather fear it will be too late. The Adjutant has twice given me a very strong hint that they intend sending me to the army of occupation—a sort of revenge, I suppose, for my being a conscript. I've got fairly used to the idea, though, and I suppose it doesn't really matter. I had hoped to gain a little happiness and freedom, but fate was against it. Don't say anything to the Yorkes about this; there is the faintest chance that if the papers went through before 30-1-19 I might get out. A. will feel rather badly when she knows; and I must tell her myself so she can re-organise her life.

Now, my dear, as to you. You must cease to worry about me; you did your best & it's not your fault. You have your troubles to contend with. I think it improbable I shall get leave before you go to hospital,[4] as they purposely keep me as long as possible, & I am not going to whine to them for special leave. You've got to consider that I am probably fixed here for many, many months to come; & you must organise your life without any thought of me. I will send you all the money I can; beyond that I can't do anything. Life has not treated either of us too well, but you've got to realise, which you still haven't, the utter soullessness of the military machine, and the impossibility of an artist securing even bare justice from it. And the harshness of that machine is the reflection of the harsh-ness of commercial civilization; you must secure some means of providing for yourself & your child. I am helpless and I am poor: you knew that six years ago;[5] whatever chance I had of "making good" has practically disappeared, and you can only rely on me for a very few pounds. When, eventually, I am discharged, I shall be scarcely able to earn a pittance for myself, as this harsh system has robbed me of whatever gifts I had. What on earth do you think I shall be worth after 2 or 3 years more of this?

There are the bare facts & you must face them. If Gray cannot or will not help you, then you must get work of some sort through your friends. What I can give will be totally inadequate.

I wish you "the best of luck"[6] in your coming ordeal; this time you go over the top[7] while I watch helplessly. If it is any good saying it I would ask your forgiveness of the pain I have caused you, as freely as I forgive the pain you have caused me.

Richard.

1. H.D. has sent Aldington a copy of his *The Love of Myrrhine and Konallis, and Other Poems* (Cleveland: The Clerk's Press, 1917). Aldington had written to Bryher on January 1, 1919: "Yes, I would like a copy of Myrrhine, as my wretched batman lost my last & only copy when we moved our quarters."

2. See Letter 83, note 2.

3. An official employer's certificate confirming occupation.

4. H.D. was planning to enter St. Faith's nursing home in mid-March in anticipation of the baby's birth.

5. That is, in 1913 when they decided to marry.

6. A jaunty phrase which recalls the curt and understated exchanges among World War I soldiers before they left the trenches to attack.

7. That is, into danger.

Between December 1, 1918, and January 29, 1919, Aldington wrote H.D. seventeen letters. It seems likely that some letters and notes were written between the end of January and February 24, 1919, but if so none of these has survived. He received his demobilization papers during the first week of February and recalled in *Life for Life's Sake* that his long trip back to England, like the experience of returning home just after the armistice in November, was a

> fantastic and uncomfortable journey, beginning with seven miles in the mess cart through deep snow. There was a slow, all-night train journey in an unlighted, unheated train, lacking window glass and doors. I had been cold in the trenches, but seldom as cold as during that interminable, frosty night [of February 8, 1919]. We sat packed together stamping our feet and beating our hands to keep them from frost-bite. At dawn we stopped at Armentières, which was a strange sight. The splintered trees and telephone wires were festooned with thick hoar frost, and the ruins looked black in the dead-white snow. We stumbled over to a shed where we were given bowls of hot soup, and the cases of frost-bite were evacuated to hospital. (199)

On February 9, 1919, Aldington reached Tournai, where he was able to write briefly to Ezra Pound:

> By enormous efforts I've managed to secure release on the very last day it was possible! Damned close shave. Am now at Tournai, which I leave tomorrow evening, for a nice 12 hour ride to the Base in frozen cattle trucks! I expect to cross on Wednesday [February 12]—then have to report to Crystal Palace [a Victorian exhibition hall in south London used as a demobilization center at this time], I should with luck be free on Friday [February 14]. Will trot along to see you. It gives me shivers to think how nearly I got caught for the Army of Occupation— never again will I trust a woman [that is, Harriet Shaw Weaver] to do anything really important.
>
> I have got a chance of one or two jobs in town, but I want to come & talk things over with you &, if possible, to re-commence our ancient war on les cuistres [the pedants]. (BL)

Aldington left Tournai on February 10, and by "late in the afternoon we detrained at Dunkirk, and we were sent to what was optimistically called an Officers' Rest Camp, which consisted of canvas tents pitched in the snow" (*Life for Life's Sake*, 199–200). On February 11, Aldington finally arrived in London and later recalled: "I walked from Charing Cross to an Italian restaurant in Soho, and as I was very tired I rented a room there for the night" (*Life for Life's Sake*, 200).[1]

Lodgings in London were if anything more difficult to come by in the months immediately following the armistice than in the months preceding it, and Aldington was compelled for a while to keep his room at the Hotel du Littoral on Moor Street across from the Palace Theatre. He felt somewhat embarrassed about the neighborhood: Moor Street is a block in length and on three of its four corners stood public houses; at Numbers 6, 9, and 14 were wine merchants; other buildings contained printers, hairdressers, a confectioner; and at Number 15 stood the Italian restaurant of Mario Missaglia. Moor Street was clearly not a residential area, and Aldington felt compromised that as a demobilized officer and a promising writer he could neither find nor afford anything better.

Aldington was also exhausted and rather disoriented. Despite the eagerness to resume meaningful work that his January letters to H.D. and his February letter to Pound reveal, he spent February 12 sleeping and attempting to wash the filth of the trenches from his body, which would take months to recover physically from the war experience. In a letter to Amy Lowell on January 5, 1920, he recalled that upon his return to England he was "covered with boils . . . through bad water, exposure &c. I was really very depressed in health. . . ." And the headaches and troubled sleep he mentioned to H.D. in letters 80 and 81 persisted.

While he recalled in a letter to Amy Lowell that on February 13, 1919, he "started work,"[2] and while he wrote to Clement Shorter on February 15 that he was "just demobilized" and eager to meet with him, Aldington left London on February 17 to spend several days at Rye in Sussex with his family. He returned to town sometime after February 21, but as letter 85 implies, he did not see H.D. during these first weeks after his release.

The terms of the Aldingtons' relationship seem very unsettled from early December, when H.D. abruptly left London for Speen (see letter 67). Subsequent letters suggest that both Aldingtons were comfortable with an intimate, ongoing professional friendship. Additionally, they were bound to each other by their shared past, and various domestic tasks continued to define H.D.'s role as she sorted through her husband's books and ran errands for him in his absence. Aldington's letters also imply their agreement that nothing about their relationship could be decided definitely until after the baby's birth (see letter 68). H.D.'s letters to Bryher during this time also imply a similar suspension: nothing about the future can be determined until after the child's arrival. Such vagueness must have been both unnerving and reassuring to the Aldingtons: neither wanted to force the other to face some ultimate rupture, while the lack of unsettled terms meant that a resolution of their difficulties was still a slim possibility. In the weeks before the baby's birth, Aldington wanted to protect H.D. in whatever way he could. In her turn, H.D. wanted Aldington to feel economically and professionally secure before any final confrontation.

Their relationship was further complicated by the differences between the experience of writing to each other and the experience of being in close proximity if not actually physically in each other's presence. Thus much of what was apparently settled between them in letters—that Aldington would never again see either H.D. or Arabella Yorke, that H.D. would expect nothing but financial assistance from Aldington (letter 49)—was in fact disregarded by both of them when Aldington returned on leave in November of 1918 and for good in February of 1919.

For her part, H.D. was almost eight months pregnant in early February and was beginning to feel cumbersome. On January 1, 1919, she wrote to Bryher about an approaching visit to London: "As you know, I am not feeling awfully fit, so would prefer, if possible, to talk with you quietly up in your little room." H.D. continued for a while, however, to make frequent trips into town, and probably called on Bryher there on February 4[3] and again the following week.[4]

The snows Aldington experienced on his way home through France also fell at Speen, and a pampered pony and its small cart were H.D.'s only means of transportation between Peace Cottage and the local railway station. By mid-February, she began to feel like staying put. On February 14, she wrote Bryher: "I feel better but still inclined to crouch a bit over the fire. Let me know about your coming. We could have a little tramp across the common + a quiet talk. . . . I am converting the big shawl—your gift—into a warm bed wrap for *myself*."

H.D. was continuing her rewarding work on new poems and translations from the Greek, work she regularly discussed with Bryher who, in turn, was sharing with H.D. chapters of her own nearly finished novel, *Development*, as well as her early attempts at translation (of Antipater of Sidon). These exchanges were emotionally as well as intellectually quickening for H.D., and her letters to Bryher during this period reveal her excitement with this fresh burst of creativity. Certainly her relationship with Bryher nurtured her artistic work; her departure from Cornwall and separation from Cecil Gray must have relieved some tensions for her, and probably her rather settled life with Margaret Pratt in Speen also encouraged her writing. In a letter to Amy Lowell on February 1, 1919, H.D. attributed her renewed energy to a release from tensions caused by the war: now that the war is over, her family is recovering from the shock of her brother's death, "and R. is safe—," she writes, "I am seriously getting back to work." The reasons she gives Lowell are surely only a half-truth (she was always guarded with Lowell), but Aldington's own renewed energy for creative work, which dominates his letters to H.D. after his return to the front in December 1918, clearly struck a responsive chord in her; however obliquely and ironically, they were once again working together.

Also ironically, it was still only with Aldington that H.D. was fully open about the now soon approaching birth. Dorothy Yorke knew Gray was the father, and it seems likely that Brigit Patmore may at this point have known, too, but

Bryher did not know. H.D., like Aldington, felt uneasy about the deep intimacy that still bound them closely to each other, yet she chose not to share with Bryher the details of their estrangement while she made clear to her new friend that she wanted to remain aloof from her husband. In late January H.D. wrote Bryher about Aldington's interest in working for *The Sphere*, commenting that he "seems duly touched and appreciative [of her efforts on his behalf]. But I must keep impersonal + detached!"[5] H.D. again wrote Bryher on February 1, 1919: "My mind is so full of ideas—and I am not at all peaceful or at one with myself."[6]

It seems clear that H.D. did not find it easy to maintain a distance between herself and her husband, yet she was wary about alternatives. Aldington's shattered nerves coupled with his self-protective determination to preserve the distance they had finally agreed upon (see letter 51) made him wary as well. H.D.'s friendship with Bryher had grown more intense between the time of Aldington's November leave and his demobilization; Aldington's relationship with Yorke had not dissolved after all, and Yorke was persistent in her desire to continue the affair and to marry him if possible. Both H.D. and Aldington had thus other potential relationships with which to replace, as it were, their relationship with each other, yet these alternative relationships were secondary to both H.D. and Aldington in February of 1919. Both Aldingtons also had chores to do: Aldington needed to reestablish himself as a writer and H.D. had to go through the process of having her baby. Both were agreed that these tasks took precedence over working out their emotional relationship.

NOTES

1. Aldington dates the stages of this journey specifically in an unpublished letter to Amy Lowell on June 17, 1920.
2. Aldington to Lowell, June 17, 1920.
3. Undated letter from H.D. to Bryher, probably written on February 1, 1919.
4. Undated letter from H.D. to Bryher, probably written in mid-February, 1919.
5. Undated letter from H.D. to Bryher, probably written on January 30, 1919.
6. Undated letter from H.D. to Bryher, probably written on February 1, 1919.

85

February 24, 1919
Hotel du Littoral
Moor St W.

Dear Astraea/

I hear you are not feeling too famously;[1] you must keep strong and hopeful, for I think you will have a good chance of a fine literary career. Let me know if I can do anything for you in the way of sending out m.s.s &c.

As to type-writer. I intend buying another second-hand so you had better keep the one you have. It still goes, doesn't it?

No news particularly. I see few people—they are all so very discouraging. But I'm sending out quite a deal of work to U.S. Dial has promised more pay. As soon as you are well I want you to write some articles for them—I know I can get them to print them.

Keep cheerful & courageous. I <u>know</u> there is happiness & a fine life for you. This is a harsh test, but remember your Greeks at Marathon![2]

Richard

1. Aldington would have heard news of H.D. from Brigit Patmore or from Bryher. Apparently there was some agreement that he and H.D. would not see each other until after the baby was born. It is not clear at this point whether H.D. is actually ill or whether she is simply feeling tired and awkward in the last weeks of her pregnancy.

2. The Greeks routed the army of Darius at Marathon in 490 B.C.E., thereby winning the first campaign of the Persian wars.

86

March 1, 1919
52 Doughty St W.C. 1.[1]

Dear Astraea/

I hope you are feeling better.[2] Brigit & Miss E.[3] let me know from time to time & I'm glad to hear you are getting better than you were. Please get well soon; I feel very miserable when I think of you lying ill.

There is so much for you to come back to; everyone speaks so admiringly of you & your work. On Friday I saw Massingham[4] and he asked me for work by you. I said I would ask you to let him see your Hippolytus;[5] so if you will ask Brigit to send it to me I will retype it & send it to him. Could you make her send it soon? This week I have some Anacreon[6] in the Nation; but you should be there too.

You must let me do anything I can for your work—it seems all I can do.

I have this studio for a month & must then find another place. And I'm very happy to be back. Please forgive my being happy when you are so ill. And please keep brave—you have a wonderful life to come back to and all the really worth-while people will stick to you.

Richard.

1. Aldington was able to rent a studio here for the month of March. This letter is addressed to H.D. at 2 Hanger Lane, Ealing W.5.; she had just moved into a pension near St. Faith's nursing home in this London suburb in anticipation of her baby's birth.

2. H.D. was ill at this time with the influenza that became epidemic after the war. The flu itself was debilitating, but brief in duration and not usually serious; the pneumonia that often developed in patients weakened by influenza, wartime deprivation, and the

harsh weather was, however, serious indeed: by 1920, the epidemic had become world-wide, and influenza and its complications were responsible for twenty-two million deaths.

3. Brigit Patmore and Winifred Ellerman.

4. The journalist Henry William Massingham.

5. See letter 72.

6. See letter 70, note 21.

By the end of March Aldington had been demobilized for six weeks and had begun to reestablish himself as a writer and to give shape to his professional future. He still had no dependable income, no "job," but he was working hard on a great many projects and publishing in a wide variety of journals. He wrote Amy Lowell on April 19, 1919, that despite his initial enthusiasm for the second Poets' Translation Series, "I feel that the translation *series* must be left for a bit. I would like to do it, but I just can't afford to!" Aldington pulled out all the stops in February and March of 1919, calling on and writing to old friends (Pound, Flint, Lowell, May Sinclair, Harold Monro) and cultivating new acquaintances (Shorter, Bryher, Sir John Ellerman, Herbert Read, T.S. Eliot) in energetic, even frenzied efforts to place individual articles, poems, and translations and to find permanent employment. His social schedule seems as a result to have been quite hectic: coming into London from a visit with his family at Rye, he dined with Shorter on February 17; he called on Henry Massingham, editor of *The Nation*, on February 24; he met with Bryher on March 10; on March 21, he dined with Sir John Ellerman at his home; on March 26 he spent the evening with Harold Monro; he spent the following evening with Shorter and Austin Harrison, editor of *The English Review*; on April 12, he dined with Frank and Violet Flint; on April 16, he attended a dinner party with May Sinclair and Hugh Walpole at the Albemarle Club.[1]

The result of these efforts encouraged Aldington. On March 31, 1919, he wrote Lowell the reasons for his essentially abandoning his Poets' Translation project:

> The attempt to get out the series was provoked first because I wanted to get back the "feel" of literature again after so long an absence & secondly because Miss Bryher & Mr. Shorter were so keen on it [in response to Aldington's own enthusiasm]. I have talked it over with them & with Hilda & am coming over to your opinion: that the attempt is ill-advised at present & probably beyond my power to carry to a successful conclusion. Hilda, W.B. & I will therefore probably publish our translations as individuals though, if possible, with the same publisher.
>
> . . . I agree with you that the whole project could be more trouble than it is worth. I see that quite well now. I didn't see it in Belgium because I was in such a condition of wretched nerves that *any* sort of hard slogging work seemed desirable.

Aldington also came to realize that his other writing was demanding nearly all of his time, and in the interests of reestablishing himself and making a living, he would need to put aside most translation work for a period. In his letter to Lowell on March 31, he described his current work:

I'm "critic of poetry" for the Pall Mall Gazette, I have got reviewing for The Anglo-French Review & I'm doing a series of articles on French poets for them; I'm doing 6 articles on life in France [during the war] for The Sphere. [Holbrook] Jackson has promised to use my work regularly in To-Day & [Austin] Harrison has promised to give me a show in The English Review.

He wrote Lowell on April 19, 1919, that his translation of Anacreon, which he had been working on in the trenches, was due to appear in parts in *The Nation, The New Age,* and *To-Day* and that *The Anglo-French Review* had accepted a set of articles on modern English poets. He wrote Shorter on March 8 that *The Express* had accepted an article and that he was considering writing something for *The Saturday Review.* His two books of poetry were also in the process of being published: early in 1919 Beaumont issued two limited editions (one of thirty, the other of two hundred copies) of *Images of War,* while Allen and Unwin issued an expanded edition in December; in June 1919, Elkin Matthews published *Images of Desire.* The Egoist Press published *Images* in September 1919, a volume which included poems in both *Images of War* and *Images of Desire.* Before the year was out the Four Seas Company in America published a similar combined volume, *War and Love (1915–1918).*

Bryher's father, Sir John Ellerman, and Clement Shorter, whom Aldington had come to know through H.D. and Bryher's family, were crucial figures in enabling Aldington to move from his prewar position as a poet associated with an influential but small, elite journal (*The Egoist* never had a circulation of more than a few hundred readers) to a position as a writer with a broad range who could produce articles as well as verse and translations for general as well as specialized periodicals with wide circulations. Shorter published six of Aldington's articles on his experiences in wartime France in *The Sphere,* but much more importantly Shorter introduced Aldington to a great number of older men, established journalists mostly of Aldington's father's generation, who were willing to take him on as a regular contributor. Probably sometime in late March or early April Ellerman wrote on Aldington's behalf to Bruce Richmond, editor of *The Times Literary Supplement,* in which Ellerman held a large block of shares. On April 19, 1919, Aldington wrote Lowell that "strictly, *entre-nous,* there is a chance of my getting on The Times in a literary capacity. But there's nothing settled." On May 5, 1919, he wrote Lowell briefly: "I've been taken on by Times Litt. Supp. as their critic of French literature."

Aldington's efforts to establish himself were in part a result of his sense that work was essential to steady him emotionally after his experiences of the war years. He was also responding naturally to the practical problem of earning a living, and part of that challenge was the hope that he might need to support not only himself but a woman and a baby.

In early March of 1919, H.D. was exhausted by her bout of influenza, but recovered steadily and amazingly rapidly. Despite her nervousness and emotional and physical vulnerability, she had deep inner resources, mental and physical, on which she could rely in times of intense stress. Throughout her life it was not so much during periods of tension and pressure as after that H.D. needed to rely on others for help. Her severe depression after the death of her baby in 1915 was characteristic of this pattern of response; similarly, it was not in the bombing of London during the Second World War that she broke down, but after the war in early 1946. In an undated letter to Bryher in March of 1919, H.D. wrote from St. Faith's that "the doctor said I have had pneumonia—of a sort—it was your fruit and flowers that persuaded me to pull through. I feel much better. . . ." Despite this gracious acknowledgment of Bryher's presents, H.D. certainly "pulled through" for many reasons. In the same letter to Bryher, who was away from London at her family's country house for most of March and April, H.D. discouraged Bryher from visiting her and wrote of Aldington's Anacreon and Bryher's novel as well as of Bryher's own health and the health of her parents. H.D. thus seems to have been in good spirits just before her baby's birth. Aldington evidently was visiting her and she recalled in *End to Torment* (41) that on March 30 Ezra Pound visited her as well.

On March 31, 1919, H.D.'s daughter, Frances Perdita Aldington, was born, a plump and healthy child to whom H.D. became immediately attached, for the baby evoked deep maternal feelings. Years later H.D. would recall: "P arrived with a bird-black mop or cap . . . she was two weeks late, so had time to grow and was a very pretty baby, really grown up."[2] Despite H.D.'s earlier decision, urged upon her in large measure it would seem by Bryher, to place the child in a nursery after leaving St. Faith's, H.D. began to nurse her daughter, though she stopped after several days, commenting to Bryher: "I think feeding Perdita weakened me a little—I have had to give it up + expect to get strong soon."[3] On April 19, 1919, H.D. again commented to Bryher about the baby: "Perdita is so very good. She stays with me most of the day. I am relieved about her 'home' [the nursery]—but don't know what I shall do." Just before she left St. Faith's, she again shared her misgivings with Bryher:

> Everything seems to be going all right, but I *will* be so glad when tomorrow is over. I grow weaker as the parting comes—but I *know* it is best to leave Perdita for the time. She gets more charming—that is the trouble. . . . I am torn between a desire for a little place with Perdita + fairy books + Noahs [sic] arks and dolls, and a wild adventure. . . .[4]

Bryher, however, was firm and clear about what H.D. ought to do: "I hope you will be sensible over Perdita and remember you were not given poetry to sit and worry over an infant in a solitary cottage. I am very jealous for your poetry and I will even fight Perdita about it. She will be much healthier and happier for the next year or two in a home. . . ."⁵

Bryher was also now demanding and directive in other ways in her relationship with H.D. While much of H.D.'s emotional and physical energy was going into the experience of motherhood and the recovery from illness and childbirth, she was also striving to come to new terms with her husband: she wrote Bryher on April 10, 1919, that once out of the nursing home, "I think I can get R. out of his bombastic Victorianism! At least I will give it a try—and if pressure from outside is too heavy, I fear I shall be forced to shout the truth to everyone! I can't stand this virtuous + abused wife business. I really can't. But I will be diplomatic for the present."

By "the truth" here H.D. apparently means the nature of the Aldingtons' "open" marriage. It seems that she has told Bryher about Aldington's affair with Arabella, in part perhaps to account for the current tensions in their marriage. H.D. wanted Bryher to understand that her husband's affair was not to be treated in a traditional ("Victorian") fashion, though of course she was deeply hurt by the extent of his feelings for his lover. On April 13, H.D. wrote Bryher that she and Aldington "had quite an interesting talk. You must not let him discourage you. He is really so interested and grateful for any intelligence—as you + I—he feels the general futility of most people + feels someone who knows Greek + Elizabethans is really a trouvaille [a find]!" On April 19, H.D. wrote Bryher again about her husband: ". . . R. came. He was in such a strange state of duality. He is so puzzling. But I want to see more of him. I can't rest now till I understand." Her future to a large degree depended on whether or not she and her husband would continue in some manner to live together, and in March and April of 1919 they were trying to define what their marriage might still be. On April 18, H.D. wrote Bryher: "R. comes tomorrow after all—so I can get future plans more definite with his help." But Bryher was growing increasingly hostile toward Aldington, forcing H.D. into a position of having to defend him and apologize for her relationship with him. Bryher was going through a difficult period in trying to separate herself from domineering parents about whose wealth and social position she felt quite ambivalent. Years later H.D. recalled that Bryher "had talked of suicide from the earliest days, when she came to see me, before Perdita was born."⁶ Bryher was also struggling to think of herself as a writer and to finish her autobiographical novel *Development*, which she was revising and completing in the early months of 1919. Her behavior with H.D. during this spring can be understood as neurotic, but was unquestionably selfish and manipulative.

H.D.'s letters to Bryher in the first weeks of April 1919 are constantly encouraging in evident response to Bryher's own self-doubt and deep insecurities; they suggest how careful and controlled H.D. had to have been to focus on Bryher and her needs at a particularly difficult time for H.D. herself. H.D.'s letter to Bryher on April 10, 1919, opens: "I think the chapter [of *Development*] excellent—really a good contrast. Do go on as well as you can. We will try to get away somewhere *as soon as possible*—then you must work. You will get ideas once away—" Bryher wanted H.D. to come away with her: to the Scillies first, then to Greece, Egypt, the United States. In the same vein, H.D. continued on April 13: "Don't get discouraged—everything *must* come right—there is a lot of work for us all. Only keep well—and have patience—" And on April 19: "I think I am getting things clear in my head— There are great times ahead, I am sure. The two chapters are *excellent*—quite in the same scale of intensity—that is what I hoped for. You have only to go ahead now. This is splendid!"

Bryher's own feelings about Aldington were clearly hostile by the time H.D. was ready to leave St. Faith's. As if to force H.D. into an increasingly dependent relationship with her, Bryher now took evident glee in alienating Shorter, who for all his Victorianism had been kind and helpful to both her and H.D., and in confronting Aldington, ironically on ground on which she was least strong and he most secure. On April 21, Bryher wrote H.D.: "I am most disturbed that Mr. Aldington is applying the pedantic method to your poems. To my eyes, at least, it lowers his mind. . . . Please don't alter a word to please him. . . . He has no right to do other than accept thankfully your poems." On April 22, the day H.D. left St. Faith's, she wrote H.D. that she had told Shorter that she was thinking of sending *Development* to a publisher other than the one to whom he had spoken at length on her behalf, after reading the manuscript and advising her about it, and continued: "I have had many pages from Clement [Shorter] who says he hates the sight of me, I have been so cruel to him, and he will never again read a line that I have written." Then she wrote about Aldington:

I have had an amusing letter from Mr. Aldington. I have evidently annoyed him very much. (This relieves my mind.) He takes refuge in saying that I shall grow wiser with age which is no right weapon to use and one feels his extreme contempt curling about the lines. But I won't give in to his theories and he can't afford to talk about wisdom increasing with years and to publish "Images of Desire" on top of it. Also one would imagine from his letter that I had never taken pen in hand before. I am so amused that he is reading the studies [Havelock Ellis's studies in sexuality]. I trust they do him good.

Bryher discounts Aldington's greater experience in life and literature on the basis of poems in *Images of Desire* which H.D. felt and must have indicated to Bryher were inspired by Aldington's relationship with Dorothy Yorke. Generously one may construe Bryher's alienation of Aldington as a misguided protection of H.D., but her tone and timing here reveal a snide cattiness and self-centeredness that have completely obscured for her any sense of what problems her nastiness to Aldington may have caused for his wife.

NOTES

1. The sources for this information are Aldington's letters to Shorter (17 and 24 February, 8 and 22 March 1919, UR); Aldington's letter to Martyn Johnson (17 February

1919, HRC); Aldington to Charles Bubb (21 February 1919, UCLA); Aldington to Frank Flint (27 March and 17 April 1919, HRC); and Aldington to Herbert Read (28 March 1919, UV).

2. H.D. to Norman Holmes Pearson, 2 March 1951 (BL).
3. H.D. to Bryher, 10 April 1919.
4. H.D. to Bryher, 21 April 1919.
5. Bryher to H.D., 22 April 1919.
6. H.D. to Norman Holmes Pearson, 26 September 1946 (BL).

87

Doughty St.[1]

Dear Astraea/[2]

I've told her.[2] It was very hard and I suffered very much, because—well, you understand. As usual after a "scene" I can't sleep—have just made a meal of eggs & tea at 4.a.m.! Shall go out when the light comes & get breakfast. Dooley, I feel terribly responsible.[3] Do you understand.

But deep down I feel calm. I wish I could go away for week-end in a motor-car.[4]

Don't worry about me.[5] I shall be all right. Only _live_!

The enclosed letter from the Nation makes one very proud—I hope it will please you a little.

Yrs

R.

1. This letter is undated, but because of the address Aldington gives, was clearly written in March 1919.
2. A great deal has happened to both H.D. and Aldington that goes unrecorded in his brief letters. Here he indicates that he has broken off his relationship with Arabella Yorke. Apparently this rupture was something he and H.D. had discussed in person and which he promised her he would do. H.D. was ill in early March with the influenza sweeping the country, but by March 8 Aldington wrote Clement Shorter that "Hilda is very much better but rather weak" (UL). On March 17, Aldington wrote Shorter again: "I saw Hilda yesterday in her new place. She is of course very very weak but I feel more hopeful about her than before. She is more cheerful. And her courage is truly wonderful; she should have been a soldier" (UL). By mid-March, then, it seems that the terms of the Aldingtons' relationship have once more shifted and they have begun to see each other again. On March 31 Aldington wrote to Amy Lowell that he had read recent poetry she had sent him "in the train going to see Hilda" (HU). Thus despite earlier resolutions Aldington and H.D. were seeing each other and developing a new closeness in the final weeks of her pregnancy.

For her part, H.D. had the added stress of her illness in early March and then the news that her father had died in the United States on March 3, 1919, partially as a result of the tensions of the war years and in response to her brother Gilbert's death in late September, 1918. She had moved from Speen to the pension in Ealing in early March, then when she developed influenza, had moved earlier than planned into St. Faith's nursing home nearby. While Bryher suggests in her memoir *The Heart to Artemis* (191–193) that H.D. in her rented room was essentially alone, deserted, and nearly unconscious and that Bryher single-handedly saved her from death, such does not quite seem to have been the case.

3. That is, responsible for the pain he has caused Yorke.

4. Aldington reiterates this desire to escape and rest in his letter to Lowell on March 31, 1919: "I'd like to go away & lie in the grass & rest & sleep for a month or two; but of course I can't" (HU).

5. Aldington is being rather jaunty. He admitted with some chagrin to Lowell on March 31, 1919: "you see I'm not at all well; my nerves have got in such a state that I have a sort of "sympathetic" neuralgia in my neck & arms; I sleep badly; I have a "trench throat" & cough; I have ague directly I get cold. This sounds a devil of a grouse, but it's true; only for Heaven's sake don't mention it to Hilda" (HU). These physical effects of the war were systemic and persisted for some time. As late as October 12, 1925, Aldington wrote Ezra Pound: "It is just three months since I got rid of the last boil on me back caused by drinking water full of corpses of several nations" (BL). Aldington was acutely aware of the war's deep psychological effect on him as well. On March 17, 1919, he wrote Shorter about his sense of dislocation:

> I wonder if you realize what a gulf there is in my generation between the men who fought and those who didn't? It's a strain being with them; I feel as if I were calling across an enormous ravine to them. Of course I've got to get used to meeting them, but honestly I shrink from it. I can't quite tell you why, except perhaps that we others have seen all the misery & pain & hunger & despair & death of the world & they, in this favoured comfortable England, have not. (UR)

Aldington remained anxious, despite his confessions to others, that H.D. not know the extent of his distress.

88

Wed. [April 2?, 1919]
Hotel du Littoral[1]

Dear Astraea/

I got the typewriter[2] all right after all; thank you for letting me have it.

I like your daughter[3] quite well; she is very attractive with her long hair and oriental features. I think you like her more than you say.[4]

Shorter has sent me duplicate proofs of two articles,[5] so I am sending them on to you.

Let me know of anything I can do for you.

Affectionately
Richard.

1. Aldington had to give up the studio flat he rented for March (it belonged to someone who needed it back), and he returned to the Hotel du Littoral on April 1.

2. Apparently the one he and H.D. jointly owned, stored in all likelihood at 44 Mecklenburg Square.

3. Frances Perdita Aldington, born March 31, 1919. Aldington clearly visited H.D. soon after the baby's birth.

4. Astutely, Aldington seems to have sensed H.D.'s mixed but essentially positive feelings about her daughter. He himself "liked" the child, despite his earlier reservations (see letter 37). Significantly, H.D. permits him to see Perdita during this early visit; when Bryher first visited H.D. after the birth, H.D. would not let her see the baby (Bryher to Brigit Patmore, 3 April 1919, BL).

5. Probably "Books in the Line" and "The Bookshop at Grenay," which appeared in *The Sphere* on April 12 and April 19, 1919, respectively, the first two of six articles Aldington wrote for *The Sphere* in 1919.

89

April 5, 1919
Authors' Club
2. Whitehall Court, S.W.1.

Dear Astraea/

Thanks for yr: note for £1. There will be lots of change![1]

I think it would be better for me to come along later next week. May S.[2] wants to see you. She has sent me a cheque saying: "Will you get H. some little thing with enclosed, considering me for the time being as a sort of aunt." It is very charming of her. So I don't think you can refuse, especially as you'll need *all* the money you can get. Will you drop May a line & tell her when to come see you? Why not make it Tuesday?[3] I'm seeing her this p.m. & will arrange that tentatively.

I will come see you Thursday,[4] if that will suit.

You are not in Nation this week.[5] Will be next I suppose.

Yrs
Richard.

1. H.D. routinely asked Bryher and Brigit Patmore to bring her envelopes and stamps; perhaps she has made a similar request of Aldington here.

2. May Sinclair.

3. April 8.

4. April 10.

5. H.D.'s translation of selected choruses from Euripides' *Hippolytus* (lines 199–233, 740–785, 1282–1296) appeared in *The Nation*, April 19, 1919, 80–81.

90

Thursday [April 17?, 1919]
Hotel du Littoral
Moor St. W.

Dear Astraea/

I don't mind abstractly what C.K.S.[1] does or says—the only thing is that the quicker & more dignified we are about it, the less conscious or self conscious, the less we shall be troubled. C'est un situation qu'il faut accepter mais dont il ne faut pas se vanter.[2]

I'm sorry W.B. worried you with it. I told $\begin{Bmatrix} \text{her} \\ \text{him} \end{Bmatrix}$! not to.[3]

I will of course try to get you a room.[4] Will a week[5] be long enough? Try to get a feeling of *leisure*. It is excellent after these years of worry. There is time enough. Anyhow I'll see what can be done.

I have been to "Times"[6] with a recommendation from Sir John.[7] They are actually considering giving me a job![8] Don't mention it to anyone—will let you know later if it "pans out." And don't be too sanguine.

Affectionately
Richard.

1. Clement Shorter.

2. It is a situation that we have to accept but which we need not boast about. Aldington was well aware that he and H.D. were friendly with Shorter in some measure because he could be so helpful to them. They could not afford to be less than polite and conciliatory. It is unclear, however, exactly what problem Shorter seems to be causing here.

3. Aldington is aware of Bryher's confusion about her sexual identity. It seems likely that H.D. has shared with him Havelock Ellis's view of Bryher's nature. On March 20, 1919, Bryher had written H.D. that she had discussed her confusion with Ellis: "we got onto the question of whether I was a boy sort of escaped into the wrong body and he says it is a disputed subject but quite possible . . ." (BL). In *Development*, Bryher writes repeatedly of her desire to be a boy.

4. At the Hotel du Littoral. Apparently it is only at this point that H.D. has definitely decided to be with Aldington after leaving St. Faith's.

5. H.D. does not intend to remain long in London after she leaves the nursing home. As soon as the baby is settled in the nursery, H.D. intends to visit Cornwall with Bryher for a few weeks. On April 19, 1919, Aldington wrote Amy Lowell of their plan:

> Hilda is better of her pneumonia & has a little daughter—very delightful little creature. But Hilda is terribly ill and thin—the strain of all these years has told on her. She comes out of hospital on Tuesday & will stay with me in town, but she will soon go to the country, probably with W. Bryher. I have to stay in town for the purpose of "getting into" these infernal periodicals.

6. The office of the *Times Literary Supplement*.

7. Sir John Ellerman, who owned a large amount of stock in *The Times* and whose name had great influence.

8. Aldington was applying for the position of reviewer of French literature, a "job" which he indeed got and held from May of 1919 throughout the twenties.

A fter Perdita's birth, Aldington visited H.D. often in the nursing home: on April 10 (see letter 89), on April 13 (H.D. to Bryher, 13 April 1919), on April 18 (H.D. to Bryher, 19 April 1919). On April 22, H.D. left St. Faith's for the Hotel du Littoral, where Aldington had found her a room as she had requested (see letter 90). H.D. was still physically weak but was feeling stronger each day. She settled Perdita in her nursery on the day she left St. Faith's. On April 23, Bryher returned to London from the country and that afternoon H.D. visited her at her parents' home at 1 South Audley Street. By April 26 (see letter 91), H.D. had left the Hotel du Littoral for the Ellermans' and had made a definite and final rupture with Aldington.

What occurred between the Aldingtons during those few days at the Hotel du Littoral was difficult and painful for them both. Sometimes less intensely, sometimes more so, they were always to regret their parting.

H.D.'s relationship with Bryher and her intense maternal feelings for Perdita contributed to her responses to Aldington during these crucial days; Aldington's responses to H.D. were influenced by the tensions which resulted from his war experiences and by his continuing if vague relationship with Dorothy Yorke. While Aldington was clear that H.D. had indeed left him, apparently he never understood quite why. When later in the twenties he heard rumors that she was afraid of him, he was shocked and mystified. On August 7, 1928, he wrote Pound, "H.D. won't know me because (so I'm told) she thinks I want to harm her— Christ knows why, since I feel perfectly benevolent and wouldn't hurt her for anything."

H.D. apparently decided to leave Aldington soon after she arrived at the Hotel du Littoral, and she was clearer about the reasons for the rupture. She had not officially registered Perdita at the time of her birth, and the issue of her legitimacy depended on Aldington's appearing as the father on her birth certificate. Aldington, always and particularly in times of stress, was a martinet about order and detail: H.D.'s work had to be perfectly spelled, punctuated, and typed; forms for demobilization had to be completed correctly and promptly; letters had to be properly addressed and stamped. With his emotional and professional life in chaos and his physical health precarious, it seems that he clung, however pedantically and irrationally, to the fact that he was not Perdita's father and that

H.D. and Perdita, taken in Kensington Gardens, probably by Bryher, late in 1919.

to claim so on an official document was illegal. Such a false claim, if discovered, could cause criminal action against H.D. by the courts or, if he chose, civil prosecution by Aldington himself, and the adultery revealed in such action would certainly be grounds for divorce, if that were what he wanted. But that was not really what he wanted. It appears that he wanted insistently to do the right thing, morally and legally, and they were not the same. In 1929 H.D. recalled their parting in a letter to Pound:

> I put down a lot of myself after Perdita's birth. I loved Richard very much and you know he threatened to use Perdita to divource me and to have me locked up if I registered her as legitimate. This you see, was after he had said he would look after us, up to the point at least, of seeing me on my feet again. I was "not on my feet" was literally "dying."

Although from all available evidence H.D.'s account here seems rather exaggerated, one can perhaps pardon the melodrama in her memory of an experience so emotionally painful. H.D. continued her recollections:

But R and A [Arabella] had told me they didn't want to marry and I suppose their turning on me afterwards [that is, in a confrontation at the Hotel du Littoral] when I was actually crippled, has put me out of touch with my own integrity. . . . suddenly they were howling at me, screaming illigitimacy and what not, and they started it. I mean I wanted A. and R. to be "happy," as R. was too forceful for me and too éxigent. . . .[1]

Amid this argument, H.D. recalled in a letter to John Cournos, Aldington "litterally called up Bryher and said 'Hilda must get out of here at once.' "[2]

In an undated letter to Pound in 1929, H.D. also tried to explain the more rational causes for her leaving her husband. She wrote that "Bryher could not stand" Brigit Patmore and

I felt she gave me nothing of the NEW and the new, I was sure then, was the only thing to save me. I have no feeling at all . . . only here I am, with a very static and "classic" and peaceful relationship with Bryher and [Kenneth] Macpherson [Bryher's husband in name and H.D.'s current lover in 1929]. I admit, I am at times, very lonely, not that they do not understand, they just ARE not of that cycle and I was made by that pre-war London atmosphere and cycle. . . . Br [Bryher], between ourselves has been in a very difficult way and is going through a trying "analysis." She is a "border line case," so that sometimes I seem actuated by weakness in giving in to her, when I alone knew what she was and what terror came into my heart at her peculiar kind of suffering. Then I had nothing anyway [in April of 1919] . . . [sic] and . . . you know as well as I, that you might as well be killed for a sheep as a lamb. Br looked after Perdita and as that seemed to be the only thing I was holding on for . . . [sic] I looked after Br. Of course, this is all very bald . . . but I am tired of mincing matters and "pretending."

H.D.'s leaving Aldington was both an emotional and to her a reasonable decision; rationally, she was willing to make the "trade-off": Bryher for Aldington. It was a decision about which she was to have mixed feelings for the rest of her life.

H.D. also, understandably, felt a measure of guilt as well as regret. She sensed the effects of the war on Aldington, but felt powerless to help him. In the above letter to Pound, she added finally, "it was madness in London [in April 1919] to see him look out at me through a strange great hulk of strange passion and disintegration." She recalled in a letter to Glenn Hughes in June of 1929 "the horrible years of the war and the dreadful break-down he [Aldington] had then, and that I in a different way, shared in."[3] She defended herself to Pound, however, in an earlier letter: "I was quite unprepared for the experience. I mean the terror of feeling that that wadge of bird-feathers and petticoats [Perdita] HAD to be protected. The freedom of my spirit . . . [sic] went. I was no longer free."[4]

Aldington did not want H.D. to leave him, but if what she wanted was divorce, he must have felt that the "facts of the case" should be clear; such a conviction seems yet another reason for his wanting Gray's name on Perdita's birth certificate. Aldington also felt caught between H.D. and Arabella. Earlier (see letter 6) he felt that he loved and wanted both women and was unwilling to choose between them; he now felt incapable of choice. In 1929 in a letter to George Plank, who had known both the Aldingtons when they were still living together, H.D. remembered that at the Hotel du Littoral, "He appealed to me, 'I shall go mad between the TWO of you, it MUST be one or the other.' It seemed feasable all round to step out completely."[5] The Aldingtons' final argument—which certainly had much to do with Bryher and Dorothy Yorke as well as with the fact of Perdita's need for a family—ultimately seems to have reduced itself to the formal and symbolic act of registering the child. In the above letter to George Plank in 1929, H.D. wrote that in 1919 "Richard had begged me to come back. . . . When I went back to R., he simply said 'now you will register this child as [Gray's] . . . I will just take that slip of paper to the court, and there will be no difficulty about divorce.' "

H.D. was aware of the irrationality of this reduction of the complex issues of their relationship, and sought advice—certainly from Bryher, also from professionals. She wrote Plank rather cavalierly, "The doctor and lawyer said the only thing was to consider it shell-shock, and get on with my life. Well . . . [sic] that was all right. Out of the frying pan into the fire. There was Br [Bryher] to look after and Perdita."[6] She also told Plank that Aldington "was, I am quite certain, all but 'certifiable' [as insane] that season just before I finally left him."[7] Bryher was surely counseling her to leave her husband; H.D. confessed to Plank that Bryher "has always been very (justly) hard on R. and I must just joke about him to the two of them [Bryher and Kenneth Macpherson], if I speak at all."[8]

Bryher insisted on referring to Aldington as "Cuthbert" throughout the twenties, a name used during the war to indicate cowardice; Bryher also suggested by it a self-centered Englishness, the stuffiness, pretension, rigidity, and hypocrisy of the quintessential English gentleman. In a letter to H.D. in 1924, Bryher wrote, "I don't like the idea of your having anything to do with Cuth—there is no trusting him."[9] Years later in a letter to Norman Holmes Pearson on March 10, 1960, Bryher wrote that she was discouraging H.D.'s idea that Aldington might accompany her on a trip to America to accept the Award of Merit for Poetry from the American Academy of Arts and Letters. Bryher felt that her role was to make H.D. feel the impossibility of their being together again; she wrote Pearson: "It is actually the repetition of the time that she cut everything and left Aldington" (BL). Bryher could be dramatic, possessive, and manipulative, and H.D. did not then feel "free," as she later wrote to Pound; she left Aldington and "cut everything" in April of 1919.

NOTES

1. H.D. to Ezra Pound, undated letter, probably written in April 1929, BL.
2. H.D. to John Cournos, dated merely February 4 and probably written in 1925, HU.
3. H.D. to Glenn Hughes, "Sunday," June 1929, BL.

4. H.D. to Ezra Pound, 20 February 1929, BL.

5. H.D. to George Plank, 4? February 1929, BL.

6. H.D. to George Plank, 1 May 1935, BL.

7. H.D. to George Plank, 4? February 1929, BL.

8. Ibid.

9. Bryher to H.D., 26? August 1924, BL.

91

April 26, 1919
Authors' Club
2, Whitehall Court, S.W.1.

Dear Dooley/

Herewith letter that came for you.[1]

I'm sorry you feel ill; but things could not go on as they were. No doubt you think me selfish and unkind. I can't help it if you do. I've done my best to be amiable all round & the result has merely been chaos. I shall see a lawyer[2] & hand the matter over; if you do the same with H.A.[3] it will save us both much worry.

Meanwhile, old thing, don't take things too damn seriously! I'm not going to have my existence poisoned by too much scrupulosity. And I *do* seriously want you to be happy somehow in your own way.

Yrs

R.

1. Aldington is forwarding H.D.'s mail to her after her precipitous departure.

2. There is no evidence that Aldington saw a lawyer at this time, although H.D. did; no plans to pursue the matter of a divorce materialized until 1937.

3. Hilda Aldington; i.e., her married self.

*I*n May of 1919, Aldington was taken on as critic of French literature at the *Times Literary Supplement*. In June, H.D. and Bryher traveled together to Cornwall and the Scilly Isles for several months; Perdita remained at a nursery in London. Unable to find other lodging, Aldington remained at the Hotel du Littoral until the end of the year; he was seeing Arabella, dining often with his old friend Frank Flint, meeting his father for occasional meals, working hard. Cecil Gray stayed in London until September, then left England for Italy. Aldington went to Cornwall for a few weeks alone in the summer of 1919; in the autumn, he and Ezra Pound, who was about to leave England permanently for Paris and then Rapallo, visited H.D. at 16 Bullingham Mansions, Church Street, Kensington, where she had taken a flat after her return from Cornwall. In autobiographical notes H.D. made in the 1950s for Norman Holmes Pearson, who was then contemplating a biography of her which he never completed, she wrote that in the fall of 1919 "Richard comes to lunch at Bullingham Mansions and Ezra drops in. I finally exclude both from flat." She recalled this meeting in writing to Pound in 1929, noting that Aldington "walked in calmly." [1] They were not to meet again for nearly ten years, and their correspondence essentially ceased, though there was some indirect communication, through Bryher or Amy Lowell, for the rest of the year and into 1920. In late 1919, Aldington left London for Berkshire. The D.H. Lawrences had lived at Chapel Farm Cottage in Newbury, and had suggested Aldington take it over when they left for Italy. In December he moved in, bringing Arabella Yorke and her mother with him. H.D. and Bryher remained in London throughout the autumn and into the winter of 1919; in February 1920, they departed with Havelock Ellis on their long-anticipated trip to Greece.

NOTES

1. H.D. to Ezra Pound, undated letter, probably written in April 1929, BL.

92

January 28, 1920
Chapel Farm Cottage
Hermitage
Newbury, Berks.

Dear H.D.,

This is just to wish you "bon voyage" and some peace in the sunlight of your Hellas.[1]

Has Constable[2] answered your letter? If they have not taken the book, tell them to send it to me & I will get it published.

What are you working at? Bring back poems from Crete. Don't ever forget that you are the "grandest of the rebel poets."[3]

Franky[4] has written a long article on poetic style, contrasting Squire[5] with H.D., to the great detriment of the former. It will appear in Monthly Chapbook for March.[6] I will save you a copy.

Yrs

R.

Thanks for the Samain—could you add "Au Jardin de l'Infant"?[7]

1. Greece. Bryher and H.D. left England for the Mediterranean on February 7, 1920, for a trip of several months.

2. Apparently H.D. was hoping that Constable, which had published *Sea Garden* in 1916 and the imagist anthologies in 1915, 1916, and 1917, would publish Bryher's novel *Development*, as indeed they did later in 1920. She may also have hoped that they would be interested in *Hymen*, but the Egoist Press finally published this volume in 1921.

3. I have not been able to trace this quotation. It sounds very like something Aldington would have written about H.D. in one of his frequent reviews, but perhaps it was only something he said about her which never made its way into print.

4. Frank Flint.

5. John C. Squire; see Biographical Appendix.

6. Flint's article, "Presentation: Notes on the Art of Writing; on the Artfulness of Some Writers; on the Artlessness of Others," appeared in *The Chapbook*, Vol. 2, No. 9, March, 1920, 17–24. In the first part of his essay Flint delineated fourteen "Axioms" about the nature of poetry, points which echoed the imagists' various manifestos. He then briefly characterized Squire's work before devoting the last two pages of the article to H.D. He praised her "sincerity" and natural form, quoted section two of "Sea Gods," and noted the precision of her word-choice and phrasing, her "sharp and fresh and clear" impressions. He concluded in words Aldington himself might well have written: "She has a secret which you are only allowed to guess at, and she calls forth the same wonder and longing that are announced by the beauty of the flowers and the seasons. She may be the most exquisite English poet we have" (24).

7. Albert Samain; see Letter 14, note 13. Published in 1893, his *Au jardin de l'Infante* was a very successful collection of sonnets and elegiac verse. Aldington is evidently still borrowing back books from their once-shared library, which H.D. still has.

Biographical Appendix

Bryher (Winifred Ellerman, 1894–1983)

Bryher was the illegitimate daughter of Hannah Glover and Sir John Ellerman, the wealthy shipping tycoon who by 1918 was also a major shareholder in *The Times, The Sphere,* and a number of other established London journals. Her parents finally married after her brother's birth in 1909. Bryher grew up a pampered child in a Victorian household, living at 1 South Audley Street in Mayfair during the winter and at Eastbourne on the southern coast of England during the summer. She also traveled extensively with her family before the war. She loved and was loved by both her parents, but her dependence on them was forced and psychologically complex. By 1918 she saw herself as a rebel, a potential writer, an avant-garde artist, but much of the competence and experience she claimed were a pose. Intelligent and eager to read widely, she had led a sheltered life. She was in fact neurotically confident and self-doubting and at the same time often petulant and aggressive. She denied her femaleness and adulthood, feeling that she was really a boy trapped in a girl's body, and by her early twenties she was clear that her sexual nature was exclusively lesbian. She was frightened of what she saw as the force of other personalities upon her; stubborn; in many ways unhappy. She responded to her insecurities by being intensely manipulative and by attempting suicide numerous times, acts which combined her tendency to overdramatize and her deep psychic distress.

Bryher met H.D. in Cornwall on July 17, 1918. An epistolary relationship developed, and by the end of the year she and H.D. had become friends. In June of 1919, H.D. and Bryher visited Cornwall together, beginning a pattern of travel in each other's company which would last the rest of H.D.'s life. While they seldom actually lived together in the same house, and while both later developed intimate relationships with other people, they remained close companions until H.D.'s death in 1961.

John Cournos (1881–1966)

Born a Jew in Kiev, Russia, in 1891 Cournos emigrated to America, where he later met and fell in love with Dorothy Yorke. In the spring of 1914 the Aldingtons met him in London, where he was working as a journalist and translator, although he contributed one poem to *Des Imagistes* in 1914 and more of

Cournos's work appeared in the imagist anthologies in 1915, 1916, and 1917. Like the Aldingtons he published work with Charles Bubb at the Clerk's Press in Cleveland. He also wrote regularly for *The Egoist* and published essays on art as well as literary criticism for other periodicals in which Aldington's and Pound's work also appeared. Although he did not contribute to either of the Poets' Translation Series, Aldington kept Cournos in mind as a potential translator of Russian and Hebrew authors. He was particularly close to H.D. and his relationship with her became especially intimate during 1916 and 1917, when they viewed each other as souls with transcendental affinities; the relationship remained "spiritual," however, not physical, although it clearly had sensual elements. He was a frequent visitor when the Aldingtons lived in Devon and introduced them to friends he knew in the area, most notably to Carl and Florence Fallas. When H.D. took a flat at 44 Mecklenburgh Square in January of 1917, Cournos moved into a room on the top floor. In the late summer of 1917, Cournos met Yorke by chance in London, where she had recently arrived from France with her mother. Yorke's feelings for him had never been so intense as his for her, but she now needed him as one of the few people she knew in London. He invited her to stay in H.D.'s large room at Mecklenburgh Square, for H.D. was on her way north at the end of August to stay near Aldington for several months while he was in officers' training near Lichfield. In October of 1917 Cournos left England as a translator with the Anglo-Russian Commission to Petrograd. When he returned in late March of 1918, Yorke told him of her affair with Aldington. He was furious and blamed both H.D. and Aldington for what he saw as the violation of a trust. His relations with the Aldingtons grew increasingly strained after late 1917, and he satirized both of them in his autobiographical novel, *Miranda Masters* (1926).

Gilbert Doolittle (1884–1918)

Two years older than H.D., Gilbert Doolittle was the brother to whom H.D. felt closest. When the United States entered the war, Doolittle enlisted in the Army Engineering Corps and was sent to France as a captain in the summer of 1918. He was killed in the Battle of St. Mihiel on September 25, 1918, and is buried at the American Cemetery near the town of Thiaucourt.

Carl Fallas (1885–1962)

The Aldingtons came to know Carl Fallas and his wife Florence through John Cournos, when the Aldingtons and the Fallases lived near each other in Devon in 1916. Fallas was a journalist, a minor novelist, and a friendly if rather passive man; his wife was livelier and very attractive. The Aldingtons and the Fallases spent a good deal of time together during the spring and summer of 1916, swimming naked in local streams and taking long walks in the countryside. Aldington began a brief affair with Flo Fallas in May of 1916, just before he was called up into the army. He and Carl Fallas enlisted together in the Eleventh Devonshire Regiment and trained and served together during Aldington's first tour in France in 1916–17. After H.D. left Devon and after Aldington returned to England in July of 1917 for officers' training, the Aldingtons' acquaintance with the Fallases essentially ceased, although Aldington maintained a sporadic correspondence with both Carl and Flo throughout his life.

John Gould Fletcher (1886–1950)

The Aldingtons came to know Fletcher in London late in the summer of 1913. He had been living on and off in England since 1910 and already knew Pound as well as T. E. Hulme and Frank Flint. As an American living abroad, Fletcher felt a particular bond with H.D., and when Amy Lowell met him in England during the summer of 1914, she developed a special affection for him. He also became a close friend of John Cournos. His work was included in the imagist anthologies of 1915, 1916, and 1917. He published *Irradiations: Sand and Spray* in 1915, an experimental attempt to join art and music with poetry, and *Goblins and Pagodas*, a collection of imaginative, even fantastic verse, in 1916. The Aldingtons soon came to feel he was a minor writer and not very dependable, and they grew apart by the end of 1917. In his autobiography, *Life Is My Song* (1937), Fletcher records not especially reliable memories of the early days of imagism and his friendship with the Aldingtons.

Frank Stuart Flint (1885–1960)

Publishing as F. S. Flint and called "Franky" by both H.D. and Aldington, Flint knew both writers well but was particularly close to Aldington and remained his one close friend and confidant throughout the war and into the twenties. Unlike other artists in the Aldingtons' circle, Flint did not support himself by his art but with various civil service jobs. His stable home life (he had two children by his first wife, Violet, who died as a result of childbirth in April of 1920; soon after he married her sister Ruth) set him somewhat apart from his literary friends; so, of course, did his steady if small income and his established literary reputation. His first book of verse, *In the Net of Stars* (1909) contained a few poems in free verse; his literary articles for *The Egoist* and other journals and publication of poems in all four imagist anthologies established Flint as a serious modernist artist. He was also a well-regarded translator and Britain's most prominent authority on twentieth-century French poetry in the years before the war. His translation, *The Mosella of Decimus Magnus Ausonius*, appeared as Number 6 in the first Poets' Translation Series in February 1916. Flint came to know the Aldingtons in London and became especially close to them during the summer of 1916, when he and his family took a cottage not far from them at Swanage in Devon. H.D.'s letters to Flint (a selection of which, edited by Cyrena Pondrom, appeared in *Contemporary Literature*, 10, Autumn 1969, 557–586) show that the two were close if jaunty friends who shared with each other details of their personal and professional lives between 1912 and 1917, after which time their relationship faded and essentially ceased after 1920. Aldington's letters to Flint are characterized by a boyish jocularity and a serious sharing of experiences, emotions, and ideas, and reveal an intimacy not found in his letters to anyone else. Aldington often wrote to Flint in other languages, privileging information as well as sharpening his linguistic skills; letters in French, Italian, and Latin occur throughout their correspondence. Flint is probably the only contemporary whom Aldington consistently admired in the teens and twenties for his professional achievement and personal qualities. Ironically, as Flint produced less and less literary work, in the twenties Aldington replaced him as England's foremost authority on French literature.

Ford Maddox (Hueffer) Ford (1873–1939)

Ford was an English novelist, poet, critic, and editor, whom Aldington first came to know well personally when he worked briefly as Ford's secretary in 1914. Ford married in 1894, but by 1908 he and his wife were estranged. In 1909 he began a relationship with Violet Hunt, but was unable to marry her since his wife would not grant him a divorce. In 1911, Ford publicized the false story that he and Hunt had married in Germany after he had assumed German nationality on the basis of his father's birth there. In 1912 his wife sued a newspaper for libel when it referred to Hunt as Ford's wife, and won the case, successfully embarrassing Ford and Hunt. In late 1914 Ford was with some difficulty naturalized as the English subject he had been since birth, in order to avoid service in the German army or internment as an enemy alien. He later served with the British Expeditionary Forces in France, about which he wrote five novels, *The Good Soldier* (1915), and the tetralogy, *Parade's End* (1950). His sensibility was modernist and he moved in London's literary circles, which included both writers of his own generation and artists of early modernism. He was influential in publishing their work in *The English Review*, which he founded in 1908, and later in the *transatlantic review*, which he founded in Paris in 1924.

Remy de Gourmont (1858–1915)

De Gourmont was a French critic, essayist, and fiction writer who held considerable prestige among the symbolists. In 1889 he joined the group that founded the *Mercure de France,* to which he contributed regularly until his death. Disfigured by lupus, he became a semi-recluse during the last years of his life and relied heavily on correspondence for his friendships. De Gourmont's encyclopedic knowledge (much like Aldington's own in his mature years) and brilliant mind were combined with eclectic curiosity. His sensitivity to language and the mysticism and sensuality in his work made him very appealing to both of the Aldingtons.

H.D., Aldington, and Pound came to know de Gourmont's work through Frank Flint, whose discovery of contemporary French literature before 1910 was initiated by his correspondence with the editors of French journals and the writers they published. In 1912 Aldington and Pound also began to exchange letters with de Gourmont. In part on the basis of conversations with H.D., N. Christoph De Nagy indicates that they began reading *Le Problème du Style* in the early months of 1912 (*Ezra Pound's Poetics and the Literary Tradition,* Basel, Switzerland: Francke Verlag Bern, 1966, 118). Pound's relationship with de Gourmont is amply discussed in Richard Sieburth's *Instigations: Ezra Pound and Remy de Gourmont* (Cambridge: Harvard University Press, 1978), but the French writer's influence on H.D. and Aldington has received little attention.

Both Pound and Aldington were instrumental in translating and publishing de Gourmont's work in his last years. Aldington developed a personal and affectionate friendship with him, and attempted to secure funds for him in his final poverty through critical praise and publication of his writing. *The Horses of Diomede,* for example, was serialized in *The New Freewoman* and *The Egoist* in 1913–14. In part through Aldington's influence, *The Little Review* even published a special de Gourmont number in March 1919, to which he as well as others contributed essays. Aldington published *Remy de Gourmont: A Modern Man of Letters* in 1928 and in 1929 his translation *Remy de Gourmont: Selections from All His Works.* He published his translation of a selection from *Lettres à l'Amazone* (1914) and the posthumous *Lettres Intimes à l'Amazone* (1928), de Gourmont's sensitive and reflective correspondence with Natalie Barney, with a substantial introduction in 1931 (*Letters to the Amazon,* London: Chatto and Windus). It is on Aldington rather than on Pound that de Gourmont had his greatest impact and through Aldington more than through Pound that de Gourmont's thought and writing reached the English and American public.

Cecil Gray (1895–1951)

Gray first met the Aldingtons in London in December of 1917. At twenty-two he was an aspiring composer and music critic three years younger than Aldington and nine years younger than H.D. Born in Edinburgh and privately educated, Gray lived with his mother in London during the war and periodically took a cottage by himself in Cornwall to work on his music at a distance from the intensity of city life. He had met the Lawrences, his country neighbors, early in 1917, and had returned to London with them in October. He visited them at 44 Mecklenburgh Square before the Aldingtons' return to London from the north in late November 1917, and continued the flirtation with Frieda Lawrence that had begun in Cornwall. In mid-March of 1918 he left London again for Cornwall, where he remained through July. He then returned to London in part to escape conscription but also under pressure from the mentally unbalanced Phillip Haseltine (Peter Warlock), who was extremely misogynistic and disapproved of Gray's retreat to the country with H.D. in bizarre, bawdy, and insistent letters to Gray throughout the spring and summer of 1918 (BM). Gray remained in London through the end of the war, never serving in the armed forces in any capacity, and left England for Italy in September 1919, as soon as continental travel, limited by the war, was again allowed.

Gray drank heavily, had many fleeting relationships with women, and was generally a passive and removed observer of experience rather than an active or successful participant. In a letter to a friend identified only as "Jack" on October 16, 1921, Gray analyzed his character: he found "drink and women, the two substantial realities of existence on this planet—. . . . my exploits and adventures have not even the justification of inner necessity. After each one a feeling of distaste and disappointment comes over me" (BM). In a notebook of random jottings, Gray continued his self-analysis in an entry in 1922:

> I experience the greatest difficulty in transmounting the gulf between feeling and action. I have never really managed it, except through alcohol. Hence, no doubt, the great hold this resource has over me. For example, I make love to a woman, but all the time the essential I is standing apart, watching, analysing, contemplating in utter detachment and isolation. (BM)

Gray's compositions were not well received, and as a music critic he was contentious, judgmental, and facetious, promoting the work of friends, principally Warlock and Bernard van Dieren. To the writers he came to know through the Lawrences he appeared at best introspective, calm, wry, and removed from passion at a time when the lives of the Aldingtons and their circle were intensely and even debilitatingly emotional. Gray was not in fact a figure of sanity, however, but a neurotically disengaged man incapable of mature commitment or deep response.

Edward Hutton (1875–1969)

The Aldingtons probably first came to know Hutton personally as a reader and translator at Constable's (where he was employed from 1913 through 1928), and they evidently worked closely with him on H.D.'s *Sea Garden* (which Constable published in 1916) and on the imagist anthologies (which Constable published in 1915, 1916, and 1917). Hutton was an author in his own right, specializing in Italian literature, history, and art, and the Aldingtons may well have been familiar with his work as early as their first trip to Italy, for he wrote several travel books on Italy in the early years of the century. Hutton served in the Foreign Office dealing with Italian affairs from 1916 through 1918, and edited *The Anglo-Italian Review* in 1918 through 1919.

David Herbert (D.H.) Lawrence (1885–1930)

The Aldingtons first met Lawrence at a dinner given by Amy Lowell in July 1914, soon after his marriage to Frieda von Richtofen Weeks, who had left her English husband and three young children for Lawrence the year before. He published *Sons and Lovers* in 1913, *The Rainbow* in 1915, and a collection of poems, *Look! We Have Come Through*, in 1917. He contributed poems to the imagist anthologies of 1915, 1916, and 1917, and came to know both H.D. and Aldington as fellow writers. After the Aldingtons left Kensington for Hampstead, the Lawrences, who themselves moved to Hampstead in August of 1915, became close friends. H.D. developed a particularly intimate relationship with Lawrence, which evidently had its source in their similar intense and spiritual response to beauty, especially in nature. They shared their poetry with each other, and when the Aldingtons moved to Devon in February of 1916, an intimate correspondence began between Lawrence and H.D. The Lawrences soon moved to Cornwall and took a cottage near Penzance, where they later met Cecil Gray. Singing German songs one evening with a light shining from improperly closed curtains, the Lawrences were accused of being enemy spies by the local authorities and were forced to leave the coastal area. The Lawrences were virtually destitute when they arrived in London in mid-October of 1917. On October 20 they moved into H.D.'s flat at 44 Mecklenburgh Square. H.D. came down from Lichfield briefly to settle them in, but they essentially occupied her room in her absence. As soon as Aldington received his commission on November 28, 1917, the Aldingtons returned to London and the Lawrences moved out of Number 44: until December 18 into Cecil Gray's mother's house in Earl's Court Square and then to Hermitage, near Newbury in Berkshire. It was through the Lawrences that the Aldingtons met Cecil Gray in December of 1917. During these weeks before Christmas, when Dorothy Yorke began flirting with Aldington, H.D. drew particularly close to Lawrence, even—if we can trust *Bid Me to Live*—indicating to him that she was willing to develop their relationship physically. He was not interested, was even perhaps already impotent as a result of his tuberculosis, and in his characteristic way withdrew from the corporeal with distinct unease. They may have corresponded during the winter of 1918 and during the time H.D. was with Gray in Cornwall. Lawrence, however, who had come to know Yorke during his weeks at Mecklenburgh Square, remained consistently fond of her, and his relationship with H.D. seems to have gradually faded away by late 1918. Lawrence left England to live permanently on the continent at the end of 1919. Aldington grew increasingly close to the Lawrences in the twenties and wrote a personal biography of Lawrence (*Portrait of a Genius But . . .*) in 1950.

Percy Wyndham Lewis (1884–1957)

Both an artist and a writer, Lewis was probably introduced to the Aldingtons by Pound and was one of the central figures in vorticism, futurism, and *Blast* in the years before the war. Lewis appeared to them as the dramatic, flamboyant, gifted, but irascible man that he indeed was. Aldington admired Lewis's art and writing, and praised his work in *The Egoist*, which published Lewis's first novel, *Tarr*, in installments in 1915. Lewis served with the British Expeditionary Forces in France during the war, for which Aldington always respected him while deploring his misogyny and his degradation of sexuality.

Amy Lowell (1874–1925)

The Aldingtons first met Lowell in the summer of 1914. She came to England because of her interest in imagism and took on the movement as a crusade, publicizing it in the United States and supporting it financially through small personal gifts to writers but particularly through her sponsorship of the imagist anthologies which appeared in 1915, 1916, and 1917. She corresponded regularly with both Aldington and H.D., primarily about literary matters, but because of their frequent letters, the Aldingtons often shared with her details of their daily life. As a large, older, socially conservative, and occasionally obtuse woman, Lowell was at times a figure of ridicule for young writers, though she was also for the Aldingtons a useful patron and a friend.

Harriet Monroe (1860–1936)

In 1912 in Chicago, Harriet Monroe founded *Poetry: A Magazine of Verse*, which she edited until her death. The journal was dedicated to modern poetry which, if it were truly good, would also, Monroe was convinced, be democratic and speak to a wide audience. Her notions of poetry and its purpose owe a good deal to Whitman, and it is revealing that among the poets she published she was especially fond of Edgar Lee Masters and Vachel Lindsay. Monroe was not enthusiastic about H.D.'s verse, but thought very highly of Aldington's work; his "Choricos" (which appeared in *Poetry* in November 1912) was a particular favorite.

Brigit Patmore (1883–1965)

Born in Ireland, Patmore married Deighton Patmore, grandson of the sentimental Victorian poet Coventry Patmore, in 1907. Her marriage was an unhappy one, and by 1918 she with her two sons was living apart from her philandering and economically irresponsible husband. Dramatically beautiful and sensitive, she enjoyed associating with artists on the bohemian fringe of London society. She had little money but was a resourceful, sensual, and dynamic woman three years older than H.D. and nine years older than Aldington. It was at a party at her house that she introduced Aldington to H.D. in early 1912. Throughout her life, Patmore would shift her sympathies back and forth between Aldington and H.D. primarily on the basis, it would seem, of erotic attachment. She and Aldington began a brief affair soon after they first met in 1912. Patmore was also, however, sexually attracted to H.D., although that relationship may never have been more than an intensely sensual friendship. When H.D. and Aldington met, Patmore may have felt that she could preserve her relationship with both poets, but as the two writers became increasingly involved with each other, she discovered that she would have to reestablish her relationship with them on new grounds. She chose to align herself with H.D. as a woman with an unfaithful husband, becoming rather hostile toward Aldington as a result. This affection for H.D. and disaffection for Aldington lasted from at least 1917 through the late 1920s, as evidenced in her letters to H.D. and Bryher during this period (BL). By 1928, she and Aldington were lovers again in a passionate affair which lasted until late 1936, when Aldington fell in love with her daughter-in-law, Netta McCullough Patmore, whom he married after H.D. finally divorced him in 1938. H.D. understandably had mixed feelings toward Brigit after 1928, and they simply ceased to correspond by the late 1930s. Aldington became very hostile toward Brigit during Netta's divorce from her son Michael, and resented the resulting legal settlement which obliged him to pay the Patmores for the rest of his life. In 1918 and 1919, both Aldingtons saw Brigit as an experienced mother and independent woman of the world who could best advise H.D. in her awkward situation.

Ezra Pound (1885–1972)

Pound first met H.D. in 1901, when he was a student at the University of Pennsylvania. She inspired early poems, later gathered into *Hilda's Book* (printed at the end of *End to Torment*, 67–84). They were periodically "engaged" during Pound's years at Hamilton, his return to the University of Pennsylvania, his brief term teaching in Indiana, and his trip to Europe in 1908–10. By the time Pound sailed again for England in early 1911, their rather vague romance was essentially over. Pound's very early influence on H.D. was intense, and he certainly influenced her ideas of poetry when she later met him in London in the autumn of 1911. There, Pound introduced H.D. to his widening circle of artistic friends, and at a party at Brigit Patmore's early in 1912, Pound introduced H.D. to Aldington. Patmore had earlier introduced Aldington to Pound.

Pound was at his best during these prewar London years, and the Aldingtons both before and after their marriage were indebted to his energy and imagination. He labeled their poems "Imagiste" in the autumn of 1912 and was responsible for their publication soon after in *Poetry*. Pound was instrumental in securing Aldington his position as literary editor of *The Egoist* in 1913, and continued to serve the Aldingtons as a sort of literary godfather through the publication of *Des Imagistes* in 1914. But before the tensions stemming from Amy Lowell's appropriation of imagism and the anthologies of 1915, 1916, and 1917, Pound was for the Aldingtons clearly a troublesome force, never quite understanding either their love for each other or their continued poetic development. They were always to feel a deep affection for him, but he became an interloper, an unmanageable enthusiast whose depressions and manic vitality they could not share. Both Aldingtons maintained an intermittent correspondence with him throughout their lives and valued his friendship and the attention he had given them. H.D. would reflect at length on her relationship with him in *End to Torment* (written in 1958); Aldington would write sensibly, perceptively, and affectionately about him in *Life for Life's Sake* (1941), concluding in words H.D. also might have written: "We have come to differ over a lot of things but . . . I can't go back on the Ezra of 1912–1914" (111).

Alec Randall (1892–1977)

Aldington first met Randall when they were both students at the University of London in 1910–1911. Randall always remained on the fringe of the bohemian and artistic circles to which Aldington introduced him. More conventional and political than Aldington, Randall nevertheless became one of his few close friends. When Aldington gave up his position as part-time secretary to Ford Maddox Hueffer (Ford) in 1914, he managed to turn the job over to Randall. Randall married in 1915, and he and his wife, Amy, a physician, took a flat at 3 Christ-church Place in Hampstead near the Aldingtons, who moved from Kensington to Hampstead in January 1915, and rented a flat at 7 Christchurch Place. The Aldingtons and the Randalls were thus neighbors as well as friends for all of 1915 until the Aldingtons moved to Devon in early 1916, and both Randalls became particularly close to the Aldingtons during H.D.'s first pregnancy and the birth and death of their child in May 1915. When H.D. left Cornwall in September of 1918, she went to stay with Amy Randall in Hampstead. From 1915 Randall served in the Foreign Office as an officer in the British Army, and after being demobilized in 1919 worked in the diplomatic service. He remained a good friend of Aldington's throughout his life.

Walter Morse Rummel (1887?–1953)

An American composer and pianist, Rummel first met H.D. in Philadelphia or at Swarthmore, where he performed during the summer of 1910. She heard him perform again in Paris late in the summer of 1911 and an acquaintance developed. When Rummel visited London in the fall, she saw him there, and she and Aldington, often together with Pound and his friend Margaret Cravens, saw him frequently in Paris during the spring and summer of 1912. When Cravens killed herself in June 1912, she sent Rummel a letter indicating that it was he she had been in love with; it had been generally supposed among their friends that Pound was the object of her affections. Rummel had announced his engagement to Thérèse Chaigneau in late May. Rummel and Chaigneau were married later in the summer, and H.D. saw them in Paris in October and probably again with Aldington in Paris during the summer of 1913. Rummel's compositions and performances influenced Pound, but while always on amicable terms with the Aldingtons, a close friendship never developed.

Clement Shorter (1857–1926)

A Fleet Street journalist of Aldington's father's generation, Shorter was aware of modernist movements in literature and art. He felt the obligation to befriend and encourage the new work of twentieth-century youth, but he was essentially old-fashioned and at best Edwardian if not Victorian in sensibility. He had strong literary tastes and hobbies, and his many editions (for instance, *The Complete Poems of Emily Brontë* and *Wuthering Heights* in 1910 and 1911) suggest his enthusiasm for facts rather than elegance of expression or critical judgment. In 1900 he founded *The Sphere*, an illustrated weekly, which he edited until his death and for which he wrote a regular literary column.

Shorter was an acquaintance of Sir John Ellerman's, and by 1918 had become a family friend. His first wife, the sentimental Irish writer Dora Sigerson, died in January 1918, and by the summer of that year he had begun his courtship of Bryher's girlhood friend, Doris Banford, whom he married in September 1920. It was through Shorter that Bryher secured H.D.'s address in Cornwall, and H.D.'s friendship with Shorter developed alongside her friendship with Bryher. Peace Cottage in Buckinghamshire, where H.D. lived during late 1918 and early 1919, was within walking distance of Shorter's country home at Great Missenden, where he had moved permanently after the death of his first wife. H.D. seems to have felt a genuine affection for the avuncular Shorter while she realized as well how useful his journalistic connections might be to both her and her husband. Shorter probably introduced Aldington to several influential journalists after his demobilization, and *The Sphere* published eight articles by Aldington between April and September 1919 (excerpts from these appear in my article, "Richard Aldington in Transition," *Twentieth Century Literature*, Vol. 34, No. 4, Winter 1988, 489–506). For a more detailed account of Shorter's friendship with the Aldingtons and with Bryher, see my article "A New Chapter in the Lives of H.D. and Richard Aldington: Their Relationship with Clement Shorter," *Philological Quarterly*, Vol. 68, No. 2 (Spring 1989), 241–262.

May Sinclair (1863–1946)

Forward-thinking and an active advocate of women's rights, the English writer May Sinclair chose not to marry but to devote herself to her art. While she began her writing career working in Victorian modes, Sinclair increasingly concerned herself in her fiction with social and psychological issues, drawing directly on Freudian notions of libido, repression, and sublimation. She was a well-established novelist by the time the Aldingtons came to know her. She was one of the first writers to whom Pound introduced H.D. late in the summer of 1911, and it seems likely that Aldington met her in 1912 through H.D. Sinclair was more intimate with Aldington than with H.D., but served both younger writers as a benevolent patron. It was May Sinclair who gave H.D.'s address in Cornwall to Clement Shorter, who in turn gave it to Bryher in the summer of 1918. The character of Richard Nicholson in Sinclair's *Mary Oliver* (1919) may well be based on Aldington, and on some level Sinclair was probably in love with him. When Aldington discovered in February of 1919 that Cecil Gray had sold a large number of his books, Sinclair comforted him with the generous gift of a life subscription to the London Library.

John C. Squire (later Sir John; 1884–1958)

As an energetic journalist and prolific writer, Squire was a well-established figure in England before the war. His work appeared in the five anthologies of *Georgian Poetry*, edited by Edward Marsh, between 1912 and 1922. He was literary editor of *The New Statesman* in 1913 and acting editor from 1917 through 1918. In 1919 he founded *The London Mercury*, one of the most important literary journals of its time, and edited it until 1934. He was also the editor of the English Men of Letters series. He published volumes of poetry in 1913, 1916, and 1918, and served briefly as London correspondent for *The Dial* under Waldo Browne's editorship in 1916. Squire was essentially conservative and hostile to early modernism, which was in turn generally hostile to him. Although T.S. Eliot praised Squire's verse in his review of the 1916–17 anthology (*The Egoist*, March 1918), Squire was among "those who especially fell into the insipid, slack, and escapist verse for which 'Georgian' became a byword" (David Perkins, *A History of Modern Poetry: From the 1890s to Pound, Eliot and Yeats*, Cambridge: Belknap Press, 1976, 206). The Aldingtons knew Squire primarily through his work, but Aldington had met him about 1915 through Harold Monro and found him "kindly, but definitely one of the world's less gifted poets" (*Life for Life's Sake*, 149).

Edward Storer (1880–1944)

Storer's books of poems, *Inclinations* (1907) and *Mirrors of Illusion* (1908), reveal early experiments in free verse, although he was not a particularly effective writer. After 1908 he had little contact with the innovations of literary modernism, and Pound was clear in a letter to Flint in 1915 that imagism was "most emphatically NOT the poetry of friend Storer" (quoted in J.B. Harmer, *Victory in Limbo: Imagism 1908–1917*, New York: St. Martin's Press, 1975, 45). After 1918 Storer lived primarily in Italy. Aldington knew him as a fellow poet and critic, a sympathetic innovator, and a man whose sensitivity to languages and competence particularly in Italian made him a potentially useful translator. His *Poems and Fragments of Sappho* appeared in October 1915, as number 2 in the first Poets' Translation Series.

Harriet Shaw Weaver (1876–1961)

The Aldingtons first came to know Miss Weaver (as she was always known to nearly everyone) when through Pound Aldington in 1913 assumed the position of literary editor of *The New Freewoman*, which in 1914 became *The Egoist*. Initially a managing editor under Dora Marsden, who founded the periodical, Miss

Weaver gradually increased her control of the journal, and she became its financial backer. Imagism and the flowering of early literary modernism, which rapidly followed Pound's first full-blown "movement," galvanized Miss Weaver. In addition to founding the Egoist Press and underwriting the works it published, she encouraged young writers and gradually focused her energies on James Joyce, eventually giving up *The Egoist* in 1919 in order to devote herself to seeing his works into print. She was by choice unmarried and a lady of "good breeding" and careful manners; her control of *The Egoist* was elegant, meticulous, and firm, particularly as she understood and became more committed to modernism. She saw Aldington as a man of boundless energy and organization, somewhat youthful and brash at times, but while he worked for her (until May of 1917) invaluable. She knew he was more reliable than Pound and could manage the editorial work his job entailed. Aldington, in turn, saw Miss Weaver as an angel who sometimes needed to be placated and as an inexperienced, unmarried woman on whose opinions his position depended. He worked well with her and respected her generosity, encouragement, and honesty.

James Whitall (1888–1954)

Brought up as a Quaker in Philadelphia, Whitall came to England just before the war. Through John Cournos, whom he had known in the United States, he met the Aldingtons in August of 1914. Whitall's independent income and his taste for traditional writers (such as George Moore, Conrad, and James) separated him from the Aldingtons, but his expatriate status and his Philadelphia roots, as well, probably, as a religious background much like H.D.'s, drew him particularly to the American poet. Aldington shared with Whitall the plan for the Poets' Translation Series in its earliest stages, and both Whitall and H.D. helped him to translate *The Poems of Leonidas of Tarentum*, which became Number 5 in the first series. Despite vague literary ambitions, Whitall never completed any original poetry or prose, but came to make his career as a translator of French and later, for a period, as a reader at Heinemann's. In *The Egoist* of August 1915, Aldington printed Whitall's translation of Judith Gautier's *Le Livre de Jade*, her translation of Chinese lyrics by, among others, Tu-Fu and Li-Po. Whitall's good friend, the American wood engraver George Plank, also became a close friend of the Aldingtons, particularly H.D. Whitall essentially lost touch with the Aldingtons after the war, but gives a warm and affectionate account of their friendship in *English Years* (London: Jonathan Cape, 1936).

Dorothy Yorke (1891–1971)

Born in Reading, Pennsylvania, Yorke first met John Cournos in 1910 in Philadelphia, where she was then living with her mother, her father having left the family some years before. Yorke and Cournos began an intermittent relationship of periodic engagements and separations. Cournos's poverty prevented their marriage, but their intimacy continued until the Yorkes' trip to Europe in late 1911. When Cournos went to England in early 1912, the two were writing each other regularly. He visited her in Paris several times, then in 1914 in New York, where the Yorkes had gone in the autumn of 1912. In April of 1914, Cournos met the Yorkes by chance in London on their way to Paris, and met them again by chance in London during the summer of 1917. Dorothy needed a room while her mother did war work in the country, and Cournos invited her to take over H.D.'s flat at 44 Mecklenburgh Square when H.D. went north to be near her husband. On the Aldingtons' return to London at the end of November, Yorke moved upstairs to another room in the same house. Cournos stresses the course and importance to him of his relationship with Yorke in his *Autobiography* (New York: G.P. Putnam's Sons, 1935).

Aldington's affair with Yorke probably began in December of 1917. It was a passionate relationship on both sides, intensified by the conflicting emotions each felt for their other partners: both Aldington and Yorke were aware of violating other ongoing relationships. H.D. portrayed Yorke as Bella Carter, John Cournos as Ivan, in *Bid Me to Live*. Yorke was dubbed "Arabella" apparently by the Aldingtons or perhaps by the Lawrences during their brief stay at Number 44 in the autumn of 1917.

An artistic woman, Yorke was a fine seamstress and periodically, probably with Aldington's encouragement, an illustrator (nine full-page fashion illustrations by Yorke appear in *The Art of Lydia Lopokova* [London: Cyril Beaumont, 1920]) and a translator (of Renée Dunan's *The Love Life of Julius Caesar*, New York: E.P. Dutton, 1931). In later years she resumed a correspondence with Cournos and, responding to the publication of *Bid Me to Live* in 1960, reflected on her experience with the Aldingtons. She objected to H.D.'s portrait of her as "an illiterate bunny-brained whore" (September 29, 1960), though she later called herself "a rather uneducated person (in fact totally so)" (October 2, 1965). She admitted, too, that H.D.'s resentment of her was understandable: "Of course I think she had plenty of cause to hate me" (September 29, 1960), but in the same letter adds her own resentment of H.D., who she felt had "no body." Yorke is also bitter in these letters toward Aldington, who left her in 1928, recalling the years in which they had lived together after the war, insisting defensively that she had "worked *for*" him, "—typed, read proofs, took dictation, cooked, washed + made his shirts to save money" (January 14, 1965). In these late letters to Cournos (from which I quote by kind permission of his step-daughter-in-law, Isabel Satterthwaite, who owns the letters), Yorke appears resentful and petty, an old and lonely woman who never had Aldington's full intellectual or emotional attention and never quite understood why. She died in a nursing home in Reading, Pennsylvania, where she spent her last years, having outlived all of her early circle of companions.

Periodical Appendix

The Dial

The Dial was edited in Chicago by Francis Fisher Browne until 1913 and after Browne's death by his son, Waldo Browne, until 1916. The Brownes had mixed feelings about modernist poetry: they wanted to encourage literature, but distinguished their journal from Harriet Monroe's *Poetry* in part by their rejection of the new movements in verse and in art generally. Characteristically, John C. Squire became their London correspondent in early 1916. Martyn Johnson took over as editor when the Brownes sold The Dial in August of 1916, and he moved the journal into the forefront of the modernist movement. The January 11, 1917, issue established the "new" *Dial* with a lead article by John Gould Fletcher, "The Secret of Far Eastern Painting," followed by Aldington's "Poet and Painter: A Renaissance Fancy," a wide-ranging discussion of the relationship between classical and later art. With the September 27, 1918, issue, The Dial began to publish verse for the first time since the turn of the century; the inaugural poem was Aldington's "Fatigues." Aldington continued to publish poetry, reviews, and essays of general commentary on literary topics throughout Johnson's tenure and after The Dial moved to New York and Scofield Thayer took over in January of 1920. H.D.'s work was first published in The Dial in November 1920, when three of her poems appeared there ("Helios," "Phaedra Rebukes Hippolyta," and "Phaedra Remembers Crete").

The Egoist

The Egoist grew out of two earlier periodicals, The Freewoman (1911) and The New Freewoman (1913), whose name became The Egoist in 1914. Initially a feminist periodical interested in theosophy and women's and gender-related topics, until the war it appeared fortnightly; from 1915 until its demise in 1919 it appeared once a month, although its final issues were sporadic. The Egoist, primarily through Pound's influence, focused increasingly on literary issues and published poems, essays, translations, stories, and installments of work by Joyce, Wyndham Lewis, and Remy de Gourmont. Dora Marsden edited the journal through 1915, when Harriet Shaw Weaver, by that time clearly in control of daily matters, took over. Aldington served as literary editor from 1914 through 1916 and jointly with H.D. from June of 1916 until June of 1917, when T.S. Eliot assumed the position. The periodical ceased publication in 1919 when Harriet Shaw Weaver decided to devote herself to the difficult task of publishing Joyce in England. Aldington and H.D. regularly published poems here, and Aldington's translations of works by de Gourmont and others appeared here often. During his time as literary editor Aldington wrote an article for each issue on literary or wider cultural matters, and the small but influential periodical served as a forum for his interests. He was paid a modest salary, but contributors were seldom reimbursed, a problem for aspiring young writers and occasionally for Aldington as an editor. *The Egoist* also served as a publisher (as the Egoist Press) in a limited way; it published the pamphlets in the Poets' Translation Series, edited by Aldington in 1915–16 and 1919–20, and later Joyce's *Ulysses* in 1922. Aldington's collection of poems, *Images*, was published by the Egoist Press in 1919 and H.D.'s *Hymen* in 1921.

The Nation

From 1907 through 1921, Henry W. Massingham edited this important weekly. It dealt with politics and current affairs from a radically liberal perspective and published as well original fiction and poetry, book and drama reviews, and literary articles. Many of the Aldingtons' acquaintances published work there, including Ford Maddox Ford, James Joyce, and Osbert Sitwell. When after the war H.D. and Aldington consciously began to seek a wider audience for their work, they naturally looked to *The Nation*. Aldington came to know Massingham professionally, and his "Faun Captive" appeared in *The Nation* on February 24, 1919, as well as portions of his translation of Anacreon in April and May of 1919. He continued to publish literary articles and poetry in *The Nation* in 1919 and into the twenties.

Poetry: A Magazine of Verse

Edited in Chicago by Harriet Monroe, *Poetry* was founded in 1912. Devoted to modern verse and its avant-garde principles, *Poetry* paid its contributors and was understandably valued by H.D. and Aldington. From late 1912 through April of 1919 Ezra Pound was its European correspondent; from the autumn of 1919 through the summer of 1921, Aldington acted in this capacity. The periodical thus served as a forum for imagism and subsequent literary movements. *Poetry* generally published a group of poems by each author it printed. Aldington's poetry appeared here in November 1912; January, February, and November 1914; October 1915; November 1918; and July 1919. H.D.'s verse appeared here in January 1913; February 1914; March 1915; and December 1919. Both writers' books were regularly reviewed here, and Aldington frequently reviewed books by others. Immediately after the war Aldington also wrote brief articles of wider scope for *Poetry:* "The Poetry of the Future" appeared in August 1919; "Recent French Poetry" appeared in October 1919; and "A London Letter" appeared in January 1920. H.D.'s and Aldington's friends also had their verse published in *Poetry:* Pound's work of course was printed here, as was poetry by Remy de Gourmont (translated by Aldington), Frank Flint, John Gould Fletcher, and Amy Lowell, for example. Even friends who were at best very minor poets had their work published: Frances Gregg's "To H.D." appeared in *Poetry* in January 1915, and three poems by Bryher appeared in December 1920.

The Sphere

Because of its editor, Clement Shorter, and Sir John Ellerman, who owned a controlling interest, *The Sphere* was particularly willing to publish work by the Aldingtons after the war. Bryher's affection for H.D. made this popular and fairly well-paying journal available, but H.D. decided not to allow her work to appear there, while Aldington wrote nine articles for *The Sphere*, all of which appeared between April and October 1919. *The Sphere*'s subtitle in 1919, *An Illustrated Journal for the Home*, suggests its wide appeal and essentially unliterary nature. During the war, it focused almost exclusively on the experience of the war and included war news and accounts of particular battles, regiments, and individual soldiers in brief articles dominated by large, well-reproduced and captioned photographs, compelling realistic charcoal drawings, and even paintings of combat and life behind the lines. "Women's Sphere," by "Olivia," was a regular feature and devoted its columns to accounts of women's war work at home and in the field and to fashion suggestions and household hints. Each weekly issue typically included a large number of advertisements, often with full- or half-page pictures, urging readers to buy cigarettes, fine men's suits, children's wear, women's hats, baby furniture, infants' food, and various elixirs for constipation and depression. The appeal was for the useful and healthy as well as the romantic and elegant.

Amid this variety, Shorter included an occasional short book review section ("Literature and Some Recent Books of the Day") and wrote a weekly column, "A Literary Letter," devoted to his interests. The paper was basically conservative, its diction patriotic, its tone sentimental, and stressed matter of popular appeal while including "highbrow" items which must have startled its readers. Shorter became interested in imagism soon after Bryher met H.D. in July of 1918, and "The Poems of Carl Sandburg—Imagist" (August 3, 1918) suggests her influence. Shorter profiled John Gould Fletcher on October 5, 1918, and reviewed at comparative length and with high praise Bryher's translation from the Greek, *The Lament for Adonis*, on November 16, 1918.

Index

Aelianus, Claudius: 166, 168n
Alciphron: 161, 162n, 166, 171, 172n, 175, 176n, 178
Aldington, Netta: 221
Aldington, Perdita: 143n, 173, 174n, 197–198, 201, 202n, 203n, 205, 206, 207, 208, 211
Aldington, Richard: childhood, 2–4; parents, 3–4, 7, 9, 18, 21, 44n, 45n, 105, 107n, 125n, 151, 152n, 211; university, 5, 24; marriage to H.D., 15; death of first child, 120, 121n; military service, x, 1, 21, 26, 27, 28, 29, 32, 33, 34, 37, 53n; shell shock, 36, 183, 190, 201n, 207, 208; library, x; on lesbianism, 122, 123n
—Works: *Death of a Hero*, ix, 3, 30, 41, 58n, 95n, 172n; *Life for Life's Sake*, ix, 2–3, 13, 16, 17, 30, 44n, 45n, 46n, 73n, 90n, 114n, 155–157, 164n, 171–172n, 189, 190, 222, 225; "Childhood," 3; *The Colonel's Daughter*, 3, 172n; *Seven Against Reeves*, 3; "Angelico's Coronation," 9; *Very Heaven*, 19, 45n; "Letters to Unknown Women," 33, 73n, 81n, 133n, 175; early verse, 43n; "Books in the Line," 46n, 176n, 202n; *D.H. Lawrence: Portrait of a Genius But*, 47n, 220; "Reverie," 53, 55n, 74n, 75n, 141n; "The Bookshop at Grenay," 58n, 202n; *Images*, 62n, 70n, 99n, 196, 230; *Images of Desire*, 62n, 70n, 196, 199; "To Atthis," 68n; "Theocritus in Capri," 70n; "The Chateau de Fressin," 70n; *War and Love*, 70n, 95n, 196; *Images of War*, 70n, 95n, 109n, 145n, 150n, 152n, 196; *Walter Pater*, 70n; *The Duke*, 72n; "To Sappho," 73n, 82n; "Choricos," 73, 74n, 75–77n, 221; "Prayers and Fantasies," 77–79n, 145n; "To the Slave in 'Cleon,' " 81n; "To Helen," 82n; "Heliodora," 82n; "To the Amaryllis of Theocritus," 82n; "To La Gross Margot," 82n; "In the Old Garden," 86, 87n; "Escape," 87–88n; "Free Verse in England," 92n; "The Art of Poetry," 92n; "Prose and Verse," 92n; "Bombardment," 93, 94, 95n; "Barrage," 93, 95n; "Dawn," 93, 95n; "Fatigues," 93, 94, 95n, 229; *Roads to Glory*, 95n; *Images of Old and New*, 95n; *War: A Book of Poems*, 95–96n; *All Men Are Enemies*, 97n, 172n; "There, violet wreathed...," 97; "The Faun Captive," 98–99, 99–100n, 117n, 140, 141n, 145, 230; "We are those...," 99n, 110; *The Love Poems of Myrrhine and Konallis*, 117n,

141n, 187, 187n; "Fantasy in Three Movements," 145; *The Viking Book of Poetry*, 164n; *Medallions*, 164n, 168n; *Women Must Work*, 172n; *Rejected Guest*, 172n; "The Poetry of the Future," 176n, 231; "Campion's 'Observations,' " 176n; *Remy de Gourmont* (biography), 217; *Remy de Gourmont* (selections), 217; "Poet and Painter," 229; "Recent French Poetry," 231; "A London Letter," 231
Alexander the Great: 86
Anacreon: 166, 168n, 175, 176n, 182, 186, 193, 196, 197, 230
Anglo-French Review, The: 144, 145n, 196
Anglo-Italian Review, The: 176n, 219
Antipater of Sidon: 179n, 191
Anyte: 166, 168n
Ariosto: 170n
Aristophanes: 113, 114n, 128n
Aristotle: 103n
Art and Letters: 185, 185n
Asclepiades: 166, 168n
Augustine, Saint: 63, 63n

Banford, Doris: 224
Barbusse, Henri: 82, 83n
Barney, Natalie: 171n, 217
Baudelaire, Charles: 70n, 171n
Beaumont, Cyril: 93, 95n, 108, 109n, 120, 121n, 145n, 196
Belloc, Hilaire: 184n
Bembo, Pietro: 166, 170n
Bion: 176n
Biron, Armand Louis de Gontaut: 93, 96n
Blake, William: 88
Blast: 220
Boccaccio, Giovanni: 166, 170n
Boiardo, Matteo Maria: 166, 170n
Bottome, Phyllis: 44n
Brooke, Rupert: 106, 107n
Brown, Edmund R.: 33, 93, 95n
Browne, Sir Thomas: 80, 81n
Browne, Waldo: 96n, 229
Browning, Robert: 62n, 113, 115n, 138
Bryher (Winifred Ellerman): x, 44n, 87n, 115–116, 116n, 123n, 126n, 128n, 133n, 138n, 139–140n, 140, 141n, 143n, 143, 144n, 144, 145n, 151n, 152n, 158–159, 160, 161, 161n, 162, 163n, 164, 165, 172n, 173, 174n, 175,

Caroline Zilboorg is Associate Professor of English at Lake Erie College. She has written numerous articles for scholarly journals on H.D., Aldington, and modernism.